GRAHAM HARMAN

# Object-Oriented Ontology:
## A New Theory of Everything

A PELICAN BOOK

PELICAN
*an imprint of*
PENGUIN BOOKS

## PELICAN BOOKS

UK | USA | Canada | Ireland | Australia
India | New Zealand | South Africa

Penguin Books is part of the Penguin Random House
group of companies whose addresses can be found at
global.penguinrandomhouse.com.

Penguin
Random House
UK

First published 2018

009

Text copyright © Graham Harman, 2018

The moral right of the author has been asserted

Book design by Matthew Young
Set in 10/14.664 pt FreightText Pro
Typeset by Jouve (UK), Milton Keynes
Printed and bound in Great Britain by Clays Ltd, Elcograf S.p.A.

A CIP catalogue record for this book is available from the British Library

ISBN: 978-0-241-26915-2

MIX
Paper from
responsible sources
FSC® C018179

Penguin Random House is committed to a
sustainable future for our business, our readers
and our planet. This book is made from Forest
Stewardship Council® certified paper.

www.greenpenguin.co.uk

# Contents

# INTRODUCTION

On 8 November 2016, as the writing of this book neared completion, the voters of the United States elected the scandal-ridden businessman and reality television star Donald J. Trump as their next President. This astonishing result came despite hundreds of controversial statements by Trump during the election campaign, including multiple incidents in which he flatly denied having made various claims despite public video evidence to the contrary. Indeed, the election's aftermath brought about such widespread shock that it led to an unusually large number of reflections by public intellectuals. As ever, one of the most contrarian positions was taken by the Slovenian philosopher Slavoj Žižek, who persisted in his pre-election claim that a Clinton victory would simply lead to more neoliberal mediocrity, while a win for the aspiring strongman Trump would at least serve to galvanize new and surprising political coalitions.[1] A more common reaction, however, was to condemn Trump's victory as the sign of a world that no longer has any respect for truth. Subtly leading the charge was no less an authority than the *Oxford English Dictionary*, which enshrined 'post-truth' as its 2016 word of the year, defining the term as 'relating to or denoting circumstances in which objective facts are less influential in shaping public opinion than appeals to emotion and personal belief'.[2] No one could miss the implied reference to a specific, newly minted American politician.

If we believe the *OED*'s definition, the best remedy for our supposedly post-truth condition would be 'objective facts'. The state of grasping objective facts is often called *knowledge*, and knowledge is taken to mean the human recognition of a truth, so that knowledge and truth generally come as a pair. In our time, the findings of science are usually recognized as the gold standard for knowledge and truth: a role once filled by the teachings of the Church, and in the future perhaps by other institutions as yet unknown. To say that we now live in a society dominated by the production of knowledge means that the success of the natural sciences and their technical application is the ultimate benchmark for what counts as truth, and hence is the possible key to opposing Donald Trump's 'appeals to emotion and personal belief'. On this view, a demagogue can only be silenced by knowledge, as in the old Leftist adage of 'speaking the truth to power'. A similar outlook was aired a few months before the election by the astrophysicist Neil deGrasse Tyson, who made the following controversial remark on Twitter: 'Earth needs a virtual country: #Rationalia, with a one-line Constitution: All policy shall be based on the weight of evidence.'[3] In other words, if only we could apply the scientific method to politics then we would finally be rid of irrational human conflict, and could perhaps make as much progress in politics as we have in our understanding of physical nature during the four centuries since the Scientific Revolution.

In this way, truth and knowledge are proposed as the

antidote to a relativism (formerly ascribed to the Left, but now fully at home on the Right) that invents whatever 'alternative facts' it pleases, to use the already infamous phrase of Trump spokesperson Kellyanne Conway. Yet somehow it is not always clear where we are supposed to find the truth and knowledge that are recommended as our miracle cure. This is especially evident in fields such as the arts and architecture, which are governed by shifting currents of taste rather than by calculative formulae: a difference that has mostly served to devalue these fields in the public eye in comparison with those that seem to produce actual knowledge, such as science, engineering or medicine. It is also unclear who possesses political knowledge, despite Tyson's call for a polity based on rational evidence. It is hard to believe, for instance, that the procedures of unusually effective politicians such as Abraham Lincoln or Mustafa Kemal Atatürk could be boiled down to a list of formulaic tips easily replicated by their successors. Nor is it always clear even where scientific knowledge can be found. Scientific theories are regularly overthrown and replaced during periods of intellectual upheaval, and the efforts by self-described 'structural realists' to claim that a permanent mathematical core endures in science despite all these revolutions have not been entirely convincing.[4] The unshakeable truths of one school of historians are dismissed as bourgeois pieties by another. Reputable engineering firms make errors of calculation that plunge hundreds of victims to death in the sea. Adherents of different religions slaughter millions of each other's followers across the centuries, and we should not forget that they are fully matched in brutality by Stalin, Pol Pot and other atheists. It would be easier to counter emotion and belief with truth and knowledge if we knew where to obtain the latter. And though the West is justly proud of its scientific tradition stretching back to ancient Greece, perhaps the greatest intellectual hero of that early period was Socrates (469–399 BCE), who claimed no knowledge whatsoever. Indeed, in Plato's dialogues we often find Socrates candidly asserting that he has never been anyone's teacher, and that the only thing he knows is that he knows nothing. Even Socrates' famous name for his profession, *philosophia*, means the *love* of wisdom rather than the possession of it. This attitude differs at its root from mathematics and the sciences, which aspire to obtain knowledge rather than merely to love it, though this difference is ignored by the many – from within the discipline and without – who urge philosophy to follow the sure path of a science.

The subject of the book now before you is Object-Oriented Ontology (abbreviated OOO, and pronounced 'Triple O'), a relatively new school of philosophy that takes Socrates at his word. No one is actually in possession of knowledge or truth, which therefore cannot be our protection against the degeneration of politics or of anything else. As OOO sees it, the true danger to thought is not relativism but *idealism*, and hence the best remedy for what ails us is not the truth/knowledge pair (which we will consider in greater detail in Chapter 4), but *reality*. Reality is the rock against which our various ships always founder, and as such it must be acknowledged and revered, however elusive it may be. Just as military commanders say that no battle plan survives the first contact with the enemy, philosophers ought not to legislate foolproof procedures for surmounting emotion and belief, but should recall instead that no theory survives its first contact with reality. Furthermore, since reality is always radically different from our formulation of it, and is never something we encounter directly in the flesh, we must approach it *indirectly*. This *withdrawal* or *withholding* of things from direct access is the central principle of OOO. The usual objection to this principle is the complaint that it leaves us with nothing but useless negative statements about an unknowable reality. Yet this objection assumes that there are only two alternatives: clear prose statements of truth on one side and vague poetic gesticulations on the other. I will argue instead that most cognition takes neither of these two forms, as is clear from such domains as aesthetics, metaphor, design, the widely condemned discipline of rhetoric, and philosophy itself. Like all of the disciplines in this list, philosophy has great cognitive value even though it is *not* a form of knowledge. And in a time like ours that quickly invokes knowledge as the cure to every ailment, this makes philosophy a potentially disruptive force, with a vastly different agenda for human advancement than the sciences. In the meantime, charlatans in politics and elsewhere are best countered not with claims to a truth that no one actually has, but with an unceasing demand that they face up to reality. How we go about detecting the gap between knowledge and reality is one of the main concerns of this book.

Barely known to the public a decade ago, Object-Oriented Ontology has emerged in recent years as one of the most provocative philosophical theories influencing the arts and humanities. Žižek has attacked the school for allowing no place in its model for the human subject, and his devotees have mostly united in rejection of OOO.[5] The French philosopher Bruno Latour has borrowed from the movement more keenly, employing the phrase 'object-oriented politics' in his recent major book on the modes of existence.[6] OOO has even been ranked by *ArtReview* among the 100 most influential forces in the international art world.[7] But perhaps its greatest impact so far has been in architecture, a discipline that is a famous early adopter of new philosophical trends. At least two organizers of major architectural conferences have stated in public that OOO is eclipsing the previous influence in architecture of the prominent French postmodernist thinkers Jacques Derrida and Gilles Deleuze.[8] In the meantime Mark Foster Gage, Assistant Dean of Architecture at Yale University, has written that 'the reason OOO is being explored by . . . architects is that it functions as an antidote not only to the Deleuzian emphasis on becoming over being, but, by extension, to architecture being justified not by its own qualities, but by its relations – its process, its internal complexity, its contextual relations . . .'[9] The charisma of this school has even captured the notice of celebrities in other fields, with the popular musician Björk having engaged in correspondence with OOO author Timothy Morton, and the actor Benedict Cumberbatch having listened attentively to one of my lectures at a private residence in London in 2014.[10]

Object-Oriented Ontology (also known as 'Object-Oriented Philosophy') dates to the late 1990s, though its extensive influence began roughly with the first conference on the topic, held at Georgia Tech in Atlanta in April 2010.[11] Along with my own books, the most prominent works in a

OOO vein have been written by Ian Bogost (*Unit Operations*, *Alien Phenomenology*), Timothy Morton (*Realist Magic*, *Hyperobjects*) and Levi R. Bryant (*The Democracy of Objects*) before his thinking took a different direction. As is always the case in an ancient discipline like philosophy, not all of the ideas of OOO are new, though they are deployed in new combinations and applied to subjects philosophers have often neglected. Some of the basic principles of OOO, to be visited in detail in the coming chapters, are as follows: (1) All objects must be given equal attention, whether they be human, non-human, natural, cultural, real or fictional. (2) Objects are not identical with their properties, but have a tense relationship with those properties, and this very tension is responsible for all of the change that occurs in the world. (3) Objects come in just two kinds: *real objects* exist whether or not they currently affect anything else, while *sensual objects* exist only in relation to some real object. (4) Real objects cannot relate to one another directly, but only indirectly, by means of a sensual object. (5) The properties of objects also come in just two kinds: again, real and sensual. (6) These two kinds of objects and two kinds of qualities lead to four basic permutations, which OOO treats as the root of time and space, as well as two closely related terms known as essence and *eidos*. (7) Finally, OOO holds that philosophy generally has a closer relationship with aesthetics than with mathematics or natural science. While some of the ideas just listed may sound challenging or even implausible, I will make every effort to explain them as lucidly as possible. My hope is that those who read this book to the end will find that a remarkable new intellectual landscape has come into view.

OOO has provoked strong reactions – both positive and negative – in such fields as African-American studies, archaeology, architecture, choreography, design, ecology, education, feminism, history, literary theory, media studies, music, political theory, psychoanalysis, social theory, theology, videogame theory and the visual arts, not to mention philosophy itself. Now, this breadth of influence might sound like a familiar song, since numerous philosophical methods deriving from the continental (mainly French–German) tradition of philosophy have already swept through the Anglophone world in the past fifty years. These trends have often been lumped together, somewhat inaccurately, under the general name of 'postmodernism' or simply 'theory', and in some quarters have been denounced as nothing but glittery frauds. Some of the first names that come to mind in this connection are Jacques Lacan, Roland Barthes, Michel Foucault, Jacques Derrida, Luce Irigaray, Slavoj Žižek, Judith Butler, Martin Heidegger and Bruno Latour – the latter two being my personal favourites in the group. But whereas many of these currents have asserted that reality is something 'constructed' by language, power or human cultural practices, OOO is a bluntly *realist* philosophy. This means among other things that OOO holds that the external world exists independently of human awareness. However bland and commonsensical this point may sound, it cuts against the grain of the past century of continental philosophy, and leads in directions surprisingly alien to common sense.

Even readers new to OOO may be familiar with the notion of object-oriented computer languages, such as C++ or Java. To avoid confusion, I should state at the outset that there is no essential link between the two: OOO merely borrowed the phrase 'object-oriented' from computer science, and was not directly motivated by developments in that field. Perhaps an expert in computing could carry out a more detailed comparison between object-oriented programming and OOO; so far this has not proven necessary, since OOO only borrows the phrase 'object-oriented' from the world of computers, rather than taking inspiration from the details of that world. Nonetheless, there are some important features common to the meaning of 'object-oriented' in both computers and philosophy. Whereas programs written in older computer languages were systematic and holistic entities, with all of their parts integrated into a unified whole, object-oriented programs make use of independent programming 'objects' that interact with other objects while the internal information of each remains hidden (or 'encapsulated') from the others. Given the independence of their parts, computer programs no longer need to be written each time from scratch, since one can make use of programming objects already written elsewhere for different purposes, bringing them into a new context without needing to change their internal structure; in other words, rather than having to create a whole new program each time, one can bring together individual programming objects to create new sets for new purposes – repurposing them in various combinations to create new uses. I want to stress the fact that these objects are opaque *to each other* and not just to the user, for the important reason that this idea is foreign to the history of Western philosophy. Over the centuries, a number of thinkers have suggested that the reality of things is ultimately unknowable to us: Immanuel Kant's 'things in themselves', Heidegger's 'being', and Lacan's 'Real' are just three examples of this tendency in intellectual history. What makes OOO different from these currents of thought – but similar to object-oriented programming – is the idea that objects never make full contact with each other any more than they do with the human mind. This is the key point missed by most of the charges that OOO is unoriginal. OOO's commitment to the mutual darkness of objects is what enables it to resist some of the fashionable holistic philosophies of our time, which hold that everything is defined purely by its relations and that the world is nothing but the total system of these relations. Against such theories, OOO defends the idea that objects – whether real, fictional, natural, artificial, human or non-human – are mutually autonomous and enter into relation only in special cases that need to be explained rather than assumed. The technical way of making this point is to say that all objects are mutually 'withdrawn', a term taken from Heidegger (1889–1976).[12] Against the assumptions of common sense, objects cannot make *direct* contact with each other, but require a third term or mediator for such contact to occur.

Having discussed the 'object-oriented' part of OOO, we now turn to the third O in its name, which stands for ontology. Here the previous borrowing relationship is reversed: for while philosophy borrowed the phrase 'object-oriented' from computer science, computer science borrowed the term 'ontology' from philosophy. In philosophy the terms 'ontology' and 'metaphysics' are so similar that some (including the author of this book) prefer to use them as synonyms. Both refer to the part of philosophy concerned with the structure of reality as such, rather than with the more specific areas covered by ethics, political philosophy or the philosophy of art. The widely accepted history of the word 'metaphysics' tells us that it was coined by the ancient editors of the works of Aristotle (384–322 BCE). Aristotle was one of the founding giants of natural science no less than of philosophy, and his *Physics* gives us a detailed account of the workings of nature. Along with the *Physics*, Aristotle wrote another work about philosophical issues lying outside or beyond those of nature: such as how individual things (or 'substances') act as a support for their changing qualities (or 'accidents'), as well as the role of God in the structure of the cosmos. It is said that Aristotle's editors, unsure of what to call these difficult writings, simply placed them after the *Physics* in the collected edition, and thus they became known as the *Metaphysics*, or the writings 'after the *Physics*'. But in Ancient Greek the prefix 'meta-' can also mean 'beyond', and thus metaphysics was widely understood as the discipline that goes 'beyond' the physical world. In the continental tradition since Heidegger and Derrida (1930–2004), 'metaphysics' is used as a highly negative term to accuse one's opponents of pursuing philosophy in what these continental thinkers regard as a naive fashion typical of Western philosophy since Plato. As for ontology, though some philosophers invest a great deal of energy in subtly interpreting the meaning of the Greek words *ontos* and *logos*, it is sufficient for our purposes to say that ontology means something like 'the study of being'. On this basis we could say that ontology appeared rather early in Greek philosophy, and even earlier in India. Nonetheless, the word 'ontology' itself was apparently not coined until the year 1613, which is practically yesterday in a slow-moving field like philosophy. By contrast with 'metaphysics', 'ontology' tends to be treated as a broadly respectable term, more rigorous and less laden with historical or mystical baggage. But in the present book as in my other writings, I will not follow this pejorative use of the term 'metaphysics', since I see no good reason to ruin a valuable term from classical philosophy. So in fact, I will use metaphysics and ontology as synonyms to allow us to avoid repetition, thereby obtaining an important stylistic resource for not dulling the reader's ears too quickly.

By the time you have finished this book, I hope to have explained the basic concepts of OOO as clearly as possible, and to have conveyed my reasons for excitement about this style of philosophy. The model I have kept in mind while writing is Sigmund Freud's *Introductory Lectures on Psycho-Analysis*, delivered by Freud to a general audience in Vienna during the First World War. Whatever one thinks of Freud's psychological theories, he is an undisputed master of the literary presentation of difficult ideas, and is well worth emulating in at least that respect. In his well-polished introductory book, Freud begins by explaining slips of the tongue, moves on to the interpretation of dreams, and then proceeds to his theory of neuroses. My method here will be similar, beginning with the simplest aspects of OOO before moving on to its more intricate details.

Chapter 1 ('A New Theory of Everything') introduces the notion of objects, which for OOO come in two and only two types: *real* and *sensual*. I will also discuss what OOO thinks is wrong with modern philosophy since René Descartes

(1596–1650) and especially Kant (1724–1804), though in one respect Kant is an important ancestor of OOO.

Chapter 2 ('Aesthetics Is the Root of All Philosophy') explains why philosophy has less in common with science than is usually believed, and more in common with the arts. Here we touch on the key cognitive role of *metaphor*, which I claim is more important for philosophy than discursive propositional statements such as 'the cat is on the mat', 'gold is a yellow metal', or 'water boils at 100 degrees Celsius', which philosophers so often take as the model for their theories.

Chapter 3 ('Society and Politics') discusses some of the implications for OOO in these fields. Some explanation is given of Latour's actor-network theory, since OOO differs greatly from this influential school in matters of social theory while tending to agree with many of its findings concerning politics.[13] In social theory OOO is more interested in the inner nature of things than in their actions, and contends that only a half-dozen or so important events befall an object before it reaches maturity, ripens, declines, and dies. In politics, OOO avoids the left/right polarization of political discourse since the French Revolution, focusing instead on the difference between truth politics and power politics, both of them in need of replacement. It also adheres to the discovery of actor-network theory that non-human entities play a crucial role in stabilizing the human polis.

In Chapter 4 ('Indirect Relations') I show why the interaction between objects, which seems like the most obvious everyday thing in the world, is more paradoxical than it sounds. There is already a long but partially obscured tradition of taking this problem seriously: first among the Arab and European Occasionalists of medieval and early modern times, and later with Kant and the important Scottish philosopher David Hume (1711–76). I will suggest that all of these celebrated figures adopt the same incorrect assumptions about the workings of causality. This will lead us to a broader discussion of the fourfold structure of objects, which serves as one of the methodological pillars of OOO. I will also ask what is left of knowledge in the wake of OOO's rejection of literalism and direct access to reality. Since Chapter 2 has already claimed that philosophy has more in common with the arts than the sciences, some might complain (and have already complained) that OOO 'aestheticizes' philosophy while leaving us sceptical as to the possibility of any actual knowledge. Yet we will see that OOO merely rejects the idea of knowledge as a direct presence of reality itself, and does not scorn knowledge *per se*.

In Chapter 5 ('Object-Oriented Ontology and its Rivals') I try to clarify the nature of OOO further by distinguishing its treatment of objects from the views of perhaps the two most dominant French thinkers of the past half-century: Derrida and Foucault, neither of them doing the degree of justice to objects that OOO itself demands.

Chapter 6 ('Varying Approaches to Object-Oriented Ontology) discusses the key authors who have worked or still work in a OOO idiom: Ian Bogost, Levi R. Bryant, and Timothy Morton. It also discusses two of the fellow travellers who have worked in proximity to OOO without accepting the exact presuppositions or methods of this school: Jane Bennett and Tristan Garcia.[14] Finally, I will briefly consider the work of several young architects and architectural theorists who have written persuasively about the role of OOO in their discipline: Mark Foster Gage, Erik Ghenoiu, David Ruy, and Tom Wiscombe.[15]

Chapter 7 ('Object-Oriented Ontology in Overview') concludes with a summary of some of the most important guiding maxims of the movement.

In writing this book I have had two primary goals in mind. The first is that any reader who continues to the end should understand OOO as well as anyone other than a few seasoned veterans. The second is that reading this book should be as pleasant an experience as possible. It has long been my view that since there are so many books one can read, and so many things that one can do besides read books, the burden is always on the author to make the topic at hand more interesting than all of these other options. I would be mortified to bore my guests at a house party, and even more so to bore thousands of readers after they have made a good-faith investment of time and money to read this book.

In closing, I would like to thank Ananda Pellerin and Thomas Penn of Penguin, who jointly persuaded me to write this volume. Jane Birdsell, also of Penguin, caught dozens of errors that I was astonished to find still lurking in my manuscript, and added a number of stylistic improvements. In deciding how to structure my chapters, I have benefitted greatly from some of the volumes already published in this series of Pelican Introductions, including but not limited to Robin Dunbar's *Human Evolution* and Ha-Joon Chang's *Economics: The User's Guide*. The helpful diagrams were designed by Professor Emeritus Michael Flower of Portland State University, who has assisted me in similar fashion in the past.

# A New Theory of Everything

In recent decades, few intellectual topics have captured the public imagination like the search for a so-called 'theory of everything' in physics. One of the best-known authors in this vein is Brian Greene of Columbia University, who views the currently popular 'string theory' as the best existing candidate for a theory explaining the composition of matter and the structure of the cosmos. As he puts it in one of his lively best-sellers: 'if you . . . believe that we should not rest until we have a theory whose range of applicability is limitless, string theory is the only game in town.'[1] The search for unifications in physics has already given humanity some of its most heroic moments. In the early 1600s, Galileo established the falsity of the ancient view that there is one kind of physics for the eternal bodies in the sky and a completely different kind for the corrupt and decaying things down here on the earth; instead, he showed that one physics governs every portion of the universe. This paved the way for the even more fateful unification announced in Sir Isaac Newton's *Principia* in 1687. In this masterpiece of the history of science, Newton demonstrated that the movement of celestial bodies and the falling of objects to the ground are governed by one and the same force: gravity, as everyone calls it today.

In the 1860s, James Clerk Maxwell was able to unify the previously separate forces of electricity and magnetism, and established further that light and electromagnetism travel at the same speed, strongly suggesting that light is simply another manifestation of the same force. In the early twentieth century, quantum theory unified various phenomena of heat, light and atomic motion by explaining them as occurring through discrete jumps rather than continuous increase or decrease. Eventually four forces of nature had been recognized: gravity, electromagnetism, the strong nuclear force (which holds atoms together) and the weak nuclear force (which governs radioactive decay). The 1979 Nobel Prize in Physics went jointly to the physicists Sheldon Lee Glashow, Abdus Salam and Steven Weinberg for their unified theory of the 'electroweak' force, while the strong force was accounted for at roughly the same time by QCD, or quantum chromodynamics. By the mid-1970s, physics had its Standard Model of Particle Physics, which was more or less completed in 2012 by the apparent discovery of the Higgs boson at CERN in Geneva. Among the remaining problems with the Standard Model is that it does not unify gravity with the electromagnetic, strong and weak forces. The pursuit of a workable theory of 'quantum gravity' continues to this day, and along with the discovery by astronomers of the still inexplicable dark matter and dark energy, the search for quantum gravity is one of the most likely triggers of the next revolution in physics.

The topic of unified theories is so exciting that physicists have created a small industry of readable popular books on the theme, with Greene's *The Elegant Universe* one of the most prominent among them. Now, I certainly agree with Greene that 'we should not rest until we have a theory whose range of applicability is limitless'. My point of disagreement will sound surprising in the current intellectual climate: I do not agree that physics, or even natural science more generally, is the right place to find such a unified theory. In my view, the 'theory whose range of applicability is limitless' can only be found in philosophy, and especially in the type of philosophy called Object-Oriented Ontology (OOO). Since I cannot be sure that Greene literally thinks that a unified theory of physics would automatically be a theory of everything else – though many physicists do display such a pride in their discipline as queen of all the others – I will invent a fictitious scientist named 'Brianna Browne' who does explicitly hold that, in principle, physics can explain everything. Though the rapid advance of modern physics has been one of the most reassuring chapters of human history, I see it as a field that excludes far too much to give us a theory of everything. Let's consider the various assumptions underlying 'Browne's' claim that physics (and string theory in particular) has limitless applicability.

String theory is not the only candidate for a 'theory of everything', but it remains the most popular, and for many the most promising. The theory has been around in some form since the 1960s, but became an especially hot topic two decades later; I still remember the first newspaper stories about 'superstrings' from 1984, which I read as an admiring high-school student. String theory postulates that matter is composed of vibrating one-dimensional strings twisting through *ten* dimensions, rather than the four dimensions of space-time that Einsteinian physics accepts. In so-called 'M-theory', Edward Witten's 1995 modification of the string landscape, the total number of dimensions was expanded to eleven. Numerous beautiful mathematical and physical results can be derived from the theory, including a possible account of the ever-elusive quantum gravity, meaning a theory of gravity that can be explained in terms of quantum mechanics just as the electromagnetic, strong and weak forces already have been. Nonetheless, a backlash against string theory began in the twenty-first century, as can be seen in the widely read critical books by physicists Lee Smolin and Richard Woit.[2] Perhaps the most frequent accusation against string theory by sceptics is that it cannot be experimentally tested, and is therefore said to be little more than a mathematical exercise of no direct relevance to physics. Another problem is that so many thousands of different string theories are mathematically possible that there is no reason to choose one in particular, except on the shaky basis that we must obviously choose the theory that fits the structure of the universe we know: for otherwise we would not be here today to have debates about it. This line of reasoning is known as the 'anthropic principle', viewed by many scientists with contempt but by others as a pivotal intellectual tool. Lastly, Smolin in particular is alarmed by the near-monopoly of string theory in the leading graduate courses in physics, which for him means that the entire profession has put all its eggs in a single, experimentally baseless basket.

# Why Science Cannot Provide a Theory of Everything

But let's leave all these objections aside, and assume that string theory will somehow manage to overcome them. Imagine that good reasons are eventually produced for preferring one variant of string theory to the others, and that someone also comes up with a brilliant experimental arrangement that confirms the truth of the theory. In this case not only would our fictitious scientist Browne be right to call string theory 'the only game in town', since it would now be something more than just one game among others; but string theory would have become textbook science, learned by students everywhere as a basic fact about our world, much like Einstein's theory of gravity or the periodic table of chemical elements. My claim is that even under this optimal scenario of maximum scientific triumph, string theory would still not be a 'theory of everything'. To see why, let's examine what I take to be the four false assumptions behind Browne's statement that string theory's range of applicability is limitless.

First False Assumption: *everything that exists must be physical*. A successful string theory would sum up everything we know about the structure and behaviour of physical matter. But this makes it a 'theory of everything' only on the condition that everything is physical. Of course, many people do not see it this way. Religion is a far weaker force in Europe than it used to be, though it remains significantly stronger in the United States, and very much stronger in other parts of the world. Among adherents of all religions, belief in imma-terial gods and souls is nearly universal. Many other people around the world, including a number of un-religious ones, still believe in ghosts and spirits. For example, in most older cities in the Western world it is a pillar of the tourist industry to offer 'ghost tours' that take visitors to sites of unredeemed murders and torments, where they are told stories about dis-turbing incidents in these places that seem to hint at a super-natural cause. In almost every country, a number of buildings stand out for their reputation as being especially haunted: one that comes to mind in America is the Skirvin Hilton Hotel in Oklahoma City, where a number of NBA basketball players have reported nights of memorable horror.[3] In more refined circles we find Jungian psychology, which affirms the existence of unconscious and immaterial archetypes shared collectively by all human beings.[4] By hypothesis, our main-stream physicist Browne will dismiss all such ideas as unsci-entific rubbish. A 'theory of everything', Browne will assert, does not mean a theory that includes all of the nonsense that gullible people *think* is real, but only a theory of what rational and scientifically minded people know to be real: the physical–material universe. Those who do believe in reli-gions, ghosts or Jungian archetypes will now simply dismiss Browne as narrow-minded, or even as a sinner destined for hell, and amidst these mutual recriminations the two sides will have nothing further to discuss. So it often goes in intel-lectual life, and perhaps it is not always a bad thing that people tend to congregate in like-minded tribes, where they are free to develop their views amidst allies rather than being hassled by mobs of dissidents. Though I for one am not particularly convinced by Jungian psychology, I do read Jung from time to time and find that he improves my imagination. And I would certainly hate to live in a world where Jungian societies were liquidated by the Rationality Police or demoralized by general public mockery. From experience I can say that a certain percentage of philosophers seem to have embarked on their careers primarily because they enjoy slaughtering the irrational fantasies of others. But I have never enjoyed spending time with these sorts of philosophers; nor have I ever been quite as cocksure as they are as to which views about our universe are the 'rational' ones.

But let's suppose we agree with the scepticism of Brianna Browne, and join her in disbelief about any gods, souls, ghosts, spirits, unconscious archetypes or other supposed non-material entities. Even if we were to walk this far down the path with Browne, and even under the supposition that string theory were confirmed by rock-solid evidence, I would still not agree with her that this meritorious theory could count as a 'theory of everything'. For we can think of plenty of things that are not physical but which are almost certainly real. In 2016 I published a book entitled *Immaterialism*, whose second half was devoted to an account of the Dutch East India Company (or 'VOC', in its commonly used Dutch abbreviation). While it might be assumed that this company was a material object, this view is difficult to sustain under questioning without having to make a number of concessions that are damaging to the materialist standpoint. For one thing, material objects always exist *somewhere*, but in the case of the VOC it is not at all clear where that place of existence would be. It was certainly not at VOC headquarters in

Amsterdam, since most of the company's operations took place in Southeast Asia; the VOC was equipped with an independent Governor-General living abroad and empowered to make decisions without first consulting shareholders back in the Netherlands. Nor was the physical location of the VOC to be found in its Asian capital, Jayakarta or 'Batavia' (present-day Jakarta, Indonesia). Only a small fraction of the ships and employees of the VOC could be found in Batavia at any given time, and at least in principle, the rules of the VOC were equally in force at all points within its territory. At any rate, it should be clear that the Dutch East India Company was not a material thing existing in a definite or semi-definite place in the same way as a quark, electron or tiny vibrating string. Beyond this, the VOC existed from 1602 to 1795, and no person (and perhaps no ship) lasted for that entire period as an enduring element of the company. For this reason, we would say that the VOC was not a piece of matter, however complicated in shape, but rather a *form* that more or less endured for 193 years despite constantly shifting its material components. There is an old philosophical paradox known as the Ship of Theseus, which poses the problem of whether the ship remains the same even when we gradually or suddenly replace each of its boards with a new one – especially if we assemble the old boards together nearby as a rival vessel to the new ship. Without going further into this paradox and its venerable history, it already serves to emphasize what I take to be a chief lesson of the VOC case study: the irreducibility of larger objects to the sum total of their material components. The Dutch East India Company was not just a collection of atoms and strings at various locations in space–time, but to a large extent was able to survive the motion and disappearance of these tiny elements while making use of others.

Second False Assumption: *everything that exists must be basic and simple*. Having read the previous paragraphs, Browne will reply that we have missed the point. For while it may be true that the VOC or the Ship of Theseus can survive despite the turnover of their material pieces, they certainly cannot exist without any material pieces at all. If over time the VOC only lost atoms and never gained any, there would finally come a point where its various ships, cargoes and officers would crumble to dust and the VOC would cease to exist. Browne will say that she never meant to tell us there cannot be higher-order objects that *seem* to endure despite massive turnover in their material components. But such objects must always be made of *some* physical matter, even if it is relatively unimportant whether one hydrogen atom or another happens to be found in the brain of the VOC's Governor-General. Beyond this, Browne will argue further that we can only speak loosely of the 'same' Dutch East India Company enduring for nearly two centuries. So many changes occur in the Company during that period that it seems rather sloppy to think it remains the same, even if such sloppiness can be tolerated in historians or everyday speakers of English, who lack the more rigorous precision of natural scientists. Perhaps we can refer vaguely to the 'same' flags, rules and slogans during the Company's entire lifespan, and pretend harmlessly that such ports as Batavia, Banten and Malacca were the 'same' in 1750 as they were in 1650. But ultimately – Browne will continue – the only things that remain the same are those tiny, durable, ultimate things that lack further internal structure: such as the strings of string theory.

But here Browne lapses into the fallacy that the philosopher Sam Coleman has termed 'smallism', as if the real elements in any situation were the tiniest components to which everything can be broken down.[5] The mid- and large-sized objects that surround us (from cups, tables and flowers to skyscrapers and elephants) seem to have independent features of their own, but according to Browne these larger objects ultimately receive all of their properties from those of their components; after all, without these small components the larger objects could never exist. What this argument misses is the phenomenon known as *emergence*, in which new properties appear when smaller objects are joined together into a new one.[6] This is visible everywhere in human life. For example, a high-school friend and I noticed one summer that girls would often walk together in groups of three, but that boys were almost always found alone or in pairs. We wondered why this was so, until my friend rather cryptically nailed it by saying that 'three boys together are already a gang'. I believe his meaning was as follows: there is something vaguely menacing in the air as soon as three young males come together, and hence this practice is subtly discouraged under normal situations, which do not provide a welcome setting for menace. If the observation is correct, then three boys together have as a vague emergent property 'gang-like threat to society' that is found neither in two boys nor in three girls. Four and a half million people together form the present-day city of Ankara, Turkey, but Ankara is obviously not just 4.5 million individuals assembled in a mass. For one thing, the city also requires a number of inanimate objects: the city would disappear if Ankara's 4.5 million residents merely stood naked together in a field. More than this, Ankara has emergent structures that belong to the city as a whole rather than to its parts, such as marriages, families, clubs, professions and political parties, not to mention the Turkish slang terms current in various age groups.

This is also true in the sciences, as can be seen with especial ease in a field such as organic chemistry: all organic compounds contain carbon, but there are millions of organic compounds, each with its own unique features. Sometimes the defenders of emergence push their luck and make unnecessary additional claims, asserting for instance that the features of organic compounds 'could not have been predicted' from the features of carbon. But quantum chemistry does allow us to predict the properties of larger molecules before they are actually created. And predictability is not even the point, since even if we could predict the features of *all* larger entities from their ultimate physical constituents, the ability to predict would not change the fact that the larger entity actually *possesses* emergent qualities not found in its components. This is equally clear in human life. Perhaps a couple is about to be married, and all of their friends see clearly in advance that the marriage will be disastrous. Now, let's imagine that the friends of the couple are completely right: not only does the marriage fail, but it fails in precisely those ways and on the exact timetable that the friends had predicted. But notice that the predictability of this marital failure does not entail that the marriage is nothing more than the sum total of the two pre-existing individuals who were married. In other words, the emergent *reality* of an object composed jointly of multiple parts (such as a married couple) does not hinge on the predictability or unpredictability of how it ultimately turns out. Emergence does not require mysterious results, but only that the married couple has joint features not found in either of the individuals in isolation. The same would hold true if the friends were completely wrong and the marriage led to eternal and blissful harmony: the point is that the *existence* of the marriage as an emergent object over and above the two individual partners has nothing to do with whether its success or failure could be foreseen.

Another prejudice infects portions of the history of philosophy in the view that only that which is *natural* truly exists. This doctrine is especially prominent in the philosophy of the German polymath G. W. Leibniz (1646–1716), who distinguishes sharply between what he calls 'substances' and 'aggregates'. Substances are simple, soul-like entities (known as 'monads'), all of them created by God at the beginning of time.[7] By contrast, aggregates are compounds such as machines, circles of men holding hands, or pairs of diamonds glued together. For Leibniz such aggregates are merely laughable stand-ins for true substances, which can exist only by nature rather than artifice. OOO rejects this view, given that machines, much like the Dutch East India Company (another example mocked by Leibniz), can be treated as unified objects no less than an atom or tiny vibrating string. In short, naturalness is no better as a criterion of objecthood than smallness or simplicity. As for the true criteria for what qualifies as an object, we will discuss them at the end of this chapter.

Third False Assumption: *everything that exists must be real*. One of the greatest fictional heroes of all time is surely the detective Sherlock Holmes, in the stories of Sir Arthur Conan Doyle. In writing these stories, Doyle tried to house his detective at a fictitious address on a real London street: namely, 221B Baker Street. Yet the very real London thoroughfare called Baker Street was later extended to go as far as the 200s, thereby putting the fictional flat of Holmes and Dr Watson within the range of real-life city addresses. Indeed, it happened that first one real building and then another claimed to be the 'true' site of the Holmes/Watson flat. It is said that some of the Sherlock Holmes fans who visit the currently accepted address, now home to a gift shop and museum, labour under the misconception that the detective was a real historical person. The retelling of this story usually provokes cruel laughter at the expense of these naive tourists. Yet there is a charming grain of truth in their ignorance: the fact that the detective is such a beloved and memorable character that one can easily imagine him resting comfortably at home on Baker Street, and picture him in a number of situations that did not actually occur in Doyle's works (as in the current television series in which Holmes, played by Benedict Cumberbatch, solves cases in present-day London). This brings us to a third objection to the global ambitions of string theory. Namely, a successful string theory would not be able to tell us anything about Sherlock Holmes, and this alone suffices to disqualify it as a 'theory of everything'. For Holmes is a fictional personage, and thus was never composed of strings or of any other physical material.

Nor is it even necessary to invoke celebrity fictional characters such as those who inhabit novels and films, since we are surrounded at all times by fictions. For example, any real orange or lemon, as I perceive it, is a vast oversimplification of the real citrus-objects in the world that are submitted to rough translation by the human senses and human brain. The real orange or lemon is no more accessible to my human perception than it is to a mosquito or dog, whose organs translate the fruits differently into their own types of experience. In this respect, all of the objects we experience are merely fictions: simplified models of the far more complex objects that continue to exist when I turn my head away from them, not to mention when I sleep or die. A successful string theory, like any fundamental theory of physics, is aimed entirely at the discovery of real physical entities rather than fictitious ones. And while it is already hard to imagine a basic physical theory adequately addressing any emergent mid- or large-sized entity (let us use 'entity' as another synonym for 'object' and 'thing'), it is even harder to imagine a successful string theory teaching us anything about the fictional objects of literature and everyday perception, a field where natural science normally does not tread. This is no small matter, since fictions are an integral part of human experience, and of animal life more generally. Along with the examples already given, recall that we humans spend much of our time worrying about things that can never happen or simply never do. We are frequently deluded about our own capacities, whether under- or overestimating them. We spend a large portion of our lives in nocturnal dreams, and despite recent criticism of psychoanalysis, it is doubtful that these dreams can be understood in purely chemical or neurological terms. All of this is to say nothing of our entertainment media, which often feature dragons, rings of invisibility, aliens assaulting the earth, or the intimate lives of characters who exist for two hours on a screen before vanishing from the cosmos forever. For many of us, artists such as Beethoven and Picasso are as worthy of esteem as Newton and Einstein, though the latter discuss such undeniable realities as light and moons while the former create pure fictions. Any 'theory of everything' that dismisses the reality of fictions, or passes them over in silence, is by that fact alone unable to reach its goal of covering everything.

Fourth False Assumption: *everything that exists must be able to be stated accurately in literal propositional language.* Here are some scientific statements, chosen at random from the three books of science nearest to hand in my living room:

1. 'Some hydrogen atoms can escape the Earth's gravity and are lost to space, [while] some meteoritic material comes in (about forty-four tons per day on average) . . .'[8]

2. 'As Schrödinger pointed out, if $M$ represents a cat and $R$ takes two possible values . . . and the decay event triggers a device that kills the cat, then the cat will be neither alive nor dead after the measurement interaction, according to the orthodox interpretation.'[9]

3. 'All other interventions, such as, for example, cold, heat, acids, alkalis, electrical currents, [the bell] responds to as any other piece of metal would. But we know . . . that

a muscle behaves in a completely different way.

It responds to all external interventions in the same way: by contracting.'[10]

These are admirably formed statements conveying information that we hope to be true, though every scientist knows that many apparently rock-solid statements are later abandoned or modified in the face of new evidence. Moreover, it is not just science that makes such statements. History does the same. I need only turn elsewhere on my living room bookshelf: 'But Mo-ch'o was growing old, and the Turks began to weary of his cruelty and tyranny. Many chiefs offered their allegiance to China, and the Bayirku of the upper Kerulen revolted.'[11] Or simply this: 'At this time, too, Venice had become the intellectual centre of Italy.'[12] All of these statements can be understood clearly by anyone with a basic secondary education. And of course we make statements of this sort constantly even in non-scholarly contexts. It is easy to state as follows: 'Leicester City stunned the sports world in 2016 by finishing on top of the English Premier League.' Or I can look at the text messages on my phone and see that my wife, a university food scientist, needs me to pick up some items for her class on sensory analysis: 'Here are the items I need before 11 o'clock. 1 pack of original Oreo cookies. 2 litres of drinking water. 1 carton of Florida Natural Original Orange Juice, with pulp.' All these examples are literal statements that convey information directly. And thus it is easy to assume that nothing can be real unless we are able to refer to it in an accurate prose statement that conveys literal properties of the thing in question. Apparently, the only alternative would be fuzzy metaphors or merely negative statements that teach us nothing.

The American philosopher Daniel Dennett is very much a literalist in this sense. I am both amused and appalled by his mockery of wine-tasting in the following passage:

> Could Gallo Brothers replace their human wine-tasters with a machine? . . . Pour the sample in the funnel and, in a few minutes or hours, the system would type out a chemical assay, along with commentary: 'a flamboyant and velvety Pinot, though lacking in stamina' – or words to such effect . . . [B]ut *surely* [note Dennett's sarcasm] no matter how 'sensitive' or 'discriminating' such a system becomes, it will never have, and enjoy, what *we* do when we taste a wine: the qualia of conscious experience . . . If you share that intuition, you believe that there are qualia in the sense that I am targeting for demolition.[13]

To summarize, Dennett thinks that the wine is literally and adequately expressed by its 'chemical assay', though his imagined machine will also add sarcastic poetic commentary at the expense of human readers who disagree with his views. Nonetheless, he holds, there is no special conscious human experience of wine that would require the elusive figurative description of a flamboyant and velvety Pinot. OOO holds that Dennett is wrong about this, and not just in the obvious sense that the taste of wine for humans resists any precise literal description. Instead, the claim of OOO is that literal language is *always* an oversimplification, since it describes things in terms of definite literal properties even though *objects are never just bundles of literal properties* (despite

Hume's view to the contrary). It is not just that the chemical assay of the wine fails to do justice to the human experience of tasting wine, but that it fails to do justice even to the chemical–physical structure of the wine. This may sound like a startling claim, since the natural sciences are generally regarded as the court of final appeal in our era, just as the Church was in the medieval period. But I will develop this anti-literalist claim throughout the present book. In so doing, I will build on the philosophical work of Heidegger, who also gives priority to poetic over literal language – though admittedly in ways that sometimes verge on Black Forest peasant *kitsch*, and though his statements against science are often needlessly extreme.[14] Thus I will make the case differently from how Heidegger did, though I agree with his basic line of reasoning: the reality of things is always withdrawn or veiled rather than directly accessible, and therefore any attempt to grasp that reality by direct and literal language will inevitably misfire. In a sense, this point by Heidegger merely develops Aristotle's ancient claim in his *Metaphysics* that individual things cannot be defined, since things are always concrete while definitions are made of universals.[15]

## Against Physicalism, Smallism, Anti-Fictionalism and Literalism

But not only natural science harbours the failed aspiration to be a potential theory of everything. Economics has increasingly claimed to be the Superman of the social sciences, and has incurred much professional resentment in doing so. But notice that even if it were possible to place all social science under the umbrella of economics, the economist obviously still could not account for the formation of stars or the role of DNA in microbial evolution. This puts the economist even further behind than the physicist, who can at least press the point (though we have seen how it fails) that there could be no economy if all physical matter were absent. Psychoanalysis as well has sometimes viewed itself as master of the human sciences, since it accounts for the hidden portion of human thought and action no less than the visible part. But here again, despite my great admiration for the insights of Freud, Lacan, and so many of their colleagues, psychoanalysis cannot take us very far beyond the sphere of human culture, and it leaves the inanimate world largely untouched. The only way to make a case for *any* of the human sciences as a theory of everything is to embrace social constructionism and try to reduce natural science to its purely socio-linguistic aspects or to some sort of power struggle. But this type of strong social constructionism is already fading away, and there is no reason to mourn its passing.

At any rate, from surveying the problems with Browne's claim that string theory could be a theory of everything, we have learned what a genuine theory of everything must avoid. The four major pitfalls faced by such a theory are: *physicalism, smallism, anti-fictionalism* and *literalism*. The main strength of OOO is its rigorous avoidance of these intellectual toxins. For the object-oriented thinker, physical objects are just one kind of object among many others, and hence we should not be in a hurry to scorn or 'eliminate' those that are not a good fit with a hardnosed materialist worldview.

Philosophy is not the handmaid of materialism any more than of religion. Against smallism, object-oriented thought holds that objects exist at numerous different scales, including the electron, the molecule, the Dutch East India Company and the galaxy. The mere fact of complexity and largeness does not make something less real than its component parts. Next, we should be in no hurry to flush fictional objects out of existence, since any philosophy worthy of the name must be able to say something positive about such beings. And remember that by 'fictional' I do not just mean the likes of Sherlock Holmes and Emma Woodhouse, but also the everyday houses and hammers that we seem to encounter directly, but which we perceive in the manner of simplified models of the real houses and hammers to which we can never gain direct access. And finally, OOO is anti-literalist, because any literal description, literal perception, or literal causal interaction with the thing does not give us that thing directly, but only a translation of it. Hence, an indirect or oblique means of access to reality is in some ways a wiser mode of access than any amount of literal information about it.

To repeat, we insist that a theory of everything must avoid physicalism, smallism and literalism, while also embracing the fictional. In this way, are we not launching an enterprise just as arrogant as those we have criticized? No, and for the same reason that a globe is not more 'arrogant' than a map. Mapmakers can be proud of the detail, accuracy and clarity of their final products, while still realizing that a globe is better at showing how the many different local maps interconnect. We must expand the analogy, of course, since OOO is not just offering a globe, but a model of both the real and fictional universes. In the words of the American philosopher Wilfrid Sellars: 'The aim of philosophy, abstractly formulated, is to understand how things in the broadest possible sense of the term hang together in the broadest possible sense of the term.'[16] We can accept this definition provisionally, with the caveat that philosophy for OOO is more about how things in the broadest possible sense of the term *do not* hang together in the broadest possible sense of the term, but maintain a degree of autonomy despite their interrelations.

## Undermining in the History of Philosophy

Some readers may already have made a silent objection in their minds, since I seem to have slipped from claiming that OOO is a theory of everything to saying that such a theory must be about *objects*. Are objects really everything that is? Even my close colleague Manuel DeLanda, an ardent realist philosopher in his own right, blows the whistle on me here: 'I am not sure why Harman wants to stick to objects. I do not deny that objects exist . . . it is just that a full realist ontology must possess objects and events, with a process being a series of events.'[17] Quite apart from the opposition between objects and events, the word 'object' seems to suggest a hard, material, solid, durable entity, which is by no means the only sort of thing found in our world. And more than this, doesn't Heidegger show that the word 'object' refers to the improper objectification of the world by the mind or by technology? Isn't this why Heidegger prefers the word 'thing'?[18] In the face of these complaints, allow me to briefly defend the 'object' part of OOO. I will deal in reverse order with the objections just made, pausing midway to defend the place of objects in Western philosophy more generally.

First, we should say that philosophers frequently modify the traditional terms they inherit from the history of philosophy. Sometimes they give these terms broader meanings than usual, other times more specific ones. For example, I mentioned earlier that I like to use the words 'ontology' and 'metaphysics' as synonyms, seeing little benefit in distinguishing them, but much to gain stylistically from treating them as synonyms. Heidegger does not agree. He uses 'ontology' in a positive way, at least in the early part of his career, but the word 'metaphysics' is one he generally treats with scorn, and even as the root difficulty of all Western civilization. The same holds for his use of 'object' and 'thing'. Heidegger employs the word 'thing' to mean the hidden thing in its own right, beyond any false objectifications of it, while 'object' is its negative inverse: the thing reduced to our perception or use of it. Heidegger is free to do this, of course, though I fail to see why we should follow him in this practice. 'Object' is a perfectly clear and flexible term that ought to be retained. More importantly, my discussion of objects is motivated less by Heidegger than by the Austrian and Polish philosophers immediately preceding him, who use the term 'object' in nearly as broad a sense as OOO: Franz Brentano, Kazimirz Twardowski, Edmund Husserl, and Alexius Meinong.[19]

The second complaint was that 'object' suggests a rock-hard, durable, inanimate entity, and is therefore too narrow a concept to include all of the transient fluxes and flows as well as the short-lived insects, sunrises, and chance collisions that give life so much of its value. My response is that OOO means 'object' in an unusually wide sense: an object is anything that cannot be entirely reduced either to the components of which it is made or to the effects that it has on other things. The first point, about objects being irreducible to their constituent pieces, is an old one for philosophers; the second point is less discussed but equally important. A philosopher such as Heidegger, for instance, would be quick to assert that a hammer is irreducible downward to the atoms and molecules of which it is composed, yet he nonetheless seems to hold that the hammer is reducible *upward* to its current place in the total system of meaningful equipment. For instance, the hammer in Heidegger's eyes is 'serviceable for building a house', and the house in turn to 'useful for providing shelter to humans'.[20] But OOO takes both forms of reduction – upward and downward – to be harmful, and reads the history of Western philosophy as an attempt to break free of this predicament, however slow and stumbling the efforts of past philosophers in this respect.

If someone asks us what something is, we might respond with millions of different sentences in an attempt to answer their question. But ultimately there are just two ways of telling somebody what a thing is: you can tell them what it is made of, or tell them what it does. These are really the only two kinds of *knowledge* that we have about things, and insofar as the human race would wither or perish without large storehouses of knowledge, this might seem to be purely a good thing. The problem is that we humans sometimes convince ourselves that knowledge is the only kind of cognitive activity worth pursuing, and thus we place a high value on knowledge (what a thing is) and practical know-how (what a thing does), while ignoring cognitive activities that do not translate as easily into literal prose terms. Among the exceptions to this reign of knowledge, art comes immediately to mind, since the *primary* role of art is not to communicate knowledge about its subject matter. Philosophy also comes to mind, despite the modern tendency to view it as the cousin of mathematics and natural science. Many people will be willing to accept that art is not a means of conveying knowledge, but fewer will concede the point in the case of philosophy. If philosophy is not a form of knowledge, then what can it possibly be? It is now worth a brief detour to consider this question.

Western philosophy and science began with the so-called 'pre-Socratics', whose intellectual activity began in the 600s BCE. Though ethnically Greek, the first pre-Socratic thinkers were located in Greek colonies on what are now the western coast of Turkey, Sicily, and the southernmost part of the Italian mainland. They were obviously not called pre-Socratics at the time, since Socrates of Athens had not yet been born. Instead they were called the *physikoi*, which can be roughly translated either as 'physicists' or 'those who are concerned with nature'.[21] It all began in Miletus, a once-thriving Aegean port whose ruins (now landlocked due to the silting effect of rivers) can still be visited near present-day Didim, Turkey. Thales of Miletus is known for a number of mental exploits, such as being the first to predict an eclipse of the sun. But his main legacy for philosophy and science can be found in his claim that water is the first principle of everything. This is thought to be the first instance in Western civilization in which the cosmos was explained by appealing to something natural, rather than to the gods or some creation myth. There followed another resident of the city named Anaximenes who held that air rather than water was the primordial element: for air is even more neutral in its features than water, being tasteless, odourless, and transparent to light. But in between Thales and Anaximenes came Anaximander, who adopted a more sophisticated-sounding position by claiming that the primordial root of everything cannot be an element, since all the different physical elements must emerge jointly from some deeper root. For Anaximander, this deeper root was the *apeiron*: a word usually left untranslated in English, but which means something like a shapeless, formless, limitless mass from which everything more specific emerges. As Anaximander saw it, over the course of millions of years all opposites would mutually cancel each other out, and the cosmos would be restored to the formless, neutral *apeiron*, an idea that later inspired Karl Marx as he wrote his doctoral thesis at Jena. Numerous other pre-Socratic thinkers offered their own theories about reality: Pythagoras, Empedocles, Heraclitus, Parmenides, Anaxagoras, Democritus, and more. Yet for all the diversity of their theories, all inclined either towards naming one or more basic elements as the root of the world or agreeing that the shapeless *apeiron* is a better way to account for all the various things that we see.

Now, whether any given pre-Socratic figure prefers to name the most basic element(s) of the world, or whether they prefer instead some version of the *apeiron* theory, all share one thing in common. Namely, all of their theories *undermine* mid-sized everyday objects. None of them think that chairs and horses have the same degree of reality as their chosen ultimate foundations; most objects are simply too shallow to be real. In the terms of the present book, the pre-Socratics are guilty of 'smallism'. In addition, they all tend to think of their chosen ultimate thing as *eternal* or at least as *indestructible*, which remained a typical prejudice in Greek philosophy until Aristotle finally allowed for destructible substances. But the real problem with undermining is that it cannot account for what we have called *emergence*. If you think like Thales of Miletus that everything is made of water, then you cannot possibly think that a lawnmower or the Dutch East India Company remain the same things over time, since these larger objects will be nothing but surface-effects of the deeper motions of water. The same holds if you think that everything is made of atoms (literally: 'uncuttables'), as Leucippus and Democritus did.

It should now be clear that the pre-Socratics were tacitly committed to all four of the basic notions that OOO rejects: physicalism, smallism, anti-fictionalism and literalism. In other words, they were committed to the same attitudes as contemporary attempts at a 'theory of everything' in physics. This is hardly an accident, since the pre-Socratics were of course the *physikoi*, the first natural scientists in the West. But in my view – admittedly a minority view – they were not the first philosophers. This honour I reserve for Socrates, for reasons to be given shortly. Because of the existence of these early thinkers, philosophers sometimes like to boast that philosophy was the parent and science was its child. But I have said that the pre-Socratics were underminers, and natural science has always been a basically undermining enterprise. Therefore, we should reverse the usual claim and say that Western science came first with the pre-Socratics, and that Western philosophy emerged later through Socrates' discovery that undermining is not a tenable method for revealing the nature of virtue, justice, friendship, or anything else. For what Socrates seeks is not a kind of knowledge, since he is interested neither in what virtue, justice and friendship *are made of* nor in what they *do*, though this has often been forgotten. Once again, the original meaning of the Greek word *philosophia* is not knowledge and not wisdom, but the *love* of a wisdom that can never fully be attained.

## Overmining in the History of Philosophy

In the modern period, though undermining remained central to the natural sciences, it decreased in popularity as a method of philosophy. The reason for this is that modern philosophy in the West is less interested in finding the ultimate substance from which everything is built than in starting from whatever *piece of knowledge* has the greatest level of *certainty*, and this means that modern philosophy is primarily concerned with what appears most directly to the human mind rather than what is buried most deeply beneath the world of appearance. One implication is that rather than viewing individual objects as too *shallow* to be the truth, modern philosophy treats them as too *deep*. This rather different way of looking at things needs a name of its own, and in opposition to the undermining technique founded by the pre-Socratic thinkers, I have coined the term 'overmining'.[22] Consider René Descartes, usually regarded as the first modern Western philosopher (though the case has sometimes been made for earlier figures, such as Nicholas of Cusa, Sir Francis Bacon, or even the fabled essayist Michel de Montaigne).[23] For Descartes there are just three kinds of substance in the world: *res extensa* (physical substance), *res cogitans* (thinking substance), and God (the sole infinite substance). With the possible exception of God, these substances are not deeply hidden things, but in principle can be understood perfectly in mathematized form. Physical matter no longer has occult or hidden qualities, but simply a size, a shape, and a position and direction of motion, which means that Descartes killed off or overmined the hidden 'substantial forms' of medieval philosophy: meaning not the forms we see when we look at things, but those which are active deep in the heart of things whether we see them or not. This makes Descartes a revolutionary figure in the history of science as well, since it spelled the end of Aristotelian substance in physics and helped put modern science on a more materialist and less metaphysical basis. Descartes' 'thinking substance' is nothing mysterious either, since with a bit of effort I can look into my mind and grasp the thoughts unfolding there with perfect lucidity. For Descartes, both the world and the self are transparently knowable, and the world is to be remade in the image of our knowledge of it: the most typical feature of modernism in every field. This tendency becomes even clearer in later modern philosophers. The extreme idealist thinker George Berkeley (1685–1753) claims that there are no autonomous things at all, since anything that exists does so only as an image in some mind, whether it be God's or our own.[24] More recently, the important philosophers Alfred North Whitehead (1861–1947) and Bruno Latour (b. 1947) have argued that an entity is nothing more than its relations or effects, so that any notion of an independent object hiding behind its effects is absurd.[25] American pragmatists such as William James (1842–1910) and Charles Sanders Peirce (1839–1914) – whose family name is pronounced 'purse', not 'pierce' – argue along similar lines, claiming that a thing is real only insofar as it makes some *difference* to other things.[26] Edmund Husserl (1859–1938) thought it absurd that an object could exist as anything other than the potential correlate of an observing consciousness.[27] Michel Foucault (1926–1984) holds that there is no way to speak about real independent things hiding behind the social formations of power in which we find ourselves at any moment.[28] And Derrida went as far as to say that 'there is nothing outside the text', however desperately his admirers try to explain away this statement.[29]

In any case, the examples just mentioned are all overmining theories that reduce things to their impact on us or on each other, denying them any excess or surplus beyond such impact. But the problem faced by all overmining theories is their inability to account for *change*. If atoms, billiard balls, watermelons, prisons or Professor Whitehead are nothing more than the sum total of their relations or effects in this very instant, then how is it that they can be doing something very different five minutes or two weeks from now? Aristotle raised this very question in the 300s BCE against his contemporary rivals the Megarian school of philosophy, who held that a thing is only what it is right now, with nothing held in reserve: a house-builder is not a house-builder unless he is building at this very instant.[30] Aristotle addressed this paradox by introducing his now famous idea of 'potentiality' (*dynamis*, the root of our English words 'dynamic' and 'dynamite'), and though there are problems with his notion of potential, his objection to the Megarians still rings true. In our own time, some defenders of overmining models will say that things can change due to mutual 'feedback loops' in which the things affect one another reciprocally. But this argument is self-contradictory, since the ability of a thing to receive and process feedback entails that it is already something more than whatever it is doing right now; receptivity is a form of potentiality, and thus borrows from Aristotle's objection even while claiming to refute it. From these considerations it should be clear that there must be some surplus in things that is both *deeper* than its effects and *shallower* than its constituent pieces. The undermined thing is not the thing itself, and neither is the overmined thing. Nor is the thing *both* what it is made of and what it does in combination, a common strategy that I have called 'duomining'.[31] For example, the natural sciences duomine by speaking of nature simultaneously as made of tiny ultimate constituents (undermining) and as knowable through mathematics (overmining). In this way, independent objects themselves are supposedly erased from the picture as obscure and superfluous.

This brings us to the verge of discussing OOO's unconventional notion of what an object is. In everyday language, the word 'object' often has the connotations of something physical, solid, durable, inhuman or utterly inanimate. In OOO, by contrast, 'object' simply means anything that cannot be reduced either downward or upward, which means anything that has a surplus beyond its constituent pieces and beneath its sum total of effects on the world. Here some examples may prove useful. Imagine that someone asks us how we can know which objects are real and which are not. How can we know, for instance, that the following compound 'object' is not real: the 1755 Lisbon earthquake, plus Dashiell Hammett's detective novel *The Maltese Falcon*, plus a bag of gumdrops, plus the five tallest Japanese passport holders. In fact, we can never know for sure, though this assemblage does not look at first glance like a promising case for reality. Why not? Because it seems to be either an undermined collection of ill-fitted components unlikely to produce anything unified, or an overmined *ad hoc* assemblage that might have a one-time accidental effect in some story or joke, but is not something that could exist outside that story or joke. That said, we can never be entirely sure which objects exist and which are merely the figments of our undermining and overmining techniques. We may never know for sure whether there was really such a thing as 'the conspiracy to assassinate President Kennedy' or 'the Yucatan asteroid that wiped out the dinosaurs' or 'the first baby with one Neanderthal parent and one *Homo sapiens* parent'. There is no direct access to the world that could permanently establish the existence of these objects, or even much simpler variants of them, for the simple reason that *there is no direct knowledge of anything*. This statement is not motivated by some sort of scepticism or hatred of reason, but is derived from Socrates' repeated assertions that he knows nothing and has never been anyone's teacher. The mistake is to think that if Socrates has no knowledge, then the only alternative is that he must be utterly ignorant: a false alternative promoted by his enemies the Sophists, and usually known today as 'Meno's Paradox'.[32]

## Objects and Events

This brings us back to my friend DeLanda's objection that he is 'not sure why Harman wants to stick to objects' while ignoring events, a claim DeLanda has partially revoked in our newly published dialogue.[33] In recent philosophy the term 'event' refers to a highly specific incident, with the frequent implication that the ingredients in an event do not have a strong independent existence outside that event. For example, the case could be made that the Beatles were an 'event', and that it is not really possible to speak of John, Paul, George and Ringo as independent entities preceding the group, given how dramatically their lives were changed by it. But according to the OOO way of looking at things, this is absurd. Instead, each of the four members of the band was an object before joining, and the group as a whole is also an object (one that was able to endure the loss of at least two members prior to the addition of Ringo). The fact that the group can have a powerful retroactive effect on its members does not entail that the members do not pre-exist the 'event' of the Beatles, which is precisely what a OOO opponent like Karen

Barad would say, given her interesting but untenable claim that the terms in a relation do not pre-exist it.[34] More generally, for OOO every real event is also a real object. It hardly matters that every event has a large number of ingredients, since the same holds for every object as well: many things happen in a hurricane, but many things also transpire in an unmoving grain of sand. Nor are events inherently shorter-lived than objects. There are long-lasting physical objects such as pulsars and granite, but also short-lived ones such as mayflies or the artificial elements high on the periodic table; by the same token, there are short-lived events such as a 100-metre dash or two people catching each other's glances, but also long-lasting events such as the reigns of the British monarchs Victoria and Elizabeth II or the stelleriferous era of the universe. For this reason, greater or lesser durability is not a good criterion for sorting things into one pile called 'objects' and another called 'events'.

To repeat, the only necessary criterion for an object in OOO is that it be irreducible in both directions: an object is *more than its pieces* and *less than its effects*. As we have seen, this does not imply that it is always easy to determine whether a given candidate for objecthood meets these criteria. During the 2008 American Presidential campaign, there was much talk of a powerful demographic group called 'soccer moms': suburban women with children, of better than average education, socially liberal but inclined to support a strong national defence. Did John McCain lose the election to Barack Obama due to his failure to win the allegiance of these soccer moms in greater numbers than he did? Can we even be sure that such a group ever existed in any meaningful sense? There is no way to know for sure, just as we can never be entirely sure that our spouse is not a government agent hired to monitor us, as reportedly happened at times in the former East Germany. But we can be reasonably sure that certain beliefs are false, and there are methods that help us sift objects from pseudo-objects with a good degree of conviction: some of them being longstanding familiar methods, others derived more recently from OOO itself.

## Flat Ontology

Before bringing this chapter to a close, it will be useful to introduce the term 'flat ontology'. It was mentioned earlier that ontology is the branch of philosophy that deals with ultimate questions of what reality and real things are. OOO uses this term in the same sense as DeLanda, referring to an ontology that *initially* treats all objects in the same way, rather than assuming in advance that different types of objects require completely different ontologies. Note that modern philosophy (from Descartes in the 1600s through Badiou and Žižek today) is emphatically *not* flat, since it assumes a strict division between human thought on one side and everything else on the other. Along with DeLanda, Levi Bryant has made productive use of flat ontology.[35] The term was used earlier by the British philosopher of science Roy Bhaskar, though with precisely the opposite meaning.[36] Be that as it may, OOO uses 'flat ontology' in DeLanda's sense, as a positive term, though it should also be noted that OOO does not see flat ontology as an absolute good. Briefly put, flat ontology is a good starting point for philosophy but a disappointing finish. For example, earlier in this chapter I argued that philosophy needs to be able to talk about everything – Sherlock Holmes, real humans and animals, chemicals, hallucinations – without prematurely eliminating some of these or impatiently ranking them from more to less real. We might well have biases that make us think that philosophy is obliged only to deal with natural objects but not artificial ones, which we might dismiss as unreal. In this case as in many others, an initial commitment to flat ontology is a useful way of ensuring that we do not cave in to our personal prejudices about what is or is not real. Yet flat ontology would also be a disappointing finish for any philosophy. If we imagine that after fifty years of philosophizing a OOO thinker were to say nothing more than 'humans, animals, inanimate matter and fictional characters all equally exist', then not much progress would have been made. In short, we expect a philosophy to tell us about the features that belong to *everything*, but we also want philosophy to tell us about the differences between various *kinds* of things. It is my view that all modern philosophies are too quick to start with the second task before performing the first in rigorous fashion.

As already mentioned, the chief benefit of flat ontology is to prevent any premature taxonomies from being smuggled into philosophy from the outside. The dominant taxonomy of the Middle Ages, of course, was the absolute difference between the Creator and what is Created. Any philosophy of that period that attempted a 'flat ontology' treating God, humans and animals in the same way would have been on thin ice, conceptually and perhaps even legally. The atheist, rationalist modern philosopher finds it easy today to laugh at the benighted medieval period with its knights, monks, feudal lords and Creator/Created dualism. Yet modern philosophy employs an equally shoddy dualism (not all dualisms are bad, just shoddy ones) by simply introducing a new and equally implausible taxonomy between human thought on one side and *everything else in the universe* on the other. While no one will be imprisoned, tortured or burned alive for claiming the contrary, experience teaches that there are other punishments in store for those who challenge the modern taxonomy. If it strikes you as implausible that human beings – however interesting we may be to ourselves – deserve to fill up a full half of philosophy, then you are already on board with OOO's critique of modern thought. It is true that humans are a remarkable species of living creature. We are able to do astounding things that even plants and animals seem unable to do, let alone inanimate matter. We have launched spacecraft, split the atom, cracked the genetic code: and these are only our most recent feats after previous millennia spent discovering the wheel, brewing, glassmaking, agriculture, using fire, domesticating animals, and developing the earliest techniques of surgery. But all these amazing achievements, even if we assume that animals cannot do anything nearly as complex, and even though we as a species are obviously of special interest to ourselves, do not automatically make human beings worthy of filling up fifty per cent of ontology. This, however, is the verdict of modern philosophy since Descartes and Kant, whose ideas entail that we cannot speak of the world without humans or humans without the world, but only of a primordial correlation or rapport between the two: a notion that

Quentin Meillassoux has justly attacked under the name of 'correlationism'.[37]

Perhaps the most important assault on this modern taxonomy has come from Latour, who defines modernism as the view that there are two permanently distinct kingdoms known as nature and culture, and that the task of modernity is to purify these two domains from each other.[38] According to this model, nature is a realm of ironclad deterministic law in which objective answers are always possible in principle, while culture is a zone of power struggles and arbitrary projections of personal value systems, and never must these two opposed categories be mixed. Latour has tried to replace this 'Modern Constitution', as he calls it, with a flat model in which all actors (whether 'natural' or 'cultural') have the same basic task. All human and non-human actors try to form links with other actors in order to become stronger or more persuasive. This approach is known as actor-network theory (ANT), and it has boomed in the social sciences while remaining mostly despised and rejected in the natural sciences, perhaps because it does favour the social sciences and is not quite as even-handed as it claims to be.[39] Yet the ANT method harbours vast potential in spite of its possible anti-realist flaws, and for this reason OOO thinkers tend to view Latour as one of the most important intellectuals of the past century. However, OOO admires him for reasons different from those for which he is often admired by others. To take just one example, Latourians are often impressed by his point that nature and culture are difficult to separate from each other because in our era so many entities are *hybrids* made up of both human and non-human entities: such as the ozone hole, which is greatly expanded by human activity but lies outside human control in the manner of a natural phenomenon. While this insight into hybrid entities remains valuable, we must avoid the assumption that *all* entities are nature–culture hybrids, since this would assume that both of the two essential modernist ingredients (nature and culture, or world and thought) must be present everywhere and at all times. Instead of hybrids we should speak of *compounds*, which might be made of purely 'natural' entities (such as the carbon and oxygen in a molecule of $CO_2$) or purely 'cultural' ones (like Europe with its mixed Greco-Jewish cultural foundation). To say that 'everything is a hybrid' would be to say that nature and culture are always mixed: an idea that must be rejected, since this preserves the very two terms that Latour meant to abandon.

Having concluded this opening discussion, we are now ready to discuss one of the key features of OOO: the unusually high value it places on aesthetic experience.

# Aesthetics Is the Root of All Philosophy

The previous chapter criticized most 'theories of everything' for displaying four basic defects: physicalism, smallism, anti-fictionalism and literalism. At this point I hope that most readers will agree that a theory of everything should be able to give an account of non-physical entities (the *esprit de corps* of a winning football club) no less than physical ones (atoms of iron). Perhaps most will agree as well that mid- to large-sized entities (horses, radio towers) need to be taken as seriously as the possibly tiniest entities (the strings of string theory). Finally, a good number of readers may also agree that a theory of everything should have something to say about fictional entities (Sherlock Holmes, unicorns) rather than simply eliminating them in favour of a discussion of their underpinnings (process, flux, neurons). Yet I suspect that the fourth point, OOO's critique of literalism, will for many readers be the bridge too far. If we give up the literal meaning of words as our privileged route to truth, then how do we save ourselves from a series of unverifiable mystical claims? At that point, why not just scream nonsense sounds while wearing animal masks in a tragico-absurd dance, as the Dadaists used to do at the Cabaret Voltaire? This is the point where rationalists often draw a line in the sand. Elsewhere

I have quoted the American rationalist philosopher Adrian Johnston on the priority of literal language, and will do so again now, since his position is so admirably clear:

> [N]umerous post-idealists in the nineteenth and twentieth centuries end up promoting a facile mysticism whose basic underlying logic is difficult to distinguish from that of negative theology. The unchanging skeletal template is this: there is a given 'x;' this 'x' cannot be rationally and discursively captured at the level of any categories, concepts, predicates, properties, etc.[1]

Pay special notice to Johnston's assertion that we either 'capture' a thing in terms of literal categories, concepts, predicates and properties, or else we are left with nothing better than 'facile mysticism' and 'negative theology'. The latter refers to a type of religious discourse which tells us that God is so far beyond human understanding that we can only say what He is not, never what He is. Yet there are problems with Johnston's brand of all-or-nothing rationalism. For one thing, 'facile mysticism' is not the true polar opposite of rationalism. For as different as the two obviously are, the mystic generally claims *direct* access to reality just as the rationalist does, even though the mystic claims to arrive there through spiritual means rather than intellectual ones. OOO rejects the priority of both of these methods equally, given our view that *indirect* access to reality is generally the best we have to work with. It should be clear enough that human statements are rarely just positive or negative about what they claim. Many of our statements allude to something in positive fashion without either spelling it out in literal terms *or* denying that any cognition is possible. We find good examples of this even in the negative theology that Johnston so disdains. One of the greatest negative theologians was the 5th–6th century author Pseudo-Dionysius, so called because he/she was originally but wrongly thought to have been Dionysius the Areopagite who appears in the New Testament (Acts 17:34). In the following passage Pseudo-Dionysius is speaking about what many critics view as the weakest link in Christianity, the three-in-one Trinity of Father, Son and Holy Spirit:

> In a house the light from all the lamps is completely interpenetrating, yet each is clearly distinct. There is distinction in unity and unity in distinction. When there are many lamps in a house there is nevertheless a single undifferentiated light and from all of them comes the one undivided brightness.[2]

While I for one do not believe in the Trinity, I nonetheless find this passage marvellous. It makes brilliant use of analogy to convey some sense of how the apparent contradiction of 'three persons in one Divine nature' might be not only possible, but even lucidly conceived. Yet for Johnston there is no room for such analogies, given his behest that we only use categories, concepts, predicates or properties to explain any topic. Metaphor more generally would be excluded from Johnston's intellectual map, though we will soon see that OOO grants it a high philosophical status.

There are numerous other examples in which indirect allusion, hint or innuendo are more powerful than direct access to the truth. For instance, it is widely recognized that a barely clothed body is more erotically charged than a completely naked one: which is why lingerie companies earn a fortune, and why nudist colonies are more of a political statement than an intriguing amorous option. The same holds for love notes and love letters, which can border on clumsy, even boring, if they are made too explicit. Threats are nearly always more effective when kept vague, as with Marlon Brando's catchphrase from *The Godfather*: 'I'm gonna make him an offer he can't refuse.' Why not replace this threat with its literal equivalent? 'If he doesn't give my friend the leading part in the movie, I'm gonna cut off the head of his racehorse and put it in his bed at night while he's sleeping. That will give him a big shock when he wakes up.' While the enactment of this threat in the film is blatantly grotesque and horrifying, it remains less ominous than the vague statement of an 'offer he can't refuse'. In the run-up to the first Persian Gulf War of 1991, there was some loose talk about Saddam Hussein's army using chemical weapons against any invading American forces. In response, Dick Cheney (who was Secretary of Defense at the time) reportedly warned Hussein that if this were to occur, 'the United States would respond promptly and decisively in a manner from which it would take Iraq centuries to recover'. However cruel and inhumane, this threat is certainly more frightening in this vague form than if it were spelled out in detail.

On another front, we can see that humour is almost always ruined by literalization as well. Consider the following, widely circulated riddle:

Q: 'How many surrealists does it take to screw in a light bulb?'
A: 'Fish.'

While reasonably amusing in this form, it is utterly ruined as humour if one is forced to explain its literal meaning, as often happens when children are listening in on adult conversation. Just imagine trying to explain it to a child: 'Surrealist artists put objects in shockingly unexpected contexts. And here they have done it again. What could be a more irrelevant answer than 'fish' when asked how many people are needed to screw in a light bulb? How typical of the surrealists to give such an incongruous reply!' Here the joke is already lost. It is true that such literalization occasionally serves as the very point of a joke, but this is the exception that proves the rule, since it is done only as a foil to the widespread expectation that jokes be other than literal. For example, a popular children's humour book during my childhood asked as follows: 'What's big and red and eats rocks?', with the answer being 'a big red rock eater',[3] beneath the illustration of a fantastic beast meeting this very description.

But perhaps the clearest example of a non-literal form of cognition is metaphor. It has been known for some time that there is no way to make a perfect translation of a metaphor into prose meaning, just as there is no way to depict our three-dimensional planet perfectly on a two-dimensional map. The literary critic Cleanth Brooks argues convincingly that the exact literal meaning of a poem cannot be determined, while the philosopher Max Black performs the same service for individual metaphors.[4]

# Metaphor

Even more important for OOO is an essay on metaphor by the Spanish philosopher José Ortega y Gasset (1883–1955).[5] Ortega is less widely read in the anglophone world than he used to be, perhaps because he was often grouped with Jean-Paul Sartre and the existentialists: a dominant intellectual movement post-World War II, but one whose prestige decreased following the rise of Derrida, Foucault and other French post-modernist thinkers. Yet Ortega has had a profound impact on philosophy in the Spanish-speaking world, and was a dazzling stylist short-listed more than once for the Nobel Prize in Literature. To my mind, his early essay on metaphor is the most important thing he ever wrote; nonetheless, it is rather atypical of his works. For one thing, Ortega composed it at the philosophically tender age of thirty-one, well before the works of his maturity. More importantly still, the philosophical spirit of the piece is rather opposed to that of his career as a whole. Ortega's most famous maxim is probably 'I am myself and my circumstances.' In saying so, he tried to oppose the idealism of modern European philosophy, which treats the thinking mind as an independent substance separate or even alienated from the world, by focusing on the interplay between self and world. Yet by countering idealism with the claim that mind and world are always mutually attached, Ortega loses all ability to account for the autonomy of things. He thereby fails to reap the rewards of a flat ontology able to treat humans and non-humans as standing initially on the same footing; in this way, he accidentally concedes the strange modern assumption that our rather minor human species deserves to occupy a full fifty per cent of ontology. But the essay on metaphor, written as a preface to a 1914 book of poems, takes the opposite tack.[6] Here the young Ortega gives us a neglected masterpiece in the *realist* tradition of philosophy, in which both humans and non-human things are treated not as correlates of each other, but as having equally rich independent lives.[7]

One of the most stirring principles of the ethics of Kant is that we should never treat people – including ourselves – merely as means to an end, but only as ends in themselves.[8] Ortega reminds us of this principle, but also gives it a fresh ontological twist. What Ortega notices, without stating it quite so plainly, is that we can broaden Kant's ethical insight in a way that takes it far beyond the realm of ethics. First, Kant forbids using *someone* only as a means to an end at the same time that he obviously sees nothing wrong with using *non-human objects* only as means to an end. Today there are those who dispute this point as well: the philosopher Alphonso Lingis argues that even inanimate objects demand that we treat them in some particular appropriate way, so that it is somehow ethically wrong to eat expensive chocolate while drinking Coca-Cola, and just as wrong to listen to popular music on headphones during a beautiful snowfall at a temple in Kyoto.[9] For the moment, however, let's agree with Kant that ethics is only about how we treat other people, and that there is no ethical dimension at all to how we treat mere things. The reason Kant views people as free agents having moral worth is because he distinguishes in his philosophy between the visible *phenomena* of our conscious experience and what he calls the *noumena*.[10] The phenomena are just what they sound like: everything that humans are able to encounter, perceive, use or think about. As Kant tells us in his 1781 major work *Critique of Pure Reason*, phenomenal experience for humans always occurs in space and time and in terms of twelve different categories of the understanding.

The noumena, by contrast, are things-in-themselves that we never experience directly, since we remain trapped in the conditions of human experience. Do space and time really exist in themselves? Are they perceived in the same way by God, superior alien races, dolphins, crows, bees and amoebas? Or are they operative only for finite human beings? Kant thinks there is no way this question can ever be answered. It is ironic that despite Kant's still overwhelming influence on philosophy to this day, only a very small number of philosophers accept the central notion of his philosophy: the ungraspable noumena or things-in-themselves; on this point OOO is one of the major exceptions. At any rate, Kant notices that humans have both a phenomenal side *and* a noumenal side. In one sense we are clearly phenomenal: we can witness each other's actions as well as our own, and it may even be possible to give complete causal explanations of each other's actions that make a mockery of any notion of free will. Perhaps I think I am free to the point of being unique and even eccentric: but then one day I read a comprehensive demographic analysis showing that all of my political and lifestyle preferences are simply those of a stereotypical married 49-year-old white American male with a doctoral degree, hailing from the Upper Midwest, and belonging to a certain family income background. A rude awakening indeed! But ethical life is possible only because I also sense a noumenal freedom deep in myself, one through which I can break away and challenge the sometimes groundless dogmas of the groups and situations to which I belong.

Now, in ethical terms Kant holds this 'noumenal' dimension to be important only for humans, since our actions have moral worth in a way that the actions of bacteria or plastic bags do not. Yet once we move outside ethics, it becomes immediately clear that all objects have a noumenal side as well. We do not have direct access to plastic-bags-in-themselves any more than we do to human-beings-in-themselves; in both cases we only encounter these things phenomenally, not noumenally. Usually the noumena are ignored in all cases other than ethics: after all, why waste time talking about things-in-themselves that lie beyond all human access? Ortega's great innovation in the metaphor essay is to show that the things-in-themselves are of crucial importance for the arts. This is something that Kant's own philosophy of art never really attempted, since Kant was obsessed with the universal structure of human taste, and was less interested in the structure of art objects themselves.[11]

Ortega notes that most of the time we encounter objects from the outside, in third-person perceptions or descriptions. In Kantian terms these experiences are obviously phenomenal, and do not plumb the depths of the things themselves. In Ortega's words: 'there is nothing we can make an object of cognition, nothing that can exist for us unless it becomes an image, a concept, an idea – unless, that is, it stops being what it is in order to become a shadow or an outline of itself.'[12] Our initial reaction might be to turn from these third-person experiences to the *first*-person kind, seeking refuge in the direct truths of inner life. Yet this is not really possible, since in introspection we also reduce *ourselves* to shadows or outlines: after all, there is no direct access to the noumenal self any more than to a noumenal house, dog or horse. Although there are still colossal battles under way in the philosophy of mind between whether first-person or third-person descriptions should have priority, Ortega in 1914 already predicts the futility of this dispute. Neither the first-person nor the third-person standpoint gets us any closer to the *true* inwardness of things beyond all description: what Ortega seeks instead is something I once called the 'zero-person' aspect of things, meaning their reality apart from any observation or introspection.[13] In the course of his argument, Ortega gains the important insight that each of us is an 'I' not because we each have a special zoological apparatus called 'consciousness', but because each of us *is* something, and that something can never be exhausted by conscious introspection any more than by outward description. It follows that every non-human object can also be called an 'I' in the sense of having a definite inwardness that can never fully be grasped. For even if we say that 'this red leather box that I have before me is not an "I" because it is only an image I have', the box is not only something phenomenal for me.[14] As Ortega puts it, in a truly radical passage:

There is the same difference between a pain that someone tells me about and a pain that I feel as there is between the red that I see and the being red of this red leather box. *Being red* is for it what hurting is for me. Just as there is an I-John Doe, there is also an I-red, an I-water, and an I-star. Everything, from a point of view within itself, is an I.[15]

But what is so important about this inward 'I' of everything if it is merely noumenal and we can never reach it? Are we left with the same 'facile mysticism' and 'negative theology' against which Johnston warned us? Ortega answers in the negative:

> Now then, imagine the importance of a language or system of expressive signs whose function was not to tell us about things but to present them to us in the act of executing themselves. Art is just such a language; this is what art does. The esthetic object is inwardness as such – it is each thing as 'I'.[16]

This is a powerful claim. Ortega is effectively saying that Kant's noumenal realm *is not* inaccessible, but that art consists precisely in giving us this noumenal realm in person. Yet he adds an important qualification: 'Notice I am not saying that a work of art reveals the secret of life and being to us; what I do say is that a work of art affords the peculiar pleasure we call esthetic by making it *seem* that the inwardness of things, their executant reality, is opened to us.'[17] He goes on to compare scientific discourse unfavourably to this aesthetic contact with inward, executant realities, though his real target is not so much science as what we have called *literalism*.

I dwell at length on this essay not only for its intrinsic interest, but because it first planted the seed of OOO in my mind at an age when I had not yet read the more famous Heidegger. On perhaps two or three occasions in a lifetime, we read something that strikes us as not just powerful and intriguing, but as harbouring a crucial paradox that contains the secret to so much else if only we could make sense of its riddle. Ortega's metaphor essay was my first such experience in philosophy, and it took no less than eighteen years of reflection to understand its implications fully. Having established why Ortega thinks aesthetics is so important, we must now look briefly at how he thinks it works, for here I believe he falls prey to a subtle but crucial error.

Since Ortega is unable to give a complete aesthetic theory in a preface to a book of poetry, he chooses *metaphor* as the topic most central to this theme: 'I say the esthetic object and the metaphorical object are the same, or rather that metaphor is the elementary esthetic object, the beautiful cell.'[18] He takes as his example a metaphor from a Spanish poet named López Pico: 'the cypress is like the ghost of a dead flame'. Since there are actually three metaphors here, Ortega discards 'ghost' and 'dead' and focuses only on the likening of the cypress to a flame. How does this metaphor work? The first thing that comes to mind is some similarity of shape between the two objects, which holds them together in a way that would not happen as easily with an example such as 'a cypress is like the ghost of a dead insurance salesman'. According to Ortega, this necessary grain of likeness in the heart of metaphor has led many theorists to wrongly see metaphor as an assimilation of real qualities between two things. He sees correctly that this is untrue: 'metaphor satisfies us precisely because in it we find a coincidence between two things that is more profound and decisive than any mere resemblance.'[19] If someone says 'a cypress is like a juniper', this may be useful botanical information about the resemblance of two species of trees, but no one would experience it *aesthetically* unless we restored the other metaphors and said 'a cypress is like the ghost of a dead juniper', which again sounds like poetry. In order for the metaphor to work, the literal basis of comparison between the two terms cannot be very important, or we will merely have a literal statement: 'Amsterdam is like Venice', 'a plantain is like a banana', or 'a hare is like a rabbit'. The reason Ortega's chosen example does work as a metaphor is because 'the similarity of linear outline in cypress and flame is so extrinsic, so insignificant with respect to each component, that we do not hesitate to call it a pretext.'[20] Once this is done, 'on the basis of their inessential identity, we assert an absolute identity. Yet this is absurd, impossible.'[21] The two objects initially repel one another. As a result, we have 'the annihilation of what [cypress and flame] are as practical images. When they collide with one another their hard carapaces crack and the internal matter, in a molten state, acquires the softness of plasm, ready to receive a new form and structure.'[22] In the case of a successful metaphor, we are able to experience a new entity that somehow combines cypress and flame.

# What Ortega's Essay Teaches Us

Though I have recommended Ortega's essay to many acquaintances over the years, some have seen nothing of interest in it whatsoever, and have thanked me for the recommendation with little more than perfunctory politeness. For my part, I find it to be one of the most important philosophical essays ever written, and crucial for ontology no less than aesthetics. What lessons does OOO draw from this forgotten classic forerunner from long-ago 1914? First, Ortega brings Kant's noumena out of the philosophical wilderness and makes them relevant again. Second, he does this by showing that we have access to noumena in a manner that is not merely facile or negative. Third, he establishes the basic mechanism of metaphor as an inessential likeness that serves to fuse two vastly dissimilar entities into an impossible new one. But there are two crucial points where Ortega comes up short; I say this not as a critic, but as someone who spent years of fascination with this essay before clearly understanding it. The first point, which Ortega gets exactly wrong, can be called the *asymmetry* of metaphor. The second, on which he is correct but only goes halfway to the goal, can be called the *theatricality* of metaphor.

We begin with the topic of asymmetry. Ortega's mistake comes in the following sentence, which details the fusion of the cypress and the flame: 'we are to see the image of a cypress through the image of a flame; we *see it as* a flame, and vice versa.'[23] But why 'vice versa'? Here he is too hasty, and fails to think through the consequences of his claim. For if

there were really a 'vice versa' between the cypress and the
flame in the metaphor, then we ought to be able to flip the
order of the metaphor without this leading to any change.
Here is the original metaphor: 'a cypress is like the ghost of
a dead flame'. And here is its inversion: 'a flame is like the
ghost of a dead cypress'. Though the second example also
works as poetry, the metaphor is clearly different. In the first
case the metaphorical object is a cypress with flame-qualities;
in the second, it is a flame with cypress-qualities. Hence the
assumption of a 'vice versa' at work in metaphor is a fatal
error. What does Ortega lose by missing out on the asymmetry between cypress and flame in his example? He misses
one of the pillars of OOO: the deep divide or tension between
an *object* and its *qualities*. As we will see later in this chapter,
the difference between an object and its own qualities is
something that comes to the forefront in many situations,
but especially in art and philosophy. For under most circumstances, we do not distinguish between an object and its
qualities. In science, for instance, the *whole point* is to replace
a proper name like 'RX J185635-3754' (a real neutron star
in the constellation Corona Australis) with a more tangible
list of definite properties of this object. As long as one has
only the proper name, one has little to offer. But the more
you do your job as a scientist, the more you are able to
replace the vague, place-holding name of this neutron star
with the fruit of definite qualities proven to belong to it: such
as being roughly 400 light years from Earth, and having a
diameter of somewhere between 4 and 8 kilometres and a
surface temperature of around 434,000 degrees Celsius. We
saw earlier that the search for knowledge is a *literalist*

enterprise that identifies an object with all of the components and effects that truly belong to it, and also noted that OOO rejects this literalism while denying that either art or philosophy are forms of knowledge. There are numerous philosophers today who try to make philosophy a literalist discipline in much the same way as mathematics or natural science, a process that has been under way throughout the four centuries of modernism. Although Hume – for example – is known as a sceptic, he actually defines objects in a way that reduces them to the correlates of possible knowledge: there is no such thing as an 'apple', but only a number of palpable qualities such as red, hard, juicy, sweet and cold, all of which seem to appear together so often that we loosely refer to this 'bundle of qualities' as an 'apple', even though there is supposedly no apple apart from all its qualities.[24]

This bundle-theory of objects, which is simply taken for granted in philosophy more often than one would expect, was first abandoned by the philosophical school known as phenomenology, founded by Husserl in 1900.[25] Husserl's line of reasoning was powerful and of lasting importance, and owes much to the initial efforts of the Polish philosopher Twardowski.[26] Husserl shows that conscious experience is not primarily about its *contents*, but about its *objects*. If I turn an apple in my hand, then toss and catch it repeatedly, I see a constantly shifting parade of different qualities. But never do I think to myself that it is a different thing each time its qualities change. Nor do I ever say or think: 'This bundle of applish qualities is 87 per cent similar to what I was seeing three seconds ago, and therefore I conclude that the family resemblances between them are sufficient to refer to all of

these images loosely as "the same apple".' In fact, as phenomenology has seen, the vaunted 'bundle of qualities' is
really just a bundle of shifting accidental appearances. The
apple itself remains the same throughout all my varying
efforts to spin and toss it.

In this respect, Ortega merely ratifies the important distinction between objects and qualities found in Husserl,
whom he admired with certain qualifications. Yet there is a
crucial difference between them, and here I must side with
the Spaniard. Unlike Ortega, who spent ten early years as an
adherent of neo-Kantian philosophy, Husserl has no patience
at all for Kant's noumena. For the mathematically trained
Husserl, it is absurd to think that there could be objects that
are not, in principle, the correlate of some consciousness
that observes them. Husserl would thus have no use for the
following passage in Ortega, which I quoted earlier in an
admiring spirit: 'Just as there is an I-John Doe, there is also
an I-red, an I-water, and an I-star. Everything, from a point of
view within itself, is an I.'[27] For Husserl there is certainly an
'I-John Doe', but only because John Doe is a thinking mind.
As for the red, the water and the star, their only role is to be
objects for the consciousness of John Doe and his fellows,
and to say otherwise would mark a slip into the controversial
'panpsychist' view that even inanimate objects can feel and
think. Of course, Ortega does not wish to claim that inanimate objects can feel and think. Rather, he anticipates and
refutes this objection in advance by saying that an object is
an 'I' not because it is conscious, but simply because it *is*. In
any case, Husserl's distinction between the object and its
qualities, such a crucial blow against Hume's bundle-theory,

belongs solely on the level of what Ortega calls *images*. Why so? Because for Husserl, if a thing is observed lucidly enough, we can eventually gain a direct vision of its essential features. This is no mystical claim, but a thoroughly rationalist one: Husserl is simply telling us that there is no impenetrable inwardness of things, since the proper intellectual attitude can give us their inwardness *directly*. The opposite holds for Ortega, just as for Heidegger, the quasi-rival to whom he is sometimes compared. For Ortega, any sort of looking at things *or* use of them automatically turns them into mere shadows and outlines of themselves. Aesthetics is so important for him precisely because neither theoretical nor practical work can ever give us the inwardness of things. In short, the Kantian notion of the concealed noumena is still active in Ortega and Heidegger, despite Husserl's intervening attempt to kill it off completely.

As a result, Husserl and Ortega actually give us two entirely different discoveries when it comes to objects and their qualities. The terminology of Ortega's essay distinguishes between the *images* of things as seen or used from the outside, and the *executant* reality of things in their own right, quite apart from how they are seen or used. But let's use instead the later terminology of OOO, which has roughly the same meaning as Ortega's own words. When speaking of objects in their own right, let's speak of *real* objects. But when speaking instead of the realm in which objects have no inwardness but are nothing more than correlates of our experience, let's speak of *sensual* objects. Consider the example of a snowmobile. What Husserl gives us is the new insight that the snowmobile is not just a bundle of snowmobile-qualities, but an enduring object that is different from the relatively small array of profiles or features that it shows in any given moment or any sum of moments. We see the snowmobile from one side or another, at a greater or lesser distance, speeding towards us or away from us, standing motionless or spinning wildly in a dangerous jump over a perilous crevice. In all of these cases, we consider the snowmobile to be the *same* thing, unless something happens to suggest that we have misidentified or confused it with a similar vehicle. In OOO terminology, Husserl splits the *sensual object* snowmobile from the *sensual qualities* of the snowmobile, since the former does not change but the latter change constantly.

Ortega's insight is different, and resembles Heidegger's own conclusions from his famous tool-analysis.[28] For Ortega, Husserl's sensual snowmobile-object is a mere image, a shadow that does not capture the inwardness of the snowmobile's 'I' – which, remember, has nothing to do with any supposed possession of 'consciousness' by the vehicle. Ortega would claim that Husserl has left out the true inwardness of the snowmobile, which is something that only aesthetics can give us. A similar argument is made by Heidegger in his famous essay on art, though in my view it is less intellectually powerful than Ortega's piece.[29] Whereas Husserl allows us to distinguish between the *sensual object* snowmobile and its *sensual qualities*, Ortega gives us a different distinction (or would have, if he had not missed the asymmetry of metaphor) between the *real object* 'snowmobile' and its sensual qualities. The reason the qualities are still sensual in Ortega's case rather than real is because while the object

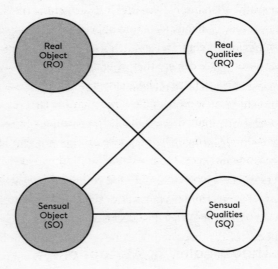

**Figure 1 — The Quadruple Object**

There are two kinds of objects and two kinds of qualities: real and sensual, in both cases. Real objects and qualities exist in their own right, while sensual objects and qualities exist only as the correlate of some real object, whether human or otherwise. Since objects cannot exist without qualities and vice versa, there are only four possible combinations, indicated by the four lines between the circles above.

'cypress' in the metaphor is deeper and more mysterious than can be summarized by listing flame-qualities, these flame-qualities are by no means hidden from the one who experiences the metaphor. We know what they are, even if sub-verbally, and simply have difficulty attaching them to a cypress. It may be handy if we now abbreviate the four terms real, sensual, objects and qualities by their first letters. Having done so, we can say that whereas Husserl discovered an SO–SQ tension, Ortega and Heidegger give us a new RO–SQ rift. This will soon become important for two reasons. First, OOO will argue that SO–SQ is the meaning of *time* and RO–SQ the meaning of *space* (more on this in Chapter 4.) And second, it suggests that we need to find names for the still undiscussed tensions of SO–RQ and RO–RQ, which are not as famous as time and space, but which find an important place in OOO's theory of objects.

## The Theatricality of Metaphor

Earlier, I said that Ortega completely missed the asymmetry of metaphor but got the theatricality of metaphor half-right. Unlike the first point, this one took me not eighteen, but *twenty-eight* years to understand! A brief discussion is in order, since theatricality will soon become important for us as well. We begin by revisiting a sentence from Ortega quoted above: 'Notice I am not saying that a work of art reveals the secret of life and being to us; what I do say is that a work of art affords the peculiar pleasure we call esthetic by making it *seem* that the inwardness of things, their executant reality, is opened to us.'[30] It is easy to grasp why Ortega hedges his bets with the word 'seem'. The noumenal inward-ness of the thing is, by definition, completely unavailable in its inwardness, and Ortega's essay is fully committed to this inscrutability of the things-in-themselves. Nonetheless, he also wants to claim that art has a special way of touching executant reality. But the word 'seem' is disappointing here, since one could think of many other ways to *seem* to grasp the thing-in-itself: simply taking a photograph might suffice, if seeming were all that mattered. So, along with Ortega we face the apparently impossible task of preserving the inaccess-ibility of the things-in-themselves while also defending the claim of art to make contact with the executant inwardness of these things: a touching without touching, so to speak.

Since Ortega led us to the formulation that art is an object–quality tension of the type RO–SQ (real objects–sensual qualities), we have the problem of knowing exactly what plays the role of RO in the metaphor 'the cypress is a flame'. By definition, the cypress in the metaphor is not the cypress of everyday experience, but the cypress in its execu-tant inwardness: the inaccessible cypress-in-itself. But this cypress *en soi* cannot be present in metaphor any more than it can be in thought or perception. Not even the vastest army of beautiful metaphors could exhaustively allude to the cypress in its inwardness. Nonetheless, since objects and qualities always come together for OOO, the metaphor only works because the flame-qualities somehow become fused with an *object*, not just with an inscrutable void where the cypress used to be. This leaves us with only one option, which we must embrace even if the consequences initially seem bizarre. For if the real cypress is just as absent from the metaphor as it is from thought and perception, there is none-theless one real object that is never absent from our experience of art: namely, *we ourselves*. Yes, it is we ourselves who stand in for the absent cypress and support its freshly anointed flame-qualities. This goes a long way towards explaining the greater forcefulness and sincerity of genuine aesthetic experience compared with even the greatest precision of discursive prose scientific statements. In genuine aesthetic experience – which means simply the kind that does not bore us – we are not just observers, but place our chips on the casino table: or rather, we place *ourselves* on that table. Ortega already showed that prose statements cannot dig down into the true inwardness of things, since prose statements work by trying to attribute true qualities to things, and since things *are not* bundles of qualities this will always have something of the superficial approximation about it. And while we may have expected Ortega to say that metaphor can do this where prose statements fail, he conceded that metaphor only 'seems' to succeed in this effort. Yet this turns out to be no great obstacle, because metaphor uses a different method than digging downward to the things themselves. Instead, it replaces the absent cypress with *us ourselves* as the real object that embraces the qualities of the flame: not digging downward but *building upward* to a higher layer. However strange this may sound, there is one professional realm where it is already a commonplace: the craft of acting, where Konstantin Stanislavski's famous system insists that one try to *become* the object one portrays as nearly as possible.[31] This theatrical structure of metaphor strongly suggests that theatre lies at the root of the other arts. For this

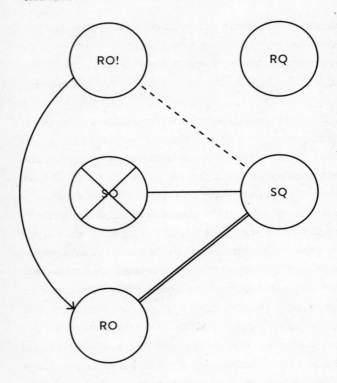

**Figure 2 — Metaphor**

In this diagram we initially have the normal case of a sensual object with its sensual qualities. By assigning improbable but not impossible new sensual qualities to the sensual object – such as the metaphorical 'wine-dark sea' rather than the literal 'dark blue sea' – the sensual object 'sea' is cancelled (hence the crossing out of SO above), being unable to uphold such unusual qualities. A mysterious real object is needed to do the job. But since sea as *real* object withdraws inaccessibly from the scene (hence the exclamation point! on the uppermost RO above), the sensual qualities of the metaphor are supported instead by the only RO that is not withdrawn from the situation: I myself, a real experiencer of the metaphor.

reason I would go so far as to hazard a guess that the *mask* was the original artwork, though the fragility of mask materials – so different from the durability of cave paintings and jewellery – ensured their disintegration and the resulting lack of evidence.

Though Ortega did not push forward far enough to see this theatrical kernel of the arts, he did come close to recognizing that we ourselves, rather than the cypress, are the real objects at stake in aesthetics. As he puts it, in a wonderfully subtle observation: 'Every objective image, on entering or leaving our consciousness, produces a subjective reaction – just as a bird that lights on or leaves a branch starts it trembling, or turning on and off an electric current instantly produces a new current.'[32] In other words, even though every image we encounter gives us just an outline or shadow of the inwardness of the thing itself, I myself am fully invested in all these experiences, and *inwardly* invested rather than as just a shadow or outline of myself. I myself am the sole real object in all experience, encountering any number of sensual things, though the tension between these real and sensual poles becomes explicit only in art and a limited number of other cases. Ortega continues the theme a bit later, saying that in art we find 'the subordination of the part of the image which looks towards the object to that part which is subjective, felt, or part of an "I" . . .'[33] It would be more accurate, however, to say that in art the part of the image which looks towards the object is subordinated to our efforts, as basically thespian beings, to become the new object generated by the metaphor.

# Five Features of Metaphor

What have we learned from this lengthy discussion of metaphor, which normally plays a fringe role (if any) in philosophical discussion? I count five lessons so far:

First, metaphor does not try to give us thoughts or perceptions about an object, since these would merely give us an external view of the thing in question. What metaphor gives us, instead, is something like the thing in its own right: the infamous thing-in-itself.

Second, metaphors are non-reciprocal, since one of the two terms is inevitably in the subject position and the other in the object position (in the grammatical sense of subject and object). It is worth stressing the point with a further example. The first page of Ernest Hemingway's *The Old Man and the Sea* introduces the fisherman Santiago, who has gone eighty-four days without catching a fish. We read the following mournful description of the sail on the old man's boat: 'The sail was patched with flour sacks and, furled, it looked like the flag of permanent defeat.'[34] But let's imagine that we are reading, instead, a dystopian novel that begins with the melancholic scene of Washington, DC sacked and conquered by an ignorant, violent, and philistine horde. The author depicts the tattered banner atop the White House – now a literal sign of permanent defeat – by saying: 'It was patched with duct tape and, furled, it looked like the flag of a decrepit, elderly fisherman.' Both metaphors work fairly well, but they are obviously not the same.

Third, metaphors are asymmetrical, a point related to the

previous one without being identical to it. In the stripped-down example of 'the cypress is a flame', we do not have a case of two objects on an equal footing, or even of two bundles of qualities on equal footing. Instead, 'cypress' plays the object role and 'flame' the qualities role. This is crucial, since for OOO the real object always withdraws from direct access. This means that the cypress disappears, and hence we would have an impossible case of disembodied flame-qualities floating in literary space with no object, if not for the next point on our list.

Fourth, given that the cypress is absent and unavailable for metaphorical purpose (despite surface appearances to the contrary), the only object prepared for duty is the real object that each of us is him- or herself. If I do not step in and attempt the electrifying work of becoming the cypress-substance for the flame-qualities, then no metaphor occurs. That might happen for any number of reasons, including the poor quality of the metaphor, the obtuseness of the reader, or even the boredom or distractedness of the reader. The successful metaphor, much like the successful joke, will occur only when the reader or auditor is sincerely deployed in living it. The metaphor is not *histrionic*, a word we can reserve for theatrical behaviour in the narrowly showboating or attention-getting sense. Instead, the metaphor is theatrical in the same sense in which living one's role on stage is theatrical. When reading the poem by López Pico, we are method actors playing a cypress playing a flame.

Fifth and finally, metaphor is an act of coupling rather than uncoupling. That is to say, the experience of metaphor is not cool or distant as the experience of knowledge is often said to be. I gain no more direct access to the cypress-in-itself from metaphor than I do from botany. I do not dig beneath my shallow everyday experiences in order to gain the truth of the cypress, which is precisely what *undermining* claims to do. The metaphor is no exercise in undermining, since in it we *attach* ourselves to the cypress more than ever, instead of claiming to wipe away those of its aspects that were 'added by the mind' and thereby give the cypress a distance from us. But now that the danger of undermining has been avoided, the attachment between me and the cypress might simply look like the opposite vice of *overmining*. For are we not simply saying that the cypress itself must be left out of the picture, so that we are now dealing only with the image of a cypress plus my sincere involvement in taking notice of it? Is this not what Meillassoux condemned as 'correlationism', a type of philosophy that remains stuck in the rut of meditating on human-world interaction, with nothing to tell us about humans or world as they are in their own right? No, neither of these objections is pertinent. All we are saying is that the real object at stake in metaphor is neither the absent cypress-object to which we never gain direct access, nor the human being who takes note of it, but rather the new amalgamated reality formed from the reader (who poses as a cypress-object) and the qualities of the flame. These are the two components of the cypress-flame. The proper term for this new sort of Frankensteinian entity would not be correlate, but *compound*. And here again we depart from the dreary anthropocentrism of modern philosophy, since innumerable compounds exist without having a human component. The metaphor that brings cypress together with flame is not knowledge about pre-existing objects, but the production of a new object.

Having summarized these points, which will not be forgotten in what follows, we are prepared to tackle other, related themes. We begin with the notion of 'formalism' in aesthetics, which generally means the view that art has an internal reality uncontaminated by its socio-political context or the biography of the artist. This focus on the non-relational autonomy of art seems to make OOO a natural adherent of formalism, as expressed in Claire Colebrook's worry that OOO will simply continue formalist business as usual in literary criticism.[35] But we will see that of the five key lessons of metaphor just cited above, only the first is compatible with aesthetic formalism. Lessons two through five would not be accepted by any formalist, and insofar as OOO adheres to them it cannot defend the formalist agenda.

## Formalism in Aesthetics

It might be wondered what the point is of giving priority to metaphorical statements over literal ones. Aristotle, the most encyclopedic mind of his age and perhaps every age, tells us that the talent for creating metaphor is the greatest gift.[36] But Aristotle's writings date to the fourth century BCE, and it may be said that we have now advanced far beyond his ideas. Is it not the case that the progress of human civilization depends on actual *knowledge*, not on a mere decorative art such as poetry? These sorts of arguments have also been used against Heidegger, a great twentieth-century philosopher who gives priority to poetic language for what he sees as its supreme profundity, and who states provocatively – though wrongly – that 'science does not think'.[37] In fact, *every* philosophical position leaves new problems in its wake, and one of the problems facing OOO is undoubtedly whether it does justice to literal knowledge, a question we will consider in Chapter 4. But let's not forget why we were driven into this predicament in the first place. Literalism is not only flawed in aesthetics, where it fails immediately in spectacular fashion: no one can tell us the literal meaning of *Hamlet* or of Edgar Allan Poe's haunting poem 'Ulalume', just as no one can translate the curved three-dimensional Russia into a perfect two-dimensional map of that country. Literalism holds that a thing can be exhausted by a hypothetical perfect description of that thing, whether in prose or in mathematical formalization. This view entails that a perfect description of the thing is 'isomorphic' with the thing itself, meaning that they have the same form. And given that almost no one thinks that, say, the perfect mathematical model of an eagle is the same thing as a real eagle, defenders of literalism are forced to have recourse to the concept of 'dead matter'. The difference between the mathematical eagle and the real one, they must tacitly or openly hold, is simply that the real eagle 'inheres in matter' while the former has been extracted from all matter – even though no one has any idea what formless matter would be. The same collection of qualities is present in both cases. But we have already seen that there are good philosophical reasons developed by Husserl, Ortega and Heidegger to doubt that objects can be deemed nothing but a collection of qualities. In fact, there is always a deep wedge between objects and their qualities, and indeed this principle is the cornerstone of OOO method in every field it has entered.

Another way to put it is to say that bundle-theories of objects are all foreground and no background. A literal statement tells you exactly what it means, neither more nor less. This is often seen as the cardinal virtue of clear propositional language, protecting it from the vague and dreamy statements of artists and con artists alike. In our time, entire branches of philosophy are obsessed with debunking the 'nonsense' or 'fuzziness' of those who speak evasively rather than directly and verifiably. Yet there is a long intellectual tradition that is fully aware of the import- ance of the unnoticed and even unfathomable background of things: a tradition perhaps culminating in Heidegger, who asks about the meaning of being beyond all visible individual beings.[38] Aristotle himself contributes a great deal to this shadow tradition, in ways that are often concealed by his opposite face as the father of Western logic. We have already mentioned Aristotle's insight in the *Metaphysics* that an indi- vidual thing cannot be defined, since a definition deals with knowable universal terms (such as 'pale', 'skinny' or 'animal'). By contrast, an individual thing is always concrete, meaning that it is never quite exhausted by a description such as 'pale skinny animal'. Just as important is his now seldom-read classic *The Art of Rhetoric*, an ancient masterpiece whose status has declined with the shallow reinterpretation of rhetoric in our time as 'mere rhetoric', treated as if it were the very opposite of a legitimate intellectual pursuit.[39] The central topic of Aristotle's work is the 'enthymeme', which means a syllogism that is in the listener's heart without the orator needing to state it explicitly. It turns out that human communication is filled to the brim with enthymemes: with things that it would be either tedious or ill-advised to state openly and literally, as with Brando's 'offer he can't refuse' or Cheney's monstrous threat to Iraq. Aristotle notes that if an orator in ancient Greece says 'this man has been crowned three times with laurel', it is not necessary to add 'because he has won three times at the Olympic games', since any Greek listener would grasp this implication immediately, and to spell it out would only be tedious or annoying. In the twentieth century, the Canadian media theorist Marshall McLuhan (long underrated in Britain) built his life's work on the notion that the background structure of technologies is more profound and important than their surface content, which is precisely what he means by his famous slogan 'the medium is the message'.[40] And as we will see shortly, the American art critic Clement Greenberg gave an influential interpretation of modernist painting that emphasized the flat canvas background in painting, while dismissing pictorial content as nothing but 'literary anecdote'.[41]

There are some obvious pedagogical implications to be drawn from OOO's distrust of literalism. History frequently shows reversals that occur over imperceptibly long spans of time. Universities were once dominated by the humanities, in a time when the sciences – and especially the applied sciences – were regarded as lesser pursuits. Today we have nearly reached the opposite extreme, in which engineering, medicine and the hard sciences are the intellectual royalty, while the humanities are widely seen as 'soft' subjects good only for those who wish to avoid greater educational rigour. As apparent dead ends in career terms (despite frequent articles to the effect that 'employers actually prefer philosophy graduates') the humanities in our time are always on the verge of major budget cuts. Sometimes successful courses are even closed outright. But if literalism is inherently flawed, as OOO suggests, then knowledge production cannot be the sole or even primary purpose of education. It will be crucial to educate students for *taste* more than currently happens: not just in order to detect 'flamboyant and velvety Pinots', but so as to become connoisseurs of the subtle background rather than the literal foreground of any situation.

But let's return to the main point of this chapter. Ortega claimed that the metaphor *seems* to give us the things themselves, rather than their pale reflection as found in perception and literal language. He called this merely a 'seeming' because we obviously cannot reach the flame-in-itself or cypress-in-itself through art any more than through science or everyday experience. We concluded that the true dose of reality in art comes from the spectator's own replacement of the metaphorical *object* (cypress), and consequent alliance with the metaphorical *qualities* (flame-qualities). This led us directly to the notion of art as primarily theatrical in nature, since the spectator in art necessarily becomes a sort of 'method actor'. But the key to Ortega's account of metaphor is its *realism*. It seeks the reality of the thing apart from its relation to the one who perceives or speaks it. The literal meaning of a thing is its meaning as exhaustively unfolded for the hearer or viewer, without surplus or residue beyond what they explicitly see of it. The aspiration of a literal statement is apparently to tell us everything known and knowable about a given thing, without any lingering unstated background, which means the thing in its *relation* to an ideal knower of that thing. By contrast, the metaphor seems to give us the thing in its autonomy from the other things to which it relates. And we have already said that in the arts, this notion that artworks should be treated as independent realities apart from any of their conditions, relations, or effects, is usually called *formalism*.[42]

## Formalism in Kant and Beyond

The roots of aesthetic formalism can be found in the philosophy of Kant. But since he only uses that term explicitly in his ethics, we should begin briefly there. Kant's primary ethical insight is that an act is only ethical if it is done for its own sake, not in order to gain some reward.[43] If I am honest only because I want others to like me, or because I plan to seek political office in later life and wish to keep my trail clean, this is not ethics but merely a means to an end. Likewise, if I tell the truth solely from fear of Almighty God in the afterlife, such behaviour on my part may be useful to society, but it cannot count as ethical if it is guided by my hopes and fears for the ultimate fate of my soul. Neither is my conduct ethical if it is performed simply out of warmth towards my fellow humans or my wonderful surplus of enthusiasm for the welfare of our species. Kant even makes a hypothetical comparison between a friendly creature of this sort and a flinty businessman who helps others only because it is right to do so while taking no pleasure in the act, and we may be startled to learn that Kant rates the latter person as more ethical than the former. He formulates the principle of his ethics in several different ways, but perhaps the easiest to remember is that ethics for Kant is a matter of duty, not of inclination. One of the things this entails is that the consequences of an action play no role in judging whether or not it was ethical. In principle, a lie cannot be justified by the fact that it happens to save ten busloads of refugees from the death squads at the border. What formalism really means in Kantian ethics is an ethical purification that separates humans from the world. Ethics plays out entirely on the side of a human being's commitment to duty, to treating others as ends in themselves rather than solely as means, and in the end the world and its objects play no genuine ethical role.

We have already discussed Latour's critique of modernity, which rejects modernism for always wanting to quarantine humans in one place and inanimate nature in another, with no impure contact permitted between the two. The greatest critic of this aspect of Kantian ethics was surely the colourful German philosopher Max Scheler (1874–1928), who spent the better part of his career developing a non-formal ethics in which our passion for the things in the world plays a crucial role.[44] Among other things, Scheler is attentive to the varying ethical vocations found in different human beings. Although he admiringly salutes what he calls the sublime and empty coldness of Kant's ethical universe, Scheler notes the highly specific ethical codes that belong only to certain people, professions or nations. For our purposes, the upshot of Scheler's insight is as follows: though formalism must be admired for its refusal to contaminate ethics with ulterior rewards and purposes, it is wrong to assume that ethics unfolds in the cavern of human being alone. The basic ethical unit is not a human being, but a human being *plus* whatever that human being takes seriously; a soul floating in empty space could not possibly be ethical or unethical. Just as metaphor results in a compound entity made up of me the reader and the qualities of the flame that is still an autonomous ethical experience unrelated to its socio-political meaning, ethics is a compound made up of me and those entities in which I take an interest: French opera, German Idealism, car engines, archery, high-risk parachute sports and gardening. The stress on autonomy found in formalism is still here, because Scheler interprets love or passion as an end in itself, even if not lying beyond all criticism. But it is no longer the autonomy of an ethical human for whom the world is just an empty backdrop; instead, it is the autonomy of compound realities such as human–parachute or human–car engine. The implications of this are immense, since the ethical person par excellence is no longer the captain of duty who lapses as seldom as possible, but rather the passionate explorer of some domain who pushes her enthusiasms all the way to the limit.

But here we are mostly concerned with formalism in aesthetics, and though Kant never uses the word 'formalism' in an arts context, it describes the core of his aesthetic vision nonetheless.[45] His arguments here are very similar to his points about ethics. Beauty must not be confused with the agreeable. I am already well aware that my love for Indian cuisine, for sweets, for the colour green, and for the Chicago Cubs baseball team need not be shared by others. I know from experience that I am one of those humans who are genetically incapable of tasting cilantro as anything other than soap, yet never would I consider others disgusting for eating it in my presence. Yet beauty is an entirely different matter, according to Kant. Here we are appalled at the insufficient taste of those who cannot appreciate the greatness of the finest products of art. A mass by Palestrina should be appreciated by anyone with aesthetic taste: not just classicists, and not just Catholics. This is possible because, for Kant, all humans have the same 'transcendental faculty of judgement', just as we all experience the world in terms of cause and effect rather than as disconnected random incidents. Yet despite this stress on the objectivity of taste, beauty for Kant is so much 'in the eye of the beholder' that he thinks the object has nothing to do with beauty at all, just as cause and effect has nothing to do with the world itself but only with the special and finite human way of organizing the world that may not be shared by angels or aliens. Here again we see the *true* meaning of formalism for Kant. It is not just a question of autonomy, but of a specific autonomy of two domains that are separate from one another: humans and world. And here as always, Kant stresses the 'human' side due to his view that the 'world' side is not directly accessible, belonging as it does to the kingdom of the thing-in-itself.

In the more than two centuries since Kant, a strong formalist tradition in aesthetics has often been visible, and has occasionally become quite dominant. An example can be found in the visual arts criticism of the late 1940s up to some point in the 1960s, especially in America, where this period was dominated by Clement Greenberg and his one-time disciple Michael Fried. The intellectual debt these two important critics owe to Kant is easy to notice in their works. But while they remain 'formalists' in Kant's sense of the term – despite their evident dislike for the word – what they give us is a backwards formalism in which the 'world' side of the equation matters more than the 'thought' side. We see this in Greenberg when he openly rejects Kant's view that the principles of art can be straightforwardly deduced from examining the structure of human thought.[46] Greenberg goes so far as to take the side of Kant's rival Hume, favouring the latter's appeal to collective human experience as a better means of discovering which works of art are the greatest. Nonetheless, Greenberg remains committed to Kant's modern taxonomy, in which everything must be decided either on the 'world' side or the 'thought' side, without ever mixing these two divergent domains. He simply gives us the opposite model, in which taste is determined through experience with artworks, and not through any overarching structure of the human mind. As a result, Greenberg's brand of formalism continues to favour Kantian disinterested contemplation over passionate engagement. It also favours an art of self-contained non-human objects uncontaminated by needless entanglement with humans and their conceptual stunts and whims. This explains his contempt for the post-formalist art of the 1960s, which he mocks as

> a row of boxes, a mere rod, a pile of litter, projects for Cyclopean landscape architecture, the plan for a trench dug in a straight line for hundreds of miles, a half open door, the cross-section of a mountain, the stating of

imaginary relations between real points in real places,
a blank wall, and so forth.[47]

Art simply moved on, choosing to view Greenberg as an
antiquated figure without ever really addressing and countering the root of his art criticism. To do this adequately
would involve, in part, a criticism of his and Kant's aesthetic
theories analogous to Scheler's critique of Kantian ethical
theory. For while many regions of the cosmos have no
need for human participation to be what they are – the
motion of planets and subatomic particles comes to mind –
art, like ethics, is a place where humans are a necessary part
of the mix.

This is more easily seen from a brief look at the work of
Fried, who idolized Greenberg as a mentor before a never
fully explained falling out between them. In an important
1967 essay, Fried makes a severe criticism of minimalist art,
one of the leading new trends – along with pop art – that flew
in the face of dominant Greenbergian formalist principles.[48]
There are two problems that Fried outlines with minimalism,
and he sees these problems as intimately linked, though
OOO holds that they are altogether different. The first is
what Fried calls the 'literalism' of minimalist art. When the
minimalists place their naked white cubes or spare wooden
rods in a gallery, what you see is what you get. We encounter
mere 'objects', a word that Fried means in the opposite sense
from OOO. Whereas objects for OOO have a depth beneath
any relation, for Fried an object is a sheer legible surface with
nothing held in reserve; indeed, Fried even ventures the
remark that minimalist sculptures strike him as 'hollow'. In

short, he finds none of the aesthetic depth in minimalism that one usually expects from the arts. And for this very reason he goes on to make a second criticism of minimalist art. Given that minimalist artworks are merely objects, merely surfaces, what they must really be aiming to do is provoke some sort of involvement on the part of the beholder. This is what Fried calls 'theatricality', and he tells us it is nothing less than the death of art.

Now, we have already seen why OOO *insists* on the theatricality of the arts. Whereas Fried rejects theatre as the necessary by-product of how minimalism reduces art to its literal surface, OOO sees theatre in an opposite light: as produced directly by the ultimate mystery of the artwork, which requires human participation to replace a real object that is permanently lost in its own depths. If, contra Fried, we assume that there is actual value in minimalist sculpture, then here as with metaphor the beholder of the work becomes the new support for the surface-features of the cube or rod left behind when the object itself went missing. More generally, Fried confuses two separate roles of the human being in any given situation. In one sense we are merely observers, the knights of anti-realism, since we reduce the things we encounter to mere caricatures incommensurable with their genuine depth. This is what Ortega was referring to when he complained about the empty shadows of things encountered in everyday perception and actions, and above all in literal language. Yet in a second sense, humans are also the knights of realism, since we are always the only real objects on the scene (despite our inability to *see* ourselves directly), given that cypresses, flames and red boxes are never directly graspable by us or by anything else. It is in this sense that theatricality is a necessary part of aesthetics, though Fried is right that every form of literalism must be excluded. One of the implications is that works of visual art involving human participation cannot be condemned for this reason alone, as happened at the hands of Greenberg and Fried, though here as in any genre of art we can find numerous cases of success along with failure.

What is great in formalism, whether in ethics or aesthetics, is its realization that the ethical deed or the work of art has an autonomous structure that cannot be explained away by the context in which it occurs. It does not follow, however, that we ought to endorse a modernist taxonomy in which a non-human artwork must be protected at all costs from any inclusion of the human factor. When the German artist Joseph Beuys films himself spending time with a coyote, this need not be a slap in the face of the autonomy of art: for there is no reason to assume that Beuys himself is less valid as an ingredient of an artwork than is a tube of acrylic pigment. Architecture need not be excluded from the sphere of fine art simply because it is always entangled with functions and purposes, though this may indeed tell us something about the dividing line between art and architecture.[49] And finally, we cannot assume that all artworks can be interpreted in complete isolation from their effects on their sociopolitical context. Picasso's anti-war painting *Guernica* is one classic example of a work that may be hard for some to approach without reference to the brutal event it depicts, and the same holds all the more for Francisco Goya's print series *The Disasters of War*. In literature, consider the case of

*Uncle Tom's Cabin*, which was not only a protest against the evils of slavery but one of the political factors provoking the war that ended it.[50] If we imagine a parallel universe where American slavery never existed, in which *Uncle Tom's Cabin* was written as a piece of pure speculative fiction, we can see how different this work would be from the real *Uncle Tom's Cabin* of our planet Earth. OOO holds no grudge against the socio-political interpretation or effectiveness of art, but simply insists that *not all* of the elements of the context of an artwork are relevant to that work, and that an artwork either admits or forbids its surroundings to enter through a fairly rigorous process of selection. The effort found in some quarters to reduce both art and philosophy to the handmaid of political revolution misunderstands the mission of art, which can include politics and anything else, but only by first aestheticizing it.

# Society and Politics

The previous chapter introduced a number of concepts drawn from the analysis of metaphor and from aesthetics more generally. There was the discovery that art is not the production of knowledge about things, but that it creates new things-in-themselves. There was the further discussion of non-reciprocal and asymmetrical relations, both points derived from the insight that things are torn between their unified nature as objects and the multiple abundance of their qualities. I concluded against Fried that aesthetics necessarily has a theatrical character. Further, I note that art does not reach the object itself by clearing away its accidental qualities, but that it actively couples the beholder to the aesthetic object so as to produce a new compound object. Moreover, we should keep in mind that some or all of these ideas may prove useful for understanding topics unrelated to art.

Yet there will still be those who see in the aesthetic realm nothing more than a secondary intellectual pastime. In Chapter 4 I will speak of those who insist that philosophy must aspire to be a form of knowledge, and who sometimes try to force the arts into these cruel fetters as well. But for now I will speak of a rather different group of opponents of OOO: those who consider society and politics to be the only subjects of any ultimate worth. As they see it, any philosophy that deals with such idle, self-indulgent topics as aesthetics and ontology 'in a time like this' is merely fiddling while Rome burns. For we are all part of a society, and a politically organized one at that. And since there are always good reasons to think that our society has reached a point of unique crisis, it will be said that any true philosopher should focus all their energies on this uniquely redeeming subject matter. For this reason, I will now pause to discuss some of the standard OOO views on social and political theory, before devoting Chapter 4 to a broader and more technical discussion of the interaction between objects and their qualities.

We have seen that up to a certain point, OOO is a 'flat ontology' which opposes the standard modernist assumption that human thought is something completely different in kind from all of the trillions of non-human entities in the universe. For this very reason, our first conclusion is that social and political theory must take inanimate objects into consideration in ways that have not usually happened in these disciplines. Thus there is no alternative for OOO but to walk the trail first cut by actor-network theory, unequalled among social theories in the attention it devotes to non-human entities. ANT has taught us a great deal about how human society would be stranded at baboon level if not for the stabilizing work performed by inanimate objects such as roads, contracts, buildings, wedding rings and fingerprinting techniques.[1] This remains the case even if many of these objects were designed or produced by humans. Our debt to such insights is too deep ever to be repaid.[2] Nonetheless, ANT also misses everything we just learned from the theory of metaphor.[3] While metaphor requires the force of the thing-in-itself, ANT discounts this notion entirely, reducing actors to their mutual effects on one another, since there is no 'substance' or any other surplus hidden behind a thing's actions here and now. For ANT relations are both reciprocal (since effects pass in both directions) and symmetrical (since there is no object separate from its qualities), though OOO insists by contrast that many relations are either non-reciprocal, asymmetrical, or both. We have also seen how important theatricality is for OOO, though this could never be the case for ANT, which recognizes no vanishing object that needs replacement by an engaged beholder who takes on the duties of the missing object. And finally, ANT cannot accommodate OOO's way of circumventing formalism through the stratagem of saying that ethics is about the compound of subject *and* object, aesthetics about me *plus* flame-qualities, and so forth. This is not because ANT insists on keeping subjects and objects pure from one another: quite the contrary, since it was Latour's critique in *We Have Never Been Modern* that first showed the defective character of such purification. Instead, what ANT would reject is the notion that compound entities are new things-in-themselves rather than just transient relational events. What interests OOO, instead, is the way that my encounter with a flame or an ethical vocation forms a *new object in its own right*, and not just an external interaction between two permanently separate entities. For this reason, we have no choice but to treat society in a way completely different from ANT.

With respect to politics, however, OOO finds itself much closer to ANT's position. We will see that both schools reject

any conception that politics is a form of knowledge masterable by scientific proof or technical expertise. While it is true
that Latourian ANT is more indebted than we would like to
the form of power politics defended by Thomas Hobbes
(1588–1679), this tendency decreases rapidly throughout
Latour's career. In fact, politics is the area in which we find
Latour's most significant concessions to the idea of a reality
beyond all knowledge, and here too that we find the only use
of the phrase 'object-oriented' in his work. Let's begin with
social theory and proceed from there to politics.

## Society

ANT has enabled a masterful advance in social theory, sup-
plying a basic toolbox for literally thousands of scholars in
anthropology, ethnography, and indeed every field in the
social sciences.[4] It allows the researcher to incorporate non-
human entities in a way not permitted by the more widespread theory of Foucault, whose primary interest is how the
human subject is shaped by various disciplinary practices.
Along with ANT's flat ontology and its promise of a more
comprehensive treatment of inanimate beings, it also provides a useful and easily memorable research motto: 'follow
the actors'. That is to say, any situation is best understood
simply by assessing which beings are having an impact, and
following them closely in all that they do instead of assuming
that we already know what they are in advance. For example,
rather than assert that Louis Pasteur was a great medical
genius who brought light into the medical darkness, we must
follow all the hygienists, vaccines, serums and chickens

present in his career to see what role each of these played in bringing about the so-called Pasteurian Revolution in medicine.[5] Instead of making grand incantations about what 'science' says as to whether the Amazon jungle is spreading or receding, let's join actual scientists on the ground and watch them as they manipulate various actors, often crudely physical ones, through a series of transformations: spreading out a plastic map with their hands, placing soil samples next to a colour bar, entering dried leaves into a storage book.[6] And finally, by focusing on the movements of these various scales of actors, we are entitled to lose faith in the gloomy master narratives which tell us that 'society' or 'capital' are everywhere oppressing us. We are forced to become much more concrete in our assertions about society. All of these principles have created a vibrant ANT school in the truest sense of the term, characterized by its unusual breadth, diligence, inclusiveness, cosmopolitanism and optimism.

But as noted at the beginning of this chapter, I also find several things missing from ANT, as usually happens when one spends a few decades with even the greatest intellectual methods. First, by interpreting things as *actors* exhaustively deployed in the effects they have on other things, ANT loses all sight of the difference between what a thing is and what it does. This makes it an overmining method, the exact inverse of materialist theories that reduce things downward and lose all sight of the difference between what a thing is and what it is made of. Yet the reader may ask why this is a problem for social theory. Are students of society not primarily concerned with what a thing *does* rather than with what it *is* in a vacuum? Not really. After all, one of the most striking features in history, politics, art, architecture, indeed any human science or aesthetic discipline is their openness to counterfactual arguments. A counterfactual exercise necessarily assumes that Pasteur, Stalin or Emily Dickinson are a surplus that exceeds whatever it was that they actually became, simply because we can imagine these human objects under a variety of alternative scenarios. Hence, we cannot simply speak of these historical figures as equal to their sum total of activities. And while ANT excels at bringing things to life that have already happened, by awakening all the surprising actors that contributed to a result now lying in the past, at the moment I cannot think of a single good example of a counterfactual analysis that has arisen within this school. Nor should this be surprising: if Pasteur is an actor who consists of a series of actions, then what sense would it make to detach Pasteur from his actual circumstances and imagine him in others? But for OOO, Pasteur – like anyone else – is an object rather than an actor, meaning that Pasteur is both more than what he is made of and less than what he does. Among other things, this means it is not difficult to imagine Pasteur in any number of situations other than the ones that actually occurred, which is precisely what counterfactual analysis achieves. Without this technique, we cannot imagine other possible histories than the one we actually have. By overestimating 'events' and underestimating objects, this tends to push us into a fatalistic attitude towards the past.

Second, ANT's theory of events is just as flat as its theory of actors, though in this case the flatness has negative rather than positive results. For ANT anything that happens, from the trivial to the momentous, is equally an event. When a hair falls from Napoleon's head on his birthday in 1807, then Napoleon as an actor has been altered to some small extent. When he is victorious at the momentous Battle of Jena, he is also a different actor post-victory than he was before. This entails the unconvincing result that there is only a difference of degree between the falling of a hair from his head and his world-historic victory on the fields of Thuringia. ANT would meet this objection by saying that of course there is a difference between the two cases: the victory at Jena mobilizes far more actors and changes their status much more than the mere falling of a human hair to the soil. Yet all events are still equally events in ANT, since an event occurs when anything affects anything else, and the difference remains only one of degree. For OOO this manner of dealing with change is insufficient due to its excessive gradualism, its inability to distinguish fundamentally between trivial and transformative events. A similar objection has sometimes been made to the Darwinian model of evolutionary biology, as in the famous theory of Niles Eldredge and Stephen Jay Gould that evolution occurs through a series of 'punctuated equilibria', or periods of rapid change followed by longer periods of biological stability.[7] But OOO is even more indebted to the work of the late Lynn Margulis, who distinguishes between moments of gradual change and moments of *symbiosis* between separate organisms, in which change leads to an organism different in kind from its predecessors.[8] In particular, the evolution from simple prokaryotic cells to the more complex eukaryotic cells seems to result from the cell's incorporation of previously independent bacteria that became permanent organelles inside the cells on which they were originally parasites. Here we have a type of relation that is not just the exchange of effects between two different actors, but the full-blown transformation of one or both entities through the incorporation of one by the other. The parasite entity gains a new home on the interior of the cell, dividing in the future whenever the cell divides. Meanwhile, the host entity gains the beneficial support of a parasite that is not just a parasite: for instance, through its superior ability to process atmospheric oxygen that might otherwise be deadly to the cell. OOO puts three additional twists on symbiosis. First, we should regard symbiosis as being primarily biographical rather than biological. It is not just a living cell that can form symbiotic relations with other entities, but institutions, historical objects, and other objects larger in size than biological individuals. Second, symbiosis need not be *reciprocal* as in Margulis' biological theory. One object can exist in symbiosis with another without the reverse being the case. Lord Byron's poetry is transformed by the Greek War of Independence without that nation really being altered by the poems; every soldier is transformed by the Vietnam War without each of them individually making much of a difference in the conflict. Third and finally, OOO stresses the *non-symmetrical* nature of symbioses. As was seen in the case of metaphor, symbiosis is not a literal case of two objects exchanging common features and benefits, but of one object stripping away the qualities of another.

A third and final problem with the social theory of OOO is that, by adhering too deeply to the notion that all events are equal in kind, ANT is unable to account for the life cycle of historical entities, one that is primarily biographical rather

than biological. That is to say, we need to be able to distinguish between the birth and death, the ripening and decadence, and the intermediate symbioses that are characteristic
of all social objects and not just biological ones. If we are to
do this, we cannot limit ourselves to treating all interactions
between objects as the mutual impact between actors, since
this will not allow us to distinguish between different kinds
of impact. A related problem is that ANT cannot allow for
any distinction between active and passive moments in the
life of an object, since it holds that all relations are both
reciprocal and symmetrical. Although this allows ANT to
escape the often excessive devotion in social theory to talk
of oppression, exploitation and domination, there is no question that such dismal relations do occur and that we must be
able to account for them. For while it may be true that workers in a salt mine only need to rearrange the various actors in
their situation in order to turn the tables and gain the upper
hand over the giant multinational mine owner – as ANT
allows in principle – we know that in practice such relations
are often heavily non-reciprocal, weighted prohibitively in
favour of the dominant actor. This sort of situation is what
the archaeologist Ian Hodder has called *entanglement*, an
important concept for which there is really no analogue in
ANT.[9] Hodder's primary focus is not so much on the human–
human oppressive relationships that are so important to
the intellectual life of the Left, but on human–thing relationships in which humans become socially and economically
entangled with often unnecessary 'stuff' – such as plastic
trinkets – that renders our long-term survival as a species
more difficult.

# The American Civil War

As mentioned earlier, in a recent book on OOO and social theory entitled *Immaterialism*, I used the Dutch East India Company as a case study. The book follows the birth, growth, decay and death of a historical object that existed for nearly 200 years, even though none of its employees (and probably none of its ships) endured along with the company from the cradle to the grave. I will now show briefly how the theory works by using a different social entity that I happen to have studied in some detail: the American Civil War (1861–5). Now, someone might begin by asking in what sense a war can be an object. Is it not, instead, an 'event' that involves a number of different objects? But recall that for OOO an object need not be physical, solid, simple, inanimate or durable; it need only be irreducible either downward to its components or upward to its effects. The Civil War is certainly not reducible to its components, however informative it may be to know them. It does help to know about the compromise found in the 1787 Constitution, in which resolving the issue of slavery was effectively postponed: the 'peculiar institution', as slavery was euphemistically termed, was permitted to exist in the Southern states but not the Northern ones. This led to deep policy divisions over such related issues as whether the people of each state should be allowed to decide its slavery policy, the 1840s Mexican–American War, and the ongoing violence in so-called 'Bleeding Kansas'. It is also useful to know about John Brown's abolitionist raid on the Harper's Ferry Arsenal in 1859, which was meant to arm slaves for an uprising, but ended with Brown and his men either shot or hanged. But in no way is the Civil War reducible to these preliminary incidents. Numerous other paths could have led to the same war at roughly the same time. More generally, it is never the case that all of the details of the history of a thing are inscribed into that thing. The world forgets a great deal, and so too does every object in the world.

Nor can we reduce the Civil War in the opposite direction, by moving upward towards its external effects or visible features. For one thing, the Civil War, like any real object, necessarily differs from any interpretation or understanding of it. Better and worse accounts of the war exist, though it is unlikely that the definitive account will ever be written, just as no final account can be written of any topic under the sun. The war cannot even be reduced to all of its future effects on America, which often seems to have failed to learn some of the most important lessons of that conflict; indeed, in 2016 we have returned to some of the same polarizations apparently settled by force of arms in 1865, and much of this political polarization can be found between precisely the same Northern and Southern states that fought each other then. Today there is even renewed talk of secession by various states, however improbable it may seem at the moment.

The first task when analysing any particular object is to establish its limits in space and time. In spatial terms this is fairly easy to do for the Civil War. Despite tense diplomatic intrigues that unfolded in London and Paris, and despite the picturesque sinking of the Confederate ship *Alabama* off the French coast in 1864, the war was more or less confined to the states and territories of the United States. The temporal limits of the conflict may seem a bit more ragged, as is often the case with historical objects. Should we date the beginning of the war from November 1860 with the election of President Abraham Lincoln, who was on record as declaring that the half-free, half-slave 'house divided' of the United States could not endure as it was? Perhaps we should date it instead to the following month, when South Carolina became the first state to secede from the Union despite Constitutional lack of clarity over whether this was a legal act. Another candidate for the war's birthdate might be the official formation of the Confederate States of America (CSA) in February 1861 with Jefferson Davis as President: the provocative formation in Richmond of a rival government to the one in Washington. Or perhaps we should embrace the dark horse option of Lincoln's own inauguration in March, since his installation in office was the fulfilment of Southern fears. But selecting any of these would make the situation more difficult than it is. When determining the birthpoint of an object, the operative principle should in fact be *literalism*, which – as always with literal questions – entails that this point in time ought to be knowable. This makes quite a contrast with the later symbioses in the life of an object, which are non-literal in character and often more interesting and consequential than its birth. We should also note that countless objects are born around us constantly: friendships, contracts, clubs, movements and other collectives, many of them utterly dull and transient. The fact that the American Civil War began did not entail that it had to amount to very much. Many expert observers expected the conflict to be over quickly, and William Tecumseh Sherman of the Union forces was viewed as something of a madman for predicting the catastrophic bloodbath that eventually ensued. There were a number of points at which the conflict might have been pre-empted, reducing it to an odd footnote of American history and preventing what became the bloodiest conflict the Western Hemisphere has ever seen. So when did the Civil War really begin? Since we are discussing the war itself, rather than the secession of states or the formation of the Confederate States of America, we need only look to when the first shots were fired after much hesitation. As is well known, this happened on 12 April 1861, when Fort Sumter off Charleston, South Carolina was fired upon and soon captured by rebel forces. The war having thus been born, it still might have ended without much consequence, however improbable this may have been in practice. The Confederates might have atoned for firing on Fort Sumter, or might have used its capture as a bargaining chip in negotiations to preserve the Union along with the guarantee of a continued Southern 'way of life'. My point in saying so is that while the firing on Fort Sumter was the watershed moment in the birth of the war, the significance of that moment was only ratified by further transformations of the conflict, of a sort that – following Margulis – we can call symbioses. Many objects are born, but few are chosen.

But things are somewhat different when it comes to the death of an object. Literalism does well enough in marking the birth of an object such as a war: fifty cannon firing from Charleston at Fort Sumter. But a higher standard than literal-ism is needed for an object to remain in existence. After all, we know it is quite possible for an object to live on in name only after the substance of the thing is dead, though it is much more difficult for something to be *born* in name only, since it is born as soon as its conditions of birth have literally been met. In *Immaterialism* I spoke about the British East India Company (EIC) as well, an institution that actually predated its Dutch counterpart but only flourished later after major reforms during the period of Oliver Cromwell. It would make no sense to say that the EIC was born at the moment when its significant impact began, since this would be to reduce the existence of a thing to the magnitude of its effect on other things, which is precisely the methodological drawback of ANT that we are trying to avoid. But once a thing has existed and flourished, literalism is no longer enough to sustain its existence. Once-great families and secret societies can drag out a miserable semblance of life for centuries after their soul has vanished. If a few hardened or ignorant Japanese soldiers still lurk in Pacific jungles in 1965, firing wildly at garrisons and tourists, this does not mean that World War II continues until the last of them is neutralized. These grizzled and deluded Japanese veterans are merely historical curiosities and perhaps an interesting subject for journalists or anthropologists. The same holds in the present case. Thus we ought to agree with the popular view that the Civil War ended on 9 April 1865 at Appomattox Court House, Virginia, with Robert E. Lee's surrender of his Army of Northern Virginia to Ulysses S. Grant's Army of the Potomac. Everything that came afterward, including Lincoln's assassination six days later, the surrender of Joseph Johnston's Confederate forces three days after that, and the further surrender of Confederate forces in Texas a good deal afterward, belongs to the aftermath of the war rather than the war itself. And if some Confederate guerrillas had retreated into Appalachia and kept up raids and sabotage for the remainder of the century, we would rightly consider this irregular campaign to have marked a new episode in American history rather than a continuation of the war itself.

We now have some rather unsurprising birth and death dates for the American Civil War: 12 April 1861 – 9 April 1865, an astonishingly brief conflict by contemporary standards. Someone might now scan the period between these two dates, assume that all the intervening events are equal in principle, and rank those events according to the amount of impact they had. But OOO does not assess objects – and remember, objects include 'events' – by their impact on other objects. Sometimes the most transformative things that occur are not the ones that have the most obtrusive external effects, just as the noisiest newspaper headlines often turn out to be of no lasting importance. As already mentioned, OOO focuses instead on several stages in the development of an object: stages triggered for the most part not by internal developments, but by symbiotic transformation. Such interaction is not the literal combination of two terms sharing something in common ('a pen is like a pencil'), which we see at the moment when objects are born. Instead, it is the half-failed combination we find in metaphor ('a cypress is a flame'). Metaphorical relations occur not when there is *no* evident resemblance between things or *significant* resemblance, but only a weak sort of resemblance. This is analogous to what the sociologist Mark Granovetter calls 'the strength of weak ties', meaning that the most transformative events in our lives tend to be opened up by casual friends or fringe acquaintances, even though the strongest emotional and financial support generally comes from those closest to us.[10] When looking for the weak ties that lay the groundwork for symbiosis, there are several criteria that can be of assistance. The most obvious one is to look for transformative and irreversible bonds rather than simply conspicuous ones, though it is true that conspicuous events are often symbiotic. Another is that the weakness of the link should be visible in the shape of certain *failures*, since when two objects fit together too quickly and easily it is usually a question of a literal combination rather than a symbiotic link.

In *Immaterialism* I began by identifying the symbioses early in the history of the Dutch East India Company (VOC), then establishing the point of maturity at which all of its symbioses were completed, then proceeding forward in time to follow the company's ripening, decadence and death. In the case of the American Civil War, it proves to be methodologically easier to work from the middle to the end, before returning to the beginning and looking for symbioses there. In many cases an object endures for a long time after the mature phase is reached: the VOC lasted for more than a century after it reached adult form. An object like a war, however, is inherently driven towards its own end – a self-destructive or suicidal object, so to speak – and thus cannot be expected to long outlast its maturity. But what do we mean by the maturity of an object? OOO social theory holds that an object is mature as soon as it has no room for further symbiosis. The previous indeterminacies as to its ultimate fate have now been resolved by committing to irreversible bonds with other objects, and such irreversibility is precisely what symbiosis means. All that remains is for the object to capitalize on what it has become by feeding on its environment; this is the ripening phase of the object. By contrast, the phase of decadence begins when an object's symbioses become overly literal, so that its various attachments become counterproductive to its own survival in a shifting environment. In the case of the VOC, its advantageous dominance in the trade of such spices as nutmeg and mace became a liability once the European market began to clamour instead for such goods as tea and chocolate, both largely under the control of the English rather than the Dutch.

The maturity of the Civil War, the moment when all impediments to its form had finally been removed, came with the final conflict between Ulysses S. Grant of the North and Robert E. Lee of the South, each a legendary commander in his own way. The actions of Grant had previously been confined to the Western theatre of the war, as President Lincoln shuffled through a long series of failed generals in the East. Conversely, the military activities of Lee had taken place solely in Virginia and the neighbouring states of the mid-Atlantic region (Maryland, Pennsylvania and what is now called West Virginia). Though Grant has often been portrayed as a clod-like butcher and Lee as an elegant gentleman tactician, this perspective on their talents can easily be reversed. From the new standpoint, Grant becomes a visionary who foresaw the crucial role of rail logistics in warfare, while Lee comes off as a less durable version of Napoleon, with numerous picturesque victories undercut by a long-term trend of attrition. In any case, once the leading commanders of the two sides in the war were finally brought into the same theatre, the development of the war was at an end, and it was simply a matter of seeing how it would turn out. Although the first battle between Grant and Lee did not take place until The Wilderness on 4 May 1864, I would argue that the mature form of the war was reached as soon as Lincoln promoted Grant to Lieutenant-General and commander of all Union armies, which happened two months earlier on 2 March. The situation already culminated on that date, even if no shots were fired until two months later. There followed the great Overland Campaign in which Grant drove towards the Confederate capital of Richmond, fighting Lee's Army of Northern Virginia in sequence at The Wilderness, Spotsylvania, North Anna and Cold Harbor, before striking in truly Grantian fashion at Petersburg, the key railway junction south of Richmond. This entire campaign can be viewed as the ripening phase of the mature Civil War, while the period of its decadence begins with the dismal nine-month siege at Petersburg, a precursor to World War I trench warfare, which ended only with the breakout and eventual defeat of Lee's depleted forces the following spring. By contrast, ANT offers us no tools to distinguish cleanly between phases, since it regards all events as equally events, even if some are conceded to be more important.

Perhaps the eeriest fact about the Civil War is that the great conflict pitting Grant against Lee had a mirror-image further to the south, where Grant's former deputy and Western successor Sherman drove towards Atlanta just as Grant drove towards Richmond. Sherman's initial opponent was General Joseph Johnston – ironically, the very man Lee had replaced two years earlier – who eventually gave way to the sometimes out-of-control John Bell Hood of Texas. After more than a dozen battles between the two armies, Hood withdrew from Atlanta on 1 September 1864, and the city was surrendered to Sherman the next day. There can be no question of the importance of the campaign in Georgia. Among other things, President Lincoln was locked in a difficult re-election campaign against his former commander George McClellan. While Grant had been stalled in trench warfare at Petersburg since mid-June, Sherman's conquest of Atlanta provided Lincoln with the clear sign of progress that guaranteed his re-election and prevented the war from 'dying' in counter-factual fashion, with a possible premature peace under a President McClellan. But the role of the Georgia campaign was more negative than positive: the war might have been lost if Atlanta had also turned into a lengthy siege, but no amount of victory or plunder in Georgia sufficed for the North to win the war. Impressive as Sherman's victories were on the road to Atlanta, and extensive though his later depredations were on his march to Savannah and upward through the Carolinas, the war had already entered its decadent phase with the beginning of the siege of Petersburg in June 1864. Everything thereafter was a matter of containment and mopping up. As mentioned previously, the death of the war came with Lee's surrender to Grant at Appomattox Courthouse, even though other Confederate forces did not immediately surrender.

Earlier I said that the birth and death of the war can simply be identified with two of its most iconic moments: the firing on Fort Sumter in April 1861, and the surrender of Lee at Appomattox in April 1865. The beginning of the mature phase was less literal than either of these, since we noted the gap between Grant's appointment as Union commander on 2 March 1864 and his first battle with Lee on 4 May of that year, sixty-three days later. Ontologically speaking, there are three different things going on here. The birth of an object will generally coincide with some literal event that can be registered somewhere in time and space, as with the artillery assault on Fort Sumter. The death of an object can sometimes precede its literal end by a good while, since it is often the case that a thing lives on in name only. But any time a symbiosis occurs – and Grant's promotion to Union commander was the final symbiosis of the war – we will find a delay between the genuine phase change and its echo in some noisy external event. Another good example would be the so-called 'Phoney War' on the Western front in World War II, when the Franco-British declaration of war on Nazi Germany after the invasion of Poland in September 1939 was followed by a staggering eight-month period with no ground battles between the ostensible belligerents.[11] Non-military examples are just as easy to find. Personal relationships, in love and work alike, quite often reach a new level before anyone is explicitly conscious of the fact. The Golden Age of German Idealist philosophy can be said to have ended with Hegel's death on 14 November 1831, though this was probably not obvious until the younger F. W. J. Schelling's late Berlin lectures proved so tepid that he lost such initially enthusiastic auditors as Friedrich Engels, Søren Kierkegaard and Mikhail Bakunin.[12]

But now we return to our main example. What about the

early symbioses, pre-1864, that helped establish the character of the Civil War prior to its reaching maturity? One clue that will be of assistance is that a symbiosis occurs between two pre-existent objects, with 'events' being only the unmistakable echo of these objects in their interaction. Though philosophy since the early twentieth century has prided itself on replacing nouns with verbs and stasis with flux, this is not the path of OOO, which sees this as a false innovation. We are looking, then, for nouns. And here there is no reason to scorn the old classroom maxim that a noun is a person, place or thing. For various reasons I suspect that most objects, of no matter what scale – and whether human or non-human – will pass through roughly a half-dozen symbioses before reaching mature form. This means that, on average, we should be looking for two symbioses belonging to each category of noun, with the symbioses being identifiable by their *irreversibility* and by their noticeable assistance in helping move the object to a new biographical stage. It need not be two people, two places and two things, of course. In the case of the Dutch East India Company I found only one individual of symbiotic stature: J. P. Coen, who successfully urged a path of violent monopoly for the Company. I also found three places whose establishment or conquest deserved to rank as symbiotic: Batavia, the eastern Spice Islands and the Strait of Malacca. Finally, I found two 'things' that had symbiotic effect: the newly created position of VOC Governor-General, and the strategic reorientation of the Company towards intra-Asian shipping from around 1625.[13] Let's now turn our energies to finding the objects with which the Civil War formed a symbiotic link.

It is perhaps easiest to begin with the 'person' category, since we have already mentioned the showdown between Grant and Lee as the climax of the war, and it is precisely these two who are the war's key people. Lincoln is surely the greatest figure of the entire period, but he was a necessary causal ingredient of the war more than a participant in it. Though his strategic conceptions were generally sound, he belongs to the background of the war in the same way as does the secession of the Confederate states, and not to the life of the war itself. Admittedly, sometimes even the pre-eminence of Grant and Lee as generals is questioned. An occasional maverick will assert that McClellan, master trainer of troops that he was, deserves greater esteem than Grant. On the Southern side there are even more contenders for the status of diamond among generals, whether it be Stonewall Jackson, future Klansman Nathan Bedford Forrest, or the Irish immigrant Patrick Cleburne, slain before his time outside Nashville. Yet we note that McClellan had abundant opportunity to transform the shape of the war and flatly failed to do so. And the other Southern generals mentioned simply never had the strategic impact of Lee. I also claimed above, in all seriousness, that an important object ought to experience some failure prior to its success, since a truly independent object ought to be somewhat out of phase with its environment rather than just a flawless spare part that accelerates that environment's efficiency. In Grant's case a number of failures came before the war, with his earlier military career ending amidst rumours of alcohol abuse, and his entry into the war being as nothing more than the leader of a sleepy volunteer company from Galena, Illinois. His rise to

symbiotic status is probably best dated to his dramatic conquest of Fort Henry and Fort Donelson in early 1862, earning
him the nickname 'Unconditional Surrender' Grant. Yet there
was a further near miss with disastrous failure at Shiloh,
Tennessee in 1862, where a Confederate attack took Grant
by surprise (and where my great-great-grandfather, Spear
T. Harman, lost a finger and took two other bullets while
fighting under Grant). Following The Wilderness in 1864, his
first battle against Lee, Grant broke down weeping in the
knowledge that he had nearly lost his entire army. There was
also Grant's own admitted culpability for the needless bloodbath of the frontal assault at Cold Harbor soon afterward.
Yet these mild to moderate failures can actually be seen to
reflect well on Grant, as signs of an incomplete fit with his
context. A more cautious general, like his predecessors,
might have avoided such failures; they also lacked Grant's
deeper understanding of the conflict, which Lincoln too
grasped so clearly.

In Lee's case the failures are largely internal to the war,
given his golden successes in pre-war life. The early months
of the conflict find Lee receiving poor reviews for his per-
formance against McClellan in what is now West Virginia,
followed by tedious coastal defence duties strengthening
various Atlantic ports. Only when Johnston was wounded
during the Peninsula Campaign of 1862 did Lee become commander of the Army of Northern Virginia; only then did Lee
first become Lee. His greatest failure in the later portion of
the war was surely his ordering of Pickett's Charge towards
the centre of the Union lines at Gettysburg in 1863, an action
that led to the utter devastation of Pickett's divisions, though

its initial success is often referred to as 'the high-water mark of the Confederacy'. Such failures, rather than being seen as downgrading the person responsible for them, are often the sign of a formidable human character at a stage when it is unable to blend into its surroundings and not yet able to master them: or in the case of Lee at Gettysburg, no longer able to master them.

We turn now from people to places, and here our choices of symbiosis may be more surprising. The Battle of Gettysburg concluded on 3 July 1863 with a Confederate defeat, ending Lee's second and final invasion of the North. It is often said that this massive three-day battle in Pennsylvania is where the war was lost for the South. Just one day later, on the highly symbolic date of 4 July, Grant received the surrender of Vicksburg, Mississippi. While less known to the public than Gettysburg, the conquest of Vicksburg was a symbiosis transforming the war in a way that Gettysburg did not. An ANT analysis of the Civil War would surely rank Gettysburg as the high point of the war, since it was the longest and most dramatic battle, and since the stakes were apparently so high. If Pickett's charge had succeeded and the centre of the Union line had crumbled, the battle could have been a Confederate rout on Northern soil, increasing the pressure on Lincoln for a negotiated settlement to the war. On the other side of the coin, if the Union commander George Meade had more aggressively pursued Lee's retreating Army and harassed their river crossing towards home, the Army of Northern Virginia might have been annihilated; Meade might one day have been President of the United States rather than being superseded by Grant in both military and political history. But none of this is relevant in symbiotic terms. Either option – Lee winning at Gettysburg or Meade destroying Lee in the aftermath – would have amounted at most to an *end* of the war rather than its further development. Vicksburg, by contrast, was a key transformation rather than an end. With the fall of that tantalizingly durable city, the North more or less gained control of the entire Mississippi River, though officially it took nearly a week for General Nathaniel Banks to mop up a final Confederate river stronghold at Port Hudson, Louisiana. Undivided Union control of the mighty river largely ended the relevance of the Western theatre of the war, and brought the conflict one step closer to its final showdown in Virginia. In the Vicksburg campaign we also find both the failures and the innovations that often accompany symbiosis. Grant failed at least a half-dozen times to take Vicksburg directly from the river, which finally led him to an ingenious alternative solution. Sailing downriver by night under the blazing guns of the city, he cut off his army from its own supply lines and ordered his men to live off whatever they could forage from the Mississippi countryside. They then marched inland to the state capital, Jackson, some fifty miles east of Vicksburg, seizing it on 14 May. Then, in what would become a lasting contribution by Grant to military strategy, he cut the supply lines to Vicksburg by marching straight down the rail lines to lay siege to the city from behind. Another innovation came during the actual assault on Vicksburg, when Generals Grant, Sherman and McPherson made what was probably the first unified start of a battle arranged by pre-synchronized pocket watches.[14]

Few historians would be surprised by the crucial role OOO gives to Vicksburg. But what other place in the war deserves to be mentioned in the same breath as this great river citadel? Here our choice is less orthodox. I have already said that it is not Gettysburg, which narrowly missed being known as the end of the war but did nothing to transform its essential character. The same holds for the unnervingly close-placed capital cities of Washington and Richmond, where the war could have ended at any time if either city had been captured. Likewise for every one of the dramatic Grant vs. Lee battles in 1864 Virginia, since I have already made the case that all symbioses were complete with Grant's achieving overall command of Union forces before he ever faced Lee. New Orleans was a sparkling naval capture for the Union, but not one that transformed the nature of the conflict. As for Atlanta, we have seen that while Sherman's victory there may have prevented re-election defeat for Lincoln, the Georgia campaign was at best a mirror image of the more central strife in Virginia. Shiloh and Antietam are both showcase battles for historians, but Shiloh was a bloody stalemate and Antietam a poor man's Gettysburg in the sense of a failed invasion of the North. That leaves us face to face with another true symbiosis: the Battle of Chattanooga, from 23 to 25 November 1863. Just as the fall of Vicksburg in the far west helped concentrate the war further to the east, the Union conquest of Chattanooga more or less ended the role of Kentucky and Tennessee as central Civil War battlegrounds, though General George Thomas later had to chase down and destroy the Confederate remnants of Atlanta in Nashville. Northern victory at Chattanooga, won by none other than Grant and Sherman (just a few months after Vicksburg) set the geographical chessboard for the remainder of the war: one campaign from Chattanooga to Atlanta and beyond, and another from The Wilderness to Petersburg. Chattanooga also features another of Grant's numerous logistical triumphs, with his opening of the so-called 'Cracker Line' to feed the starving Union forces. There was also General Hooker's theatrical victory over the Confederates on Lookout Mountain, and Sherman's initial success on the right flank of Missionary Ridge. But when Sherman's advance became stalled on the right, Grant ordered a distracting movement by General Thomas towards the Confederate centre. He was shocked when Thomas's men continued their charge up the mountain, and even more shocked when they comically won the battle in this way. As we have seen, these sorts of mistakes and failures often accompany important moments of symbiosis. Confederate forces fled into Georgia, and once Grant was summoned to the East by Lincoln, Sherman's destiny was to roll through Georgia all the way to the sea.

One peculiarity of the four symbioses mentioned so far – Grant, Lee, Vicksburg, Chattanooga – is that three of the four involve Grant. While I would not call this a coincidence, it is certainly not a necessity, but more a side-effect of the compressed spatial and temporal scales of the Civil War as an object. In the case of the Dutch East India Company, for instance, the outstanding individual was J. P. Coen, who by no means intervened in every spatial symbiosis of the VOC, unlike Grant in the 1860s. It is conceivable that others besides Grant might have conquered Vicksburg and Chattanooga, though in that case these others would have likely been the ones who were summoned eastward to fight General Lee. Although Tolstoy's *War and Peace* makes a wonderful case for war as a chaos beyond the control of any supposedly ingenious general, history teaches that war is one of those events in which the strategic decisions of individual leaders matter more than in most cases. This is why generals in wartime are so often fired and so often raised from obscurity to greatness, though in times of peace such things happen rarely. The same is true in a watered-down form of the coaches of sports teams, who resemble wartime generals in their unusual degree of influence over the course of events.

Having named two people and two places as sites of transformative symbiosis for the war, I now conclude by adding a single 'thing' to the list. During a tour of Civil War battlefields in the 1990s, I stopped near Sharpsburg, Maryland, site of the fabled Battle of Antietam. The ranger in charge of our tour made a case for Antietam, the bloodiest single day in American military history, as the most important battle of the war. While such a case can certainly be made, this is not because Antietam was a crucial geographical place. Instead, the importance of this battle was because the Union victory – or tie – at Antietam enabled Lincoln to issue the famous Emancipation Proclamation from a position of strength, which he did on 1 January 1863. Though slavery can be viewed as the root cause of the Civil War, it was initially not to the advantage of either side to raise this issue directly. The case for the Confederacy was more palatable if made in terms of 'states' rights' and against the tyranny of the central government; indeed, 'states' rights' remained the special battle cry of the American Right until quite recently, when anti-Trump liberal states began to assert their independence from federal immigration orders. As for the Union cause, to begin the conflict by calling it a war to end slavery might have spelled strategic disaster, since Lincoln needed if possible to retain the loyalty of four slave states that were not in rebellion: Missouri, Kentucky, Maryland and Delaware. The Emancipation Proclamation did not announce the end of slavery on principle: that would have to wait for the 13th Amendment to the Constitution, eight months after Lincoln's death. Instead, the Proclamation ordered the liberation of slaves only in those states *still in rebellion*, purely as a military punishment. This was a clever way of shifting the political burden of ending slavery on to the secessionists themselves, while legally freeing such a large majority of American slaves that leaving the remainder in bondage after the war's end would hardly be plausible. For it is absurd to imagine a post-war United States in which slavery had been militarily abolished in its heartland of the Deep South while remaining legal in the middle region of Missouri, Kentucky, Maryland and Delaware, along with parts of Tennessee and southern Louisiana (areas already occupied by the North at the time of the Proclamation). The Emancipation Proclamation counts as a symbiosis because it transformed the nature of the war by broadening its goals and further uncovering its ultimate outcome. The 13th Amendment, although far more principled in its rejection of slavery, was effectively a post-war phenomenon despite Lincoln's not living long enough to see it through Congress.

Much more could be said about these issues. A OOO

interpretation of the Civil War could easily run to hundreds of pages, and perhaps some day I will attempt it. But I hope the reader has noted the central point: that there is a *qualitative* difference between different events rather than just a quantitative one. The loudest and most dramatic events are not always the most crucial ones. The judgement and action of individuals is often more important than the structural analyses of social scientists allow. Even the most blatant conflicts often need to unfold in several steps before their underlying character takes shape.

## Politics

We have now seen that OOO approaches social theory in a manner almost the opposite of actor-network theory. Unlike ANT's 'actors', the objects of OOO are always a surplus deeper than whatever they are doing now or will ever do. Whereas ANT sees all relations as being of the same kind, differing only in terms of their quantitative size and strength, OOO notes several qualitative differences between various types of relation. Symbiosis marks an irreversible change in the life of an object, and must therefore be distinguished from relations that change nothing. This is impossible for ANT, which holds that *every* relation in which a thing is engaged necessarily changes it. Indeed, it does not make much sense in ANT to ask about the life-cycle of an actor at all, since an actor does not really endure across time, but is 'perpetually perishing' (Whitehead's phrase) and replaced in every instant by a close successor. OOO also allows for *non-reciprocal* relations, meaning that one object can relate to another without the other relating back to it in turn, which ANT does not permit. Finally, OOO allows for *asymmetrical* relations, meaning that an object relates only to the *qualities* of another object rather than to that object directly; this is what makes metaphor possible.

Yet somewhat surprisingly, there are two points where ANT converges with OOO on the need for a surplus in reality. The first of them comes in Latour's remarkable and surprisingly little-read critique of materialism.[15] Traditional materialism was the idea that nothing exists other than tiny physical particles speeding through a void. Everything else that seemed to exist was to be reduced to such particles, and everything immaterial was to be mocked ruthlessly on this basis. In recent years, materialism has again come back into fashion. But it now has little to do with tiny material particles, and serves instead to cover a motlier range of intellectual commitments. In the words of Levi R. Bryant: 'materialism has become a *terme d'art* which has little to do with anything material. Materialism has come to mean simply that something is historical, socially constructed, involves cultural practices, and is contingent . . . We wonder where the materialism in materialism is.'[16] Though Latour is more occupied with the failings of the earlier form of materialism than with that of the present day, he would surely agree with Bryant on this point. In Latour's eyes, the real problem with traditional materialism is that it starts off by assuming it *knows* what matter is – hard physical stuff occupying a discernible point in space and time – and then uses this supposed knowledge to eliminate everything in the universe that does not fit the materialist model. The problem, however, is that no one really knows what matter is. We become philosophers rather than aggressive ideologues by always being *underway towards* discovering what everything is. If ANT is too quick to think it knows what objects are – by identifying them as actors, performers of actions – its critique of materialism takes a more Socratic turn by insisting on our ultimate ignorance of what everything is really made of.

The same is true, even more importantly, of Latour's political philosophy. Though his political thinking passes through several phases, he ultimately reaches the point of contending that there is no such thing as political *knowledge*. This is the first pillar of Latour's political philosophy, which we will review in a minute. The second pillar, no less important than the first, is his insight that politics is not primarily about humans. Latour and Shirley Strum had already written about the fact that human society surpasses baboon society primarily through the human use of inanimate objects as stabilizers. Unlike baboons, we humans do not need to renegotiate our social positions every day, but find those positions firmed up with birth certificates, driving licences, bank accounts, job titles, fixed residential addresses, and so forth. While this might seem obvious once stated, it seems to have escaped previous political thinkers, who focused either on the evil machinations or the innate goodness of human beings. Thomas Hobbes (in *Leviathan*) and Niccolò Machiavelli (in *The Prince*) speak only peripherally of the role of non-human entities in politics. Jean-Jacques Rousseau (in *Discourse on the Origin of Inequality*) does speak of agriculture and metallurgy alongside human nature, but only as factors corrupting and degrading that nature. More generally, conservatives and progressives tend to debate too much whether human nature is fixed or malleable, as if human nature were the primary factor in politics. Latour thinks it is not, and this puts him in the same camp as another important sociologist-philosopher for whom he has little affection: the German thinker Niklas Luhmann (1927–98).[17] We will return later to this theme of the role of non-humans. For now, let's return to the first pillar of Latour's mature political philosophy, his recognition of the impossibility of political knowledge.

The dominant political distinction of the modern era is that between Left and Right, referring originally to the opposite sides of the assembly during the French Revolution. Even if some politicians may seem difficult to place on the Left/Right divide, and even if we occasionally dream of a more satisfying map of the political spectrum, the opposition between Left and Right continues to dominate our political imagination: the former emphasizing change for the better and the malleability of human nature, the latter seeking to preserve those fragile institutions we have while assuring us that the basic human passions and defects have not changed since the dawn of history. In *Bruno Latour: Reassembling the Political*, I argued that lying behind the Left/Right division is a more profound modern divide that crosses both sides of the spectrum: Truth Politics vs. Power Politics. Truth Politics claims to have the political truth, which could be incarnated here on earth if not for the meddling obstructions of competitive inequality, the class interests of the bourgeoisie, or the mental weakness of the masses. When thinking of Truth Politics one usually thinks first of the Left, whether of Rousseau's *Discourse on the Origin of Inequality* or *Capital* by Karl Marx. But it can also be found on the Right, particularly among those Straussians – followers of the political philosopher Leo Strauss (1899–1973) – who stress an eternal hierarchy of human types that does not advance over time.[18] One famous consequence of the Straussian view is that philosophers supposedly need to hide their true 'esoteric' views from the mob, pretending that they are harmless and religiously devout patriots even though true philosophy works like a corrosive acid against mainstream views.

Power politics holds, by contrast, that 'truth' is whatever the winner decides it to be. There are numerous instances of power politics on the political Right. Machiavelli's *The Prince* gives us numerous hints on how to overpower or outfox the enemy, but only rarely does this work speak of a difference between noble and base actions. In the *Leviathan* of Hobbes, we are told that civil peace requires an absolute monopoly on authority by the central state, with neither religion nor science permitted to contradict the sovereign by appeal to some higher truth. In the works of Carl Schmitt – widely respected, despite his allegiance to Hitler – we learn that a 'state of exception' can be decided by the sovereign, as in his short work *The Concept of the Political*. In this state of exception, the difference between friend and enemy is decided, and the views of the enemy are no longer considered; we do not aim to annihilate the enemy, as Schmitt accuses liberals of doing, but simply must defeat him in an existential struggle. But there also exist Left versions of Power Politics, especially those postmodernist philosophies which view truth as relative, and only wish to assert the oppressed rights of various marginalized groups in order to empower them. Friedrich Nietzsche's *Beyond Good and Evil* is one of the founding ancestors of this sort of thinking, though Nietzsche himself was closer to what we would call today the Right, rather than the Left.

For all their differences, what Truth Politics and Power Politics have in common is that both claim to have political *knowledge*: the first in the shape of its own preferred political truth, the second in its certainty that force is the only truth. In this respect, both claim to be a 'science' of politics, and have little to do with Socrates's permanent uncertainty as to the meaning of justice, virtue and friendship. Latour's first major contribution to political philosophy is his restoration of the awareness that political knowledge cannot be obtained: politics is a matter of coalition and of temporary exclusion for those whose views are rejected. It should be noted, however, that it took him quite a long time to reach this position. In his early career, up through 1991, Latour was a remorseless power politician, his youthful writing filled with lively praise for Machiavelli and Hobbes. No figure in Latour's early work is treated as more pathetic than the moralist: the one who opposes 'right' to 'might' while making no effort to obtain the needed might. This phase only ends with *We Have Never Been Modern*, a turning point in Latour's career. The opening sections of this now classic work closely consider *Leviathan and the Air-Pump*, an important book in the sociology of science by Steven Shapin and Simon Schaffer. These authors consider the dispute between Hobbes and his contemporary, the scientist Robert Boyle, concerning Boyle's air-pump. Does the pump give us direct access to a truth about nature, as Boyle contends? Or is the truth of nature subordinate to the political decisions of the sovereign, as Hobbes believes? After a wonderfully fair presentation of both sides of the story, Shapin and Schaffer conclude that Hobbes was right, since the definition of what counts as good science is decided by society. In his earlier years, Latour could only have agreed with this conclusion, but suddenly a new door opens in his brain, and he declares bluntly: 'No, Hobbes was wrong.'[19] If the supposed scientific truth of the air-pump is going to be deconstructed and shown to result from the labour of various concrete *actors* such as scientists, witnesses, candles, mice and air-pumps, then it is equally necessary to deconstruct the political concepts of 'power' and 'force'. After all, these have no more obvious, immediate, unquestionable truth than do the declarations of science.

Following this moment of insight, one can feel Latour shifting his views away from power throughout the 1990s. In his 1999 book *Politics of Nature*, he even grants an important political role to the moralist, previously an object of ridicule. Namely, the moralist must detect people who have been unfairly excluded from the current polis (for example, undocumented immigrants), just as the scientist performs the same work for unrecognized non-human objects (for example, global warming). Yet this development of Latour's political thought truly reached a new stage as a result of the important 2005 doctoral dissertation by Noortje Marres at the University of Amsterdam, 'No Issue, No Public', for which Latour served as co-advisor. Marres returned to the old and famous debate between the philosopher John Dewey and the prominent journalist Walter Lippmann, both of them Americans of the early twentieth century. Lippmann's book *The Phantom Public* (1925) challenged the American ideology that citizens must be educated in order to rule themselves, cynically observing that the American education system produces its fair share of robotic fools who pay no attention to the nuances of public policy. As a result, Lippmann thought, America was destined to evolve into a technocracy governed by councils of experts. Dewey's important book *The Public and its Problems* (1927) appreciated the letter of this critique if not its spirit, and put a more positive spin on Lippmann's observations. Expecting the citizenry to be fully engaged on all important political issues is setting the bar too high, Dewey claimed; even Lippmann, the best-informed journalist of his day, could never hope to meet such a standard. Instead of asking all members of the public to weigh in wisely on every political concern, Dewey asks us to conceive of a new and limited public arising with every issue. The issue of dairy subsidies might mobilize one group of stakeholders, national defence policy another, and immigration law still another. This is the meaning of Marres's title 'No Issue, No Public', a formula that her advisor Latour enthusiastically embraced. This pushed Latour the final step of the way to his mature political philosophy, as later expressed in the politics chapter of his major work *An Enquiry Into Modes of Existence*. Political knowledge is not obtainable or even desirable. Politics arises whenever an issue arises, and takes the form of a dispute between various stakeholders, a dispute that must eventually achieve closure with some sort of decision. Since no knowledge results from this decision, the losing position can only be excluded on a temporary basis. Politics consists of coalitions lined up around the boundaries of an issue whose exact nature can never be determined.

This is what Latour calls 'object-oriented politics', and he was right to borrow this metaphor from OOO, which feels very much at home with this model of the political. This is more or less where Latour remains politically to this day. It is true that his recent work on Gaia and global warming often seems to revert to the power politics of his early career, as when he draws on Schmitt to say that the time for debate with climate change sceptics is past and that they now must simply be defeated.[20] Latour has also expressed increasing fondness for the conservative political philosopher Eric Vogelin (1901–85).[21] My sense is that this does not signal a move by Latour away from the object-oriented model of a politics without knowledge. Instead, he simply seems to be following his own directive that 'it is a common thing in political philosophy, that reactionary thinkers are more interesting than the progressive ones . . . in that you learn more about politics from people like Machiavelli and Schmitt than from Rousseau.'[22] Though we have seen that reactionary thinkers are just as apt as progressives to assume that political truth or power can be obtained, reactionaries do often have the positive trait of scepticism towards the human ability to change reality simply by wishing it to change. Though this attitude can easily slip into a fatalism that listens too closely to the past, it does have the upside of not assuming that the world is the same as what we think it is: a valuable kernel of realism sometimes lost by progressives amidst their fervour for a better world.

# The Two Major Features of Modern Political Theory

Modern political theory has two major features. First, it claims to have political *knowledge*, even if it is only the knowledge that there is no truth and everything is a ruthless struggle for power. Latour counters this claim with his object-oriented politics, initiated by his break with Hobbes and cemented by his adoption of Dewey's interpretation of Lippmann. The second major feature of modern politics is its obsession with human beings. With the secularization of post-medieval thought, and in the wake of the discovery of New World 'savages', political theorists become obsessed with what humans are like in the 'state of nature', prior to the emergence of civilization. As a general rule, those of the Left (like Rousseau) imagine the state of nature as a time of equality and co-operation, while those of the Right (like Hobbes) conceive it as a brutal war of all against all. Another difference is that the Left often views human nature as highly malleable under differing historical conditions, while the Right sees a continuity of human nature that can easily be gleaned even from the Bible and the ancient Greeks. Latour's answer to both of these groups is to suggest that human nature is somewhat beside the point, since humans are just one of many actors in the political network. Whether or not you think humans are naturally good, the printing press is a bigger political actor than any human, so too is the atomic bomb, and – we are soon to discover – so is the melting of the polar ice caps. In short, along with Latour's politics of uncertainty that rejects claims to knowledge, he gives us a politics of *agglomeration* in which non-humans play as crucial a role in structuring the polis as Caesar, Danton or Lincoln. We can certainly speak of political networks, but since 'network' implies a philosophy like Latour's in which everything is determined by its relations, I will introduce the term political *chain* – in honour of Leibniz, who worked in the early 1700s on how separate substances can link together in chains to form physical bodies.[23] If there is one most typical weakness of actor-network theory in dealing with chains or networks, it can be found in the unspoken assumption – stemming from Latour's early years as a Hobbesian power politician – that networks become stronger by becoming *larger*, by assembling *more* allies. Yet counter-examples are not difficult to find. Adding a fifth guest to dinner often creates the famous 'fifth wheel' social problem. Mid-sized corporations are often more agile and hence often more profitable than large ones. And Rousseau explains in his dedication to the *Discourse on the Origin of Inequality* why he would not wish his home city, Geneva, to be any larger than it is. The important theme of the optimal size of any given political chain is simply ignored by ANT, given its largely unaddressed prejudice that size equals strength. Along the same lines, Granovetter's work on weak ties has also shown that a *looser* connection between two actors often has greater benefits than a strong one: for instance, we are more likely to learn of promising job opportunities from fringe acquaintances than from our closest friends, even though the latter provide much more loyalty and emotional support.

In addition to the theme of optimal political size, there is also a topological question that ANT never raises, given its assumption that relations are always reciprocal. For ANT, Entity A in relation to Entity B entails that entity B is also in relation to Entity A, as in Newton's law that every reaction yields an equal and opposite reaction. Yet often enough the political entanglement occurs in one direction only, as Hodder has shown. If we reserve the term 'chain' for cases in which political influence flows in just one direction, we can use 'loop' for those instances when influence is reciprocal. And since one object can be involved in many chains, when considering it in this respect we can call it a 'cluster'. But when we consider a single object as the meeting point of many reciprocal loops, we will find a structure like that of a clover leaf, and thus we can refer to the object as a 'clover' rather than as a cluster.[24] On this basis, a number of different types of political chains can be described, though this is not the place to enter into the topic in detail. One thing to be kept in mind, however, is that Latour's two most important political insights work against each other to some extent. The theme of chains made up of humans and non-humans tends to emphasize the relational, networked character of actors. But the theme of an object-oriented politics without knowledge stresses the degree to which political issues *are not* straightforwardly accessible, but resist direct comprehension. In the terminology of OOO, political chains include real objects, not just sensual ones. Understanding how this is possible is the key to further development of the non-modern political theory outlined by ANT.

Let us conclude with the core points about OOO and politics. We have seen that object-oriented politics rejects all claims to political knowledge. An obvious implication is that OOO cannot be sympathetic to most forms of radical politics, since these are invariably based on the claim to a radical knowledge that warrants rapidly tearing down our historical inheritance. Radical politics as we know it is an outgrowth of modern philosophy with its modern idealism, and hence is unlikely to survive much longer than modern philosophy itself. We have also seen that OOO cannot be sympathetic to any form of human-centred politics, which treats the political sphere as if it were the product of human nature and a purely human history. Object-oriented politics also means that non-human objects are crucial political actors, and that the 'state of nature' would no longer be politically relevant even if it had ever existed. Several things follow from this. The first is that if political transformation wants to be grounded in reality, then it is more likely to be driven by environmental or technological changes than by manifestoes and courageous stands at the barricades. It is interesting that this is precisely where Latour sees Donald Trump as a failure: not because he is a 'fascist' (this strikes Latour as an anachronism), but because he is an *escapist*. That is to say, Trump wants to pretend that the two looming crises of our time – the climate and the growing wave of refugees – can simply be ignored.[25] As a form of realism, object-oriented politics joins with Latour against any form of escapism, environmental or otherwise.

# Indirect
# Relations

Having paused to discuss the implications of OOO for social and political theory, we return once more to the aesthetic discussions of Chapter 2. There I claimed that aesthetic phenomena result whenever a wedge is driven between an object and its qualities. To be more specific, it was a matter of *real* objects – withheld, inaccessible, concealed – vanishing from the scene while their qualities remained visible, accessible, and always revealed. As a result, the aesthetic beholder was required to step in to replace the missing real object, giving rise to a *theatrical* model of aesthetics: the reader of Homer's metaphor 'wine-dark sea' behaves in the manner of a method actor who replaces the withdrawn sea in its absence and takes on all its various purported wine-dark qualities. In this way, aesthetics gives us a rift between real objects and what we have called their sensual qualities, a rift never made explicit in the normal course of everyday experience. Yet we also noted the existence of sensual objects and real qualities as well. Taken together in all their possible combination, the two kinds of objects and two kinds of qualities yield four separate types of rift between objects and their qualities. This quadruplicity of objects and things is one of the two main themes of the present chapter. The other is the question of how objects can touch at all. Since real objects exceed the grasp not only of all human theory, perception and practical action, but of every sort of direct relation, then I wonder how it is possible for one entity to influence another in any way. Obviously, I do not question the existence of such influence, but only wonder about the mechanism behind it. Given that real objects are by definition incapable of touching each other, we need to find a way in which they *touch without touching*, through some sort of indirect contact. This concept is known in OOO as 'vicarious causation'. It owes much to a medieval Islamic and early modern European current of thought called 'occasionalism', according to which no two created objects are able to make contact unless they pass through the mediation of God.[1] But ultimately OOO cannot accept the findings of occasionalism: not because we wish to mock religious currents in the history of philosophy, but because *no entity at all* – whether God, the human mind or anything else – should be permitted arbitrarily to make direct contact with other objects when this is forbidden in principle to everything else. Let's discuss these two themes in turn, beginning with the fourfold structure of objects.

## The Tensions in Objects

It is remarkable how often the number four turns up in both Western and non-Western philosophy. But we need to be careful not to assume that all such quadruple structures are alike, since the only thing that fourfolds usually share in common is that they result from two separate principles of division. Here is an extremely simple example: if we combine the north–south distinction with the perpendicular east–west distinction, we can divide any map into four quadrants – northwest, northeast, southwest and southeast. This shows that the mere existence of a fourfold structure does not prove that anything interesting has been discovered – which would require that the two axes of division are both relevant to their subject *and* somewhat surprising in their conclusions. For example, in Chapter 3 we noted that the usual distinction between Left and Right in modern politics is crossed by a separate distinction between Truth Politics and Power Politics that is usually left unnoticed. As a result, we were able to identify four basic – though unobvious – families of modern political theory: left-wing Truth Politics (Rousseau, Marx), right-wing Truth Politics (Strauss), left-wing Power Politics (various postmodernists: Foucault, Butler), and right-wing Power Politics (Machiavelli, Schmitt).[2] The concluding value of this exercise was to show that all four families of political theory are wrong: both because they claim a non-existent political knowledge, and because their conception of politics has too much to do with human beings and too little to do with everything else. In any case, there are as many other examples of quadruple structures in intellectual history as we have the patience to seek. The notion of a fourfold structure of things was an idea floated by Heidegger in his 1949 lecture 'Insight Into That Which Is', though in such an obscure poetic form – earth, sky, gods, mortals – that even his most loyal disciples have made little headway with the concept.[3] In *The Quadruple Object, Heidegger Explained*, and elsewhere,

I ventured an interpretation of Heidegger's fourfold, trying to show how it both resembles and differs from the fourfold of OOO.[4] Since there is no need to explain the details of Heidegger's quadruple object philosophy in this book, we will now discuss only the OOO version of the fourfold.

When considering the aesthetic case of metaphor, we became familiar with a situation in which an object seems to vanish behind its surface-qualities, forcing the beholder (who is also an object) to step in and theatrically replace the missing object. In the early years of OOO, much attention was paid to the tool-analysis found early in Heidegger's 1927 classic, *Being and Time*. Heidegger had been the star disciple of Husserl, and was expected at first to carry the banner of Husserl's phenomenology onward into the future, until he took an unexpected path. The basic principle of phenomenology is that philosophy should not speculate on hidden causal mechanisms or mysterious things-in-themselves, but should simply describe what *appears* to us in all its magnificent subtlety. Husserl thought it absurd that anything might exist that would not be, at least *in principle*, the object of some mental act. The rebellious genius of Heidegger's tool-analysis was to show that Husserl was wrong: for the most part, dealing with things consciously is a relatively rare and derivative scenario. More common is the experience of simply taking things for granted, not noticing them until they go wrong. The floor in our home, the air we breathe, the grammar we immediately understand, or the bodily organs upon which we silently rely: all of these objects tend to function unobtrusively while our consciousness is occupied elsewhere. Heidegger focuses on the case of using a hammer;

normally we do not notice this tool until it fails to function and is suddenly exposed to our conscious gaze. Another of his prominent examples is a covered railway platform, which is not just an assemblage of physical materials, but tends to vanish from view in favour of our tacit wish to remain dry during rainfall. In sum, Heidegger sees the world as made up of a constant reversal between 'tools' (referring not just to tools in the strict sense, but to anything that operates without our noticing it) and 'broken tools' (referring to anything that becomes explicitly noticeable for any reason). We should also notice that just because a tool becomes 'broken' does not mean it also becomes nakedly present before us; the now-visible form of the tool is still just a translation of the deeper life of the hammer. In any case, given that Heidegger's hammer is always deeper than anything we see or say about it, and that it ought to exist whether or not we are using it – though Heidegger's own views on this point are not so straightforward – his hammer is not a Husserlian phenomenon, but a *real object* that silently labours in the depths.

But before continuing with Heidegger, let's turn for a moment to Husserl, who was dismissed somewhat unfairly by Heidegger's critique in the tool-analysis – even if we are deeply impressed by the force of that critique. For the fact remains that Husserl discovered at least two things about objects that his student Heidegger never seems to have grasped. Before discussing these two insights, we should begin with a more obvious point. Phenomenal experience shows us numerous different qualities by which we distinguish between different things. That reddish and spherical thing to my right looks edible in a way that the hard and greyish square beneath my feet does not. When we hear Homer's metaphor of the wine-dark sea, the object 'sea' seems to vanish under the pressure of its unlikely wine-dark qualities, but these qualities remain in our consciousness: in such moments we do not experience a blank void, but wine-dark qualities, however difficult these may be to describe precisely. In other words, along with the real object we have sensual qualities, and these two can be handily abbreviated as RO and SQ.

However, we have not yet considered Husserl's greatest philosophical insight, one that laid the very foundation of phenomenology. Empiricists such as Hume saw little evidence for the existence of unified things called 'objects'. Instead, Hume maintained, what we encounter are 'bundles of qualities'. Supposedly none of us has ever seen an object called 'the White House' in Washington, but only a rectangular shape of generally off-white colour, with a combination of semi-circular and columnar shapes in the centre. Since these qualities seem to remain together in stable fashion, and since everyone apparently agrees about this, we form the habit of speaking of a unified object called 'White House', even though the 'object' part of it does not seem to add anything to our perception of the bundle of its various qualities. Husserl's genius was to completely invert this empiricist way of looking at things, and to lay stress on the object rather than its qualities. His reason for doing so was that the qualities of every object are shifting every instant due to changes in sunlight, as well as our shifting distance and angle as we approach the object, not to mention our minuscule changes in mood as we go about perceiving it. I never have exactly the same perception of the White House in two different instants, and yet it never occurs to me to see my differing perceptions as multiple different things that simply resemble each other very closely. Instead, what I say is that I perceive the *same* White House with slightly varying qualities at each and every moment: Husserl uses the term 'adumbrations' for these changing perceptions of one and the same thing. Nonetheless, this enduring unified White House which remains the same through all my various perceptions of it is not the *real* White House. Husserl was horrified in advance by what I am now saying, since if the White House I perceive is not the same as the real White House, the problem will arise as to how these two different White Houses are connected. This is why he denied the existence of any real objects apart from the sensual ones (which for historical reasons he called 'intentional' objects).[5] Yet the fact remains that Donald Trump does not live in my perception of the White House, but inside the White House itself – however badly I wish this were only happening in my mind. By the same token, what burns is a flame, rather than our perception of the flame. More than this, some of the objects of experience simply do not exist, including hallucinations, dreams, and the non-existent objects of our most groundless anxieties. While real objects exist regardless of whether we perceive or think of them, *sensual* objects exist only as the correlate of our acts of consciousness. Along with RO and SQ, we must speak of SO as our abbreviation for the sensual object. It is interesting to note that neither Husserl nor Heidegger had a clear conception of the existence of SO. For Heidegger, the realm of presence was a place of qualities not in tension with a distinct and visible object-pole; meanwhile, for Husserl there was never any kingdom of the real, and hence just one kind of object (the sensual) rather than two.

The attentive reader will now correctly predict that we are about to introduce real qualities – RQ, for short – since after all that is the final blank space in the fourfold grid. But far from being the arbitrary filling in of an empty spot, we are led to affirm the existence of RQ by another subtle insight of Husserl's. If we return to the case of the White House, we have already seen the difference between the sensual object and its sensual qualities. This historic building is always viewed as a *specific* hue of white, depending on the quality of the sunlight or spotlights in which it is observed. It is always seen from a *specific* angle and distance, and in a mood subtly different from any other through which we have ever lived. Obviously, none of these details is necessary to the experience of the White House: we might just as easily have seen it from the other side, at half or twice the distance, and on a much sunnier afternoon than was in fact the case. By varying all of these inessential details of the experience or mentally subtracting them, we are led to notice the difference between the sensual object and its sensual qualities. However, it is also the case that not *all* of the qualities of the White House can be removed from our experience of it. There are certain qualities so pivotal for this sensual object that, if they were removed, we would not be experiencing this object at all but something else instead. If the building were burnt down to nothing, as very nearly happened during the War of 1812, then obviously it would not be the White House anymore. But what about lesser forms of damage, renovation or historical desecration? What is the uncrossable line that the White House cannot trespass without becoming something altogether different? Through mental exercises of this sort, we approach the *real qualities* that the phenomenon needs in order to be itself. Husserl claims another important difference between sensual and real qualities: while the former can be known through the senses, the latter can never appear sensually, but only to the intellect. Our 'intuition of the essence' of an object is never a sensuous intuition; perception is always saturated with accidents, not just with objects in their own right. OOO counters Husserl by denying that intellectual intuition can grasp things as they are any better than sensual intuition does. This is a rationalist fallacy that arises when Husserl denies the gap between real and sensual objects. Despite Husserl's claim that RQ can be grasped by direct intellectual intuition, we object that it is no more possible to have a direct vision of RQ than of RO itself. These real qualities, too, can only be known by indirect allusion or innuendo.

## The Fracture in Things

Yet we are interested not only in the four poles of real objects, real qualities, sensual objects and sensual qualities in isolation, but primarily in the bonds or tensions between them. Here again there are four basic permutations, of which the first (RO–SQ) was the topic of my aesthetic discussion in Chapter 2, and again in my account of Heidegger's tool-analysis earlier in the present chapter. Even so, my more general name for the RO–SQ tension is neither 'aesthetics' nor 'tool', but *space*. The reason for this is that space means both proximity and distance, just as is true of RO–SQ. Whatever is in space is removed from us and ensconced in its own private place, but also belongs to the same spatial arena as we do, and is positioned at a *determinate* distance from us that might be overcome if sufficient energy were expended: for example, it takes significant effort for me to travel from my home in Dubuque, Iowa, to Hong Kong, but it is physically possible to do so as long as the financial resources are available. In similar fashion, the sensual qualities of a real object remain both bound to it and separated from it, as the case of the broken hammer makes clear. The dented hammerhead or damaged wooden handle do not express the whole of the hammer – which forever withdraws from view – yet they do belong to the hammer in some loose way.

The next tension (SO–SQ) is central to Husserl's phenomenology, since it marks the difference between an enduring sensual object and its shifting parade of qualities from one moment to the next. This tension can be named *time*, in the sense of our *experience* of time rather than that of objective time passing on a clock. Just as space requires both proximity and distance, time entails both endurance and change: if we encountered nothing but a strobe-like kaleidoscope of constantly changing properties, this would be an experience of derangement rather than of time. What time gives us, instead, is the experience of constant flickering change amidst a more slowly shifting background of enduring sensual objects.

Yet OOO speaks not just of a duality of space and time, but of a quadruplicity. By showing that space and time do not just emerge arbitrarily from nowhere, but result from two kinds of object–quality tension, OOO is in a position to place two other terms on the same footing as space and time. The first of these concerns Husserl's insight that sensual objects do not just have shifting sensual qualities, but indispensable real qualities as well. This is the tension called SO–RQ, which we call *eidos*, borrowing Plato's ancient Greek term for his perfect forms of whiteness, justice, horses, or anything else: a term that Husserl himself loved. Here we encounter the strange fact that a sensual object (which exists only as a correlate of our paying attention to it) nonetheless has real qualities (which exist whether we are aware of them or not).

The remaining tension is RO–RQ, which cannot be wished out of existence even though neither pole is directly visible to us. After all, Leibniz correctly noted in the Monadology that every real object is a single unit, but also that all such objects must have a multiplicity of qualities, since otherwise they would be indistinguishable from all others. The name for this tension is *essence*, since it concerns the real qualities that belong to a real thing. Thanks to the influence of postmodern philosophy, the term 'essence' is often dismissed as politically repressive. But this critique only works against those who claim to have *knowledge* of the essence of a thing: that is, only if they claim to *know* that the essence of the Middle Eastern peoples is to require autocratic rule, or to *know* that the essence of femininity is to put family before career.[6] It should never be forgotten that OOO renounces all claims to know the essence of anything directly. Yet this does not entail that nothing *has* an inner

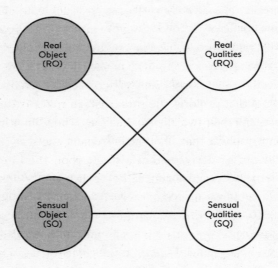

**Figure 1 — The Quadruple Object**

There are two kinds of objects and two kinds of qualities: real and sensual, in both cases. Real objects and qualities exist in their own right, while sensual objects and qualities exist only as the correlate of some real object, whether human or otherwise. Since objects cannot exist without qualities and vice versa, there are only four possible combinations, indicated by the four lines between the circles above.

nature, and that therefore everything would be wilfully performed or socially constructed rather than having an inherent character that resists all our efforts to plumb its depths. Since essence is the only one of the four tensions made up of two real terms and no sensual ones, it is admittedly also the most difficult of the four to investigate. This seems like a good place to review Figure 1 from earlier, as a reminder of how the four poles of the OOO fourfold interact.

Let this suffice for a basic overview of *ontography*, the part of OOO that explores the rifts between the two kinds of objects and their two kinds of qualities. The main principle of ontography is that all of the movement and stasis in the world can be derived from a single root: the interplay between objects and their qualities. As such, OOO is opposed to any form of realism that thinks the real object or its real qualities can be directly obtained. Such realisms can be found even among the friends of OOO: for instance, in the New Realism of Maurizio Ferraris (Turin) and Markus Gabriel (Bonn).[7] Ferraris and Gabriel are particularly concerned with the rampant spread of relativism throughout European philosophy, and for this reason they are committed to a realism able to obtain *knowledge* about the real. This obviously differs from OOO, which sees knowledge as a duomining result that turns the things into caricatures of themselves, however important knowledge remains for the advance of the human species.

# Causation

The reader might now be wondering about possible permutations of objects and qualities that we did not mention. What about qualities interacting with qualities, or objects with objects: does this play no role in OOO? Of course it does, and in a way that leads to interesting results, as long as we can avoid feeling stupefied by the alphabetic monotony of our abbreviations. The conjunction of sensual qualities (SQ–SQ) is not difficult to understand, since any real or sensual object is a support for multiple sensual qualities at the same time: the everyday Mediterranean on which we now sail is glowing and roaring and shimmering, while Homer's mysterious wine-dark sea also has multiple sensual qualities for the reader to enjoy and to ponder. The same holds for real qualities (RQ–RQ), which are also joined through the medium of some real or sensual object. The Eiffel Tower is a real object with multiple real features, but the Eiffel Tower is also a sensual object with multiple real features without which it would not be the tower that it evidently is. Nothing changes if we ask about RQ–SQ, which simply indicates that the same object – whether real or sensual – has both real and sensual qualities at the same time and serves as the basis for both.

But it becomes more interesting when we turn to the relations among objects. If we ask about the possible connection between real objects and sensual ones (RO–SO), we find that this is the only link that needs no mediator. The real object that I myself am is directly confronted by sensual objects, looking straight through the qualities by which they are announced so as to encounter various fruit, trees, people, animals and stones. It is admittedly true that if there were no sensual qualities I would not be able to experience sensual objects, just as it is true that a boat could not exist without atoms. But if phenomenology achieved anything at all, it was to show us that experience consists primarily of objects, and only secondarily of the qualities of those objects. As for the other two possible kinds of links between objects, they do require mediation. Two sensual objects (SO–SO) can be seen to meet in the experience of a single real one, as we just saw in the example of sensual fruit, trees, people, animals and stones, all of them experienced by me simultaneously. But given that sensual objects only exist as the correlate of the one who experiences them, there is no other way for them to meet than through being experienced simultaneously by one observer. And by the same token, it is also the case that two real objects (RO–RO) only meet through a sensual one. Although this entails a rather bizarre-sounding theory of causation, it is one to which OOO enthusiastically adheres: for according to this theory, two real objects in the world make contact not through direct impact, but only by way of the fictional images they present to each other. One real rock strikes the sensual version of another, in such a way that there are retroactive effects on the real. This is what OOO calls vicarious causation. But it is not as strange as it sounds, since more than a millennium's worth of the history of philosophy has already been leading in this direction.

Despite this history, we have to admit that vicarious causation is not a mainstream philosophical concept. If we consult a good overview on the topic of causality, such as Stephen

Mumford and Rani Lill Anjum's *Causation: A Very Short Introduction*, we find that the authors simply never raise the question as to whether two things are able to affect each other directly. Nonetheless, the problem is not altogether new. The speculations of early Islam already led such important figures as Abu al-Hasan al-Ash'ari (874–936) and al-Ghazali (1058–1111) to claim that God alone was the source of all *causation* and not just all creation: fire might *appear* to burn cotton, but in reality only God burns it.[8] This view, which was often associated with other, somewhat reactionary religious tenets, initially did not penetrate into European philosophy. It was not until the seventeenth century, in such great figures as Descartes, Nicolas Malebranche (1638–1715), Spinoza, Leibniz and Berkeley, that causation was finally placed in the hands of God. As already mentioned, this theory is known in the West as occasionalism, though the use of this word is often artificially restricted to cover only Malebranche and some of his contemporaries.

From the standpoint of secular Western civilization in the twenty-first century, it feels all too easy to laugh at philosophies that imagine the intervention of God in every least event in the world, from the burning of cotton balls to moving my own hand once I decide to do so. But if we look at contemporary philosophy, we will find that it accepts a surprisingly similar claim. By 'contemporary' I am referring to a very long period, one that begins at the earliest point in history when we have philosophers whose views do not provoke laughter today if taken literally. In mainstream secular-academic circles, we would be subjected to immediate ridicule if we were to make a *literal* defence of Descartes's idea of God as bridging the gap between mind and body, or Spinoza's identification of God with nature, or Leibniz's doctrine of countless tiny monads in pre-established harmony such that they seem to interact without really doing so. Even Berkeley's view that everything exists only as an image in some divine or human mind, though it is always taken seriously as an argument that ought to be refuted, would be mocked as soon as someone actually seemed to believe it sincerely rather than just use it in a game of devil's advocate. The historical point where laughter currently subsides can be dated to the eighteenth century, since even now one can be a *literal* disciple of Hume or Kant without becoming an academic laughing stock. Now, Hume and Kant certainly do not agree with the occasionalist view that causation must always have God as a mediator. But what they do share in common with occasionalism is the view that *one special entity in particular* is the site of causation: namely, the human mind. Hume argues that the only place we encounter causation is through the 'customary conjunctions' of experience, and the habits we form on the basis of such conjunctions. Kant tells us, even more ardently, that causality is a transcendental structure of the human understanding, not something that can necessarily be ascribed to the world outside human experience. Kant, Hume and the occasionalists all agree that causation is a problem, and that the right way to solve the problem is to ground all causation in the structure of a single ultra-important entity.

It was Whitehead in the 1920s who dared to resume the classical occasionalist tradition, with his claim that the relation between any two entities passes through God as the site of the 'eternal objects' that any entity draws upon in order to objectify or translate any other entity into perceptible form. But it was only Latour, to my knowledge, who insisted that all causality must be mediated *locally* rather than by calling upon some omnipotent God or omnipotent human mind to do all of the work of causation. Latour's classic example of local mediation can be found in *Pandora's Hope*, in his account of how the physicist Frédéric Joliot made the first connection in France between politics and neutrons. Though I argued in *Prince of Networks* that Latour's model still contains flaws, this does not prevent my admiring him for being the founder of a *secular occasionalism*, the first one known in the history of Western philosophy. A variant of Latour's approach can be found in OOO's preoccupation with giving a sufficient account of how two real objects interact through the mediation of a sensual object.

Before moving on, we should note another artificial limitation that is often placed on discussions of causality. The contemporary French thinker Quentin Meillassoux claims that the laws of nature can change at any moment for no reason whatsoever. Thus, the contingency of laws is something that happens across *time*, so that the laws can change from one moment to the next without anyone expecting it. Indeed, this is usually what we mean when we discuss cause and effect: the way that two entities meet and affect one another in the medium of time, or 'diachronically'. But cause and effect can also happen in a single moment, or 'synchronically', as in the part–whole structure of any given thing: for example, a chunk of gold is caused by the atoms and molecules inside it, no less than by the supernova explosion in which those particles were forged. Although Meillassoux boldly challenges the assumption that the laws of nature either hold eternally or change only for some understandable reason, he tells us nothing about whether several large systems of gold molecules must all result in lumps of gold, or whether some of them might produce silver, wheat or clouds instead. For OOO, this compositional sense of causation is the primary one, since it holds that any relation between separate things produces a new composite object. While it is obvious how the relation between a number of components can form a new object, this effect is often concealed if we consider a rapidly forming object that quickly decomposes again into its constituent parts. An example I once discussed was the mid-air collision of two planes, which OOO interprets as the formation of a new collision-object with a very brief lifespan, followed by a serious retroactive effect on its two component objects, followed in turn by the decomposition of the collision-object into its initial components.[9] Another example would be the break-up of a couple, whose relationship forms a new object that disintegrates, though not without lasting effect on both partners.

## Knowledge

Earlier in this book, OOO was distinguished from the two basic forms of knowledge: what a thing is made of, and what it does. More than this, I suggested that philosophy and the arts are forms of cognition without being forms of knowledge. This may have been startling to some readers, since we live in an era in which the production of knowledge is the basic organizing principle of society, and also serves as the root of our wounded but lingering faith in historical progress. Science in particular has become the final court of appeal in the dominant way that once belonged to the Church. Admittedly, there is good reason for this dominance. The Scientific Revolution that began in seventeenth-century Europe is a good candidate for the most important event in human history, even if we have become more serious these days about tallying up its drawbacks along with its benefits. Where knowledge is lacking, the people perish; without the promise of an increase in knowledge, our hopes for the future darken. For this reason, even if OOO's argument that knowledge is always an imperfect translation of its object, whether through under- or overmining, were accepted, surely there is still a difference between having a better or worse handle on that object? If diagnosed with an advanced case of cancer, we would surely seek out the hospital ranked highest in oncology rather than entrust our treatment to poets. When driving across the United States, we are sure to use a GPS system rather than consult the inexact maps of the early explorers Lewis and Clark. People spend years amassing knowledge and expertise in their respective subjects; surely OOO will not belittle such mastery by saying that it is all nothing more than translations of an unknowable essential core hidden in the things themselves? The issue is obviously important.

In asking what knowledge is, we can use our previous discussions to narrow down the field of possible answers. Above all, OOO is completely opposed to the idea of knowledge as direct access to the real; we do not even think physical causation consists of direct contact between two entities, and will certainly not grant such a power to 'minds' any more than to 'bodies'. We also know that knowledge cannot be metaphorical in character, since that is the medium in which both aesthetics and philosophy operate; knowledge, by contrast, must ascribe genuine qualities to the entities it knows. We should not expect art to provide us with knowledge, and by the same token should not expect beauty from the sciences, despite the historical irony that scientists now speak of beauty more frequently than artists. We must also rule out the notion that knowledge is an 'asymptotic' approach to reality, one that approaches the world ever more closely without quite reaching it, which seems to be Heidegger's intention with his concept of 'unveiling' or 'unconcealment'. The problem with this approach is that it assumes one can move quantitatively closer to the real as one gains knowledge of it, though this is ruled out from the start by the absolute gap between real and sensual as affirmed by OOO. In what sense does Einstein's theory of gravity 'more closely' resemble the truth than Newton's, if – as OOO holds – every theory is separated from every reality by an unbridgeable chasm? Whatever the difference between better and worse medicine may be, it cannot consist in good medicine having a more accurate picture of reality than bad medicine does: for between any picture and the reality it depicts, the gulf is absolute.

Another alternative comes to mind: philosophers have often claimed that knowledge means 'justified true belief'. From a OOO standpoint the word 'true' in this phrase does not inspire confidence, since truth implies a direct grasp of reality. Yet it is not entirely clear how such a direct grasp is possible, given that the relation between the arms I perceive and my withdrawn real arms already gave rise to difficulties, and OOO is more generally committed to the imperfect translatability of any form from one place to another: including from reality to any knowledge, thought or perception of it. But perhaps the word 'justified' is more promising, so that better knowledge would mean beliefs that have better justifications. Though the literature on this topic is hopelessly vast, it will prove useful to consider a few basic points that commentators have made on the matter. As a final reminder before starting, here is what we are looking for when seeking the nature of knowledge. Since knowledge cannot be metaphorical – for this is the realm of both aesthetics and *philosophia* – it must be literal, which means that it must be a question of articulating the qualities or effects of an object in overmining/undermining fashion. And since knowledge cannot be 'truth', which would imply an impossible direct revelation of the world, it needs to have some sort of contact with *reality*, though not contact of a *direct* sort, which we have seen to be impossible. But unlike in aesthetics, the point of knowledge is not to experience the unknowable uniqueness of a real object, but to attain some sort of partial grasp of the features of a sensual object that is already in our midst. This means that whereas aesthetics brought *real objects* into play, knowledge must somehow bring *real qualities* into the picture.

# Meno

Let's begin our discussion with Plato's *Meno*, which is often viewed as an ideal introductory work for students of Plato, though to my mind it is something much more: one of the most important pieces of philosophy ever done. Here I will exclude two interesting parts of the dialogue as lying beyond our immediate concerns: (a) the attempt to show, with an uneducated slave boy, that knowledge is recollection of things already known before birth, and (b) the foreshadowing of Socrates' eventual trial and death through his provocation of the patriotic Anytus.

Meno begins the dialogue by asking Socrates whether virtue can be taught: an already interesting question that becomes even more interesting if we recall that the word for virtue in Greek (*arete*, ἀρετή) has a much broader meaning than the primarily moral sense it has in English. In other words, Meno's question can be widened into one of whether anything can be taught at all. Socrates' response is more interesting than it seems: 'If I do not know what something is, how could I know what qualities it possesses? Or do you think that someone who does not know at all who Meno is could know whether he is good-looking or rich or well-born, or the opposite of these?'[10] Now, the status of 'knowledge' will remain up in the air until the end of the dialogue, and perhaps even following its end. More interesting for our purposes is the distinction Socrates draws between what a thing is and what qualities it possesses. The pre-aesthetic, pre-philosophical experience of common sense tends to operate according to a 'bundle of qualities' model under which a thing is no different from its traits. Socrates unfortunately softens the force of the problem somewhat by shifting from the question of what virtue is to the knowledge of who Meno is. Yet the latter case is not especially troubling, since we can come to know 'who Meno is' simply by asking someone to point at him: and once they have done so, many of his qualities become visible to us by the same stroke, such as whether he seems good-looking or not. But the difference between virtue and its qualities is a more interesting theme, and we could easily make Meno just as interesting if we were to ask not just who Meno is, but 'deep down, what is Meno all about?', or 'what makes Meno tick?' For these are questions about Meno as a withdrawn reality never fully expressible in his traits, not simply the question of how to recognize him on the street.

Meno's failed responses to the question of what virtue is follow the same pattern we find in other interlocutors in Plato's Dialogues. He begins by merely offering *examples* of virtue, which he holds are different for a woman, child, elderly man, free man and slave: 'There is virtue for every action and every age, for every task of ours and every one of us – and, Socrates, the same is true for wickedness.'[11] When Socrates notes that examples are not yet a definition, and that all these numerous virtues must have something in common that makes them virtues, Meno finally tries to offer a definition of this term. In this task he makes two separate attempts, both of them miserable failures. First he tells us that virtue is the ability to rule other people, to which Socrates responds that ruling others is not a virtue in 'a child or a slave'.[12] Surely Meno must mean ruling others *justly*? In the present day, for instance, it would obviously not be a virtue for an untrained person to perform heart surgery or fly an airplane, although these are obviously forms of ruling other people. Meno assents to the condition that rulership must be just, but before long he offers another absurdity in his second attempt at a definition: 'virtue is to desire beautiful things and have the power to acquire them.'[13] Following some prodding from Socrates, Meno specifies some examples of beautiful things: health, wealth, gold, silver, and honours and offices in the city.[14] Yet there are at least two possible problems with such a definition. One is that we normally would not consider the *theft* of gold and silver to be virtue, and thus again we can only speak of the *just* acquisition of beautiful things. But even if we imagine an amoral narcissist with no qualms about unjustly seizing the goods of others, we still need to draw a distinction between what *seems* to be beautiful and good and what is actually so. If someone considers heroin to be a good and beautiful thing and has sufficient power to use it without legal punishment, they are likely to destroy their health by using it anyway. For this reason, we cannot have virtue without having the *wisdom* to distinguish between the truly beautiful things and those that only seem so. Yet again, Meno's definitions of virtue in terms of its supposed qualities have failed, becoming subordinate to terms such as 'justice' and 'wisdom' that will turn out to be no easier to define than 'virtue' itself was. We seem to be reaching a conclusion that is not uncongenial to OOO: none of the concepts for which Socrates seeks a definition seem to be paraphrasable in discursive or literal terms. It is strangely appropriate that Meno used the word 'beautiful' in one of his definitions, since beauty for Kant can never be defined or spelled out in exact words. Given that in all of Plato's Dialogues Socrates never succeeds in finding a definition of anything, we should stop ascribing such failures to his insatiable irony, and wonder instead if *anything at all* can be defined in literal terms. In other words, we seem to have another confirmation of the close relationship OOO claims between philosophy and aesthetics.

Next, in one of the most famous passages of the dialogue, Meno is stunned and confused by his multiple failures to define virtue. He endorses an argument that Socrates then openly rejects, and which is often known today as 'Meno's Paradox'. The argument is as follows: there is no point searching for the definition of anything, because if you already know it then you would not need to look for it, and if you do not already know it then you cannot recognize it when you find it.[15] But this is the same all-or-nothing definition for which I criticized Adrian Johnston above, and which is also found among many other philosophers of idealist inspiration. Socrates' moving rejoinder amounts to this: learning is not an all-or-nothing question. We are partly in the truth and partly in the untruth, so that 'nothing prevents a man, after recalling one thing only – a process men call learning – discovering everything else for himself, if he is brave and does not tire of the search, for searching and learning are, as a whole, recollection.'[16] Here 'recollection' refers to the famous Platonic theory that the soul had knowledge of the things prior to birth, and later lost that knowledge due to the distracting pleasures and pains that arise from being in a body, but can still be stimulated to recall it once again. But the details of this theory of the soul need not be accepted to preserve its essential value: the insight that we are neither fully ignorant nor fully knowledgeable of anything.

The close of the dialogue gets under way when Meno insists on an answer to his initial question of whether virtue can be taught. Though Socrates would rather have continued to ask what virtue is, he yields to Meno's impatience and offers a new line of inquiry to assist with his question. Namely, 'if virtue is a kind of knowledge, it is clear that it could be taught.'[17] For as Socrates puts it, 'I have often tried to find out whether there were any teachers of [virtue], but in spite of all my efforts I cannot find any. And yet I have searched for them with the help of many people, especially those whom I believed to be most experienced in this matter.'[18] Through a series of questions he then leads Meno to the same conclusion: there are no teachers of virtue, because it is not a form of knowledge.[19] What is virtue, then, given that it is not a kind of knowledge? The alternative to knowledge turns out to be 'true opinion', also called 'correct opinion' or 'right opinion'. Socrates' famous example concerns the road to Larissa in northern Greece. A man who knew the way to Larissa would obviously be able to tell others the correct route. Yet there is also another, more interesting case: 'What if someone had had a correct opinion as to which was the way but had not gone there nor indeed had knowledge of it, would he not also lead correctly?'[20]

Socrates proceeds to assert that true opinion is not inferior to knowledge in terms of the results it yields, but Meno is not ready to accept this sweeping claim. As Meno responds: 'But the man who has knowledge will always succeed, whereas he who has true opinion will only succeed at times.'[21] When Socrates makes the clever response that the man with true opinion will always succeed in those cases when his opinion is true, Meno wonders aloud why knowledge is more honoured than true opinion. Socrates explains why with a reference to the mythical sculptures of his supposed ancestor Daedalus, said to be so lifelike that they would run away if not tied down.[22] Knowledge, Socrates continues, is like a tied-down form of true opinion that cannot run away. He adds that 'one ties [it] down by [giving] an account of the reason why', such as the reasons one can be sure that this is the real road to Larissa.[23] A stranger moment occurs when he immediately adds: 'And that, my friend Meno, is recollection, as we previously agreed. After they are tied down, in the first place they become knowledge, and then they remain in place.'[24]

Yet none of this is tidy enough. First of all, it does not make much sense to equate tied-down knowledge with recollection, which was originally introduced as a middle ground between knowledge and ignorance, not as a source of knowledge. Second, though the passage seems to speak in praise of tied-down knowledge, we know that Socrates is no great advocate of knowledge or of the teachers who claim to possess it. He is known, primarily, for (a) stating that he knows nothing and has never been anyone's teacher, and for (b) systematically making a fool in public of anyone who claims to know anything. Philosophy is nothing if not the permanent practice of 'learned ignorance', as the important German religious thinker Nicholas of Cusa would call it in the 1400s.[25] If we try to think up good examples of what could count as *knowledge*, mathematics comes to mind. And while it is true that Socrates uses a geometry problem to attempt to prove the power of recollection in a slave boy, and though Plato's admiration for mathematics was legendary, there is little chance that either Socrates or Plato would accept mathematics as the equal of philosophy, let alone its superior. We need only recall the famous fourfold 'divided line' in Plato's *Republic*, in which shadows are at the bottom, sensory objects just above them, mathematical objects one step higher, and the forms sought by philosophers the highest of all.[26] Far from denigrating virtue when he calls it true opinion, Socrates is thereby able to call it 'a gift from the gods' that cannot be taught, much like metaphor for Aristotle.[27]

Here is what we can take from the *Meno* before moving on. First, Socrates does not think that knowing a thing is the same as knowing its qualities. Whatever the status of knowledge ultimately is for *philosophia*, it is important to note that Socrates rejects the 'bundle of qualities' theory of objects. Second, Socrates refuses the idea that we either know a thing or we do not. The reason for introducing the theory of recollection is to show that there is a way in which we can know something without knowing it, just as indirect language is able to say something without saying it. Much like the first point, this one gives us a reason to reject the idea that the way to grasp a thing is to paraphrase its attributes literally. Third and finally, virtue – like *philosophia*, or anything else for which there are no teachers – is not a form of knowledge, but a 'gift from the gods'. The point of calling philosophy a gift is not to make it the elite province of chosen geniuses, but to say that it cannot be reduced to rules and criteria any more than the fine arts can.

## Other Views on Justified True Belief

Let's look at a handful of other views on these questions before striking directly towards a conclusion as to the nature of knowledge. One of the most famous philosophy articles since World War II is Edmund Gettier's celebrated 1963 piece, 'Is Justified True Belief Knowledge?' I will let the reader decide which is more remarkable: the fact that this article is only three pages long, or that its famous author never published anything else. Gettier notes that many philosophers have tried to define knowledge as justified true belief, and that Plato's *Meno* seems to be the ultimate source of this view.[28] What Gettier does in his article is demonstrate the simple point that 'justified true belief' is not a sufficient condition for something being knowledge. He offers two examples, of which one will suffice for our purposes. Imagine that two men named Smith and Jones have applied for the same job. Smith has already heard from the president of the company that Jones will get the job. For some strange reason, Smith also took the opportunity to count the coins in Jones's pocket, and found there were ten of them. On this basis, Smith is justified in believing as follows: 'The man who will get the job has ten coins in his pocket.' But unbeknownst to Smith, the company has actually decided to hire Smith himself rather than Jones. And again unbeknownst to Smith, who has not even counted his own coins despite his strange action of rummaging through Jones's pocket, he too has exactly ten. Thus, when Smith is suddenly and surprisingly hired for the position, then ceremonially counts his own coins, he will find it was true that 'the man who will get the job has ten coins in his pocket.' Smith's belief in advance of the decision *was* both justified and true: he had good evidence for it, and it turned out to be correct. Nonetheless, it was correct purely by luck, and thus we would never call it knowledge. There has been a hurricane of responses to the article in the more than half a century since it was published. But we need not consider them here, since for now we are only interested in Gettier's conclusion: being both justified and true is not a sufficient condition for a belief being counted as knowledge.

But are 'justified' and 'true' even *necessary* conditions for knowledge? Let's consider first whether justification is needed. This question was answered in the negative in a 1992 article bluntly entitled 'Why Knowledge is Merely True Belief' by Crispin Sartwell, whose title already announces its conclusion. That is to say, Sartwell gives us a strategy for eliminating justification and defining knowledge simply as 'true belief'. In doing so he also makes a pre-emptive strike against the opposite possibility of mere 'justified belief', as in his critique of William Lycan's appeal to such criteria as elegance, economy and evolutionary advantage in his definition of knowledge. But if truth is unattainable, then justification will have to do. And if truth means a correspondence between our beliefs and reality, or some subtler variant thereof (such as Heidegger's partial 'unveiling'), then OOO – unlike Sartwell – cannot possibly accept truth as a criterion of knowledge. Knowledge, which in OOO terms means undermining, overmining or duomining, will have to be defined as 'justified untrue belief', since truth is not possible in the usual sense. What makes 'justified untrue belief' so interesting in the case of OOO is that our account of aesthetics showed it to be the opposite: a form of 'unjustified true belief'. After all, we grasp the wine-dark sea in the moment of theatrically enacting it, although there is certainly no scientific justification for asserting that the sea is dark in the same way as wine. The resemblance between them is not quite literal, since if it were, we would have a mere prosaic statement of identity without any aesthetic effect: 'a pen is like a pencil'. But given that aesthetics now seems to be an inverted form of knowledge – unjustified true belief, as opposed to justified untrue belief – perhaps it is also the case that we can understand knowledge from a OOO standpoint by inverting its theatrical model of metaphor.

As a reminder, metaphor worked in the following way (aesthetic experience more generally can be explained in analogous fashion). The sea and the wine are brought into proximity through the words of Homer. They are put into a definite order: wine-dark sea, not sea-dark wine. This means that the sea as an object takes on the darkness-qualities of the wine, and by implication some of its other qualities, such as disinhibition and oblivion. We now have SO (sea) and SQ (wine-qualities). Yet it is impossible for us to ascribe wine-qualities literally to the sea, or we would simply have a literal statement as in the failed pen/pencil example above. As a result, though the wine-qualities remain largely familiar as they have always been, the sea becomes a mysterious sea, capable of holding wine-qualities in its orbit. Another way of putting it is that SO (sea) is replaced by RO (sea). Thus, the metaphor *should* work to combine RO (sea) and SQ (wine-qualities). But now we come to the final stage. RO (sea) cannot possibly participate in the metaphor, since every RO withdraws or is withheld from any access or relation whatsoever. This, in turn, should have the implication that SQ (wine-qualities) is floating in space, attached to nothing. But the most important lesson we learned from phenomenology is that there is no bundle of qualities unattached to an object. And since RO (sea) is permanently unavailable, it is replaced by RO (beholder). I myself, as the reader of the poem, must perform the metaphor by standing in for the absent sea, or else no metaphor results. Rather than burrowing downward towards the reality of the sea, the metaphor builds a new theatrical sea-reality upward, *on top* of the sensual qualities of the wine. There is no 'justification' for believing in a wine-dark sea, since it is not built from a literal comparison. And yet this belief cannot possibly be untrue, because *it creates its own object in the very act of believing it*. This is why it makes sense to call aesthetics a case of 'unjustified true belief', though one that is not a form of knowledge, as Sartwell's 'true belief' boldly claims to be.

## Justified Untrue Belief

But what about knowledge, which is apparently the inverted case of aesthetics: 'justified untrue belief'? Something similar happens here, though in this case it is the sensual *qualities* rather than the sensual object which get cancelled and replaced. Let's consider a particular known, sensual object, such as the sun. In normal everyday experience, we do not draw a distinction between the sun as an object (SO) and the sun as its qualities (SQ); we tacitly operate with a 'bundle of qualities' theory in which the sun is taken to be nothing more than the sum of its sensual traits. But once we are focused on gaining *knowledge* about the sun, its sensual qualities are cancelled as being no longer enough, since we seek a knowledge lying deeper than first appearances. For example, we know that the apparent tiny size of the sun as a visual phenomenon is simply the result of its great distance from us. In this example as in others, we want to know what the *real* qualities of the sun are, even though ironically we are concerned here with the sensual sun (SO) rather than the real sun (RO), since the latter is the concern of aesthetics rather than science (what does science care about objects that withdraw from all direct access?). Husserl would handle this situation by telling us to ignore our senses and focus on what our intellect tells us, on the basis that the intellect should be able to give us RQ (sun-qualities) rather than SQ (sun-qualities). However, it turns out that the intellect cannot grasp RQ any better than the senses can; the sensual vs. intelligible distinction in Husserl turns out to be no more profound than the practical vs. theoretical distinction to which Heidegger falls prey when explaining his tool-analysis. In fact, RQ (sun-qualities) is not directly attainable by any means, just as RO (sea) was not attainable in the case of metaphor. Recall that in the latter scenario, the ungraspable RO (sea) was theatrically replaced by RO (beholder). In the present case, we seek a replacement for RQ (sun-qualities), but obviously this replacement needs to be a qualities term rather than an object term, and hence the theatrical solution of metaphor will not work.

We therefore must ask: what RQ is already available on the scene in the same way that RO (beholder) was when it stepped in and saved the day for metaphor? The RQ (sun-qualities) cannot be directly known, since contra Husserl's belief in the transcendent powers of the intellect, they withdraw every bit as much as does RO (sun). Nor can the needed RQ be found in any of the other things surrounding the sun in experience, since these too are sensual objects manifesting nothing but sensual qualities. Once again the beholder must do the job, yielding a combination of SO (sun) and RQ (beholder-qualities). To repeat, this is not *theatrical* work by the beholder in the metaphorical manner in which RO (beholder) is combined with SQ (wine-qualities), since we are not ourselves stepping in as objects the way we did when replacing the absent sea of Homer. Instead, it is somehow the case that real qualities drawn from us are lent to SO (sun), in a way we will try to clarify shortly. This is why knowledge does not require the same degree of personal absorption as aesthetic experience: we can look on dispassionately at a riddle of knowledge rather than constantly sustaining it with our own being as we must in aesthetics. As soon as we are bored the artwork is no longer an artwork, but boredom in matters of knowledge is not a rare case at all, and by no means does it destroy the object of knowledge.

Let's summarize the features, just listed, that are needed to fulfil a OOO model of knowledge. We have said that direct or even partial revelation of a thing is impossible, and that it

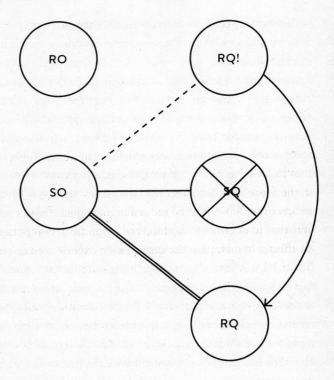

**Figure 3 — Knowledge**

This diagram functions in a manner similar to Figure 2 (p. 84). We begin again with the normal case of a sensual object and its sensual qualities. Just as with Husserl's phenomenology, the evident qualities of a thing are too shallow to provide us with genuine knowledge (hence the crossing out of SQ above). But whereas Husserl thinks the real qualities of an object can be known by the intellect even though the senses fail, OOO holds that real qualities – no less than real objects – withdraw from both sensual and intellectual experience: hence the exclamation point ! on the uppermost RQ above. For this reason, the sensual object SO can combine only with the substitute RQ that I myself as the knower bring to the table.

is therefore less a question of 'truth' than of some sort of *indirect* contact with reality, which means with the real rather than the sensual. Extending this point, we also said that the reality in play in knowledge – unlike in aesthetics – would be real qualities rather than a real object. After all, knowledge (unlike aesthetics) concerns a *sensual* object rather than a real one, but also aims to arrive at the *real* qualities of its sensual object rather than any sensual qualities. We also said that knowledge cannot be metaphorical but must be literal, in the sense that the object of knowledge – such as SO (sun) or any other SO – *must* be reducible to its qualities in such a way that it amounts to nothing but a bundle of components or effects. In metaphor the qualities are experienced directly but orbit a mysterious object; in knowledge the object is before us directly, but is built of a bundle of mysteries. Finally, we said that knowledge must be 'justified untrue belief'. The 'untrue' part is easy, since it is clear that we are dealing with a reality that eludes us rather than a directly accessible truth; the 'justified' part is less immediately clear. And above all, the real qualities grasped in knowledge cannot come from the object itself, but must come from the beholder, whose reality (just as in the aesthetic case) is the only one there on the scene rather than withdrawn.

## Knowledge Without Truth

The time has come to make a slight change to our previous terminology, and draw a distinction between 'knowledge' and 'truth'. Previously we have treated these two words as more or less interchangeable: namely, as forms of 'overmining' that

reduce objects to their direct accessibility to human awareness, with no remaining surplus of reality. It was in this connection that we spoke fondly of Socrates's claim that there is
no knowledge: for if there were knowledge then we ought to
be able to find someone to teach it, and one of the chief lessons of the *Meno* is that there are no teachers – least of all
Socrates himself. But from this point forward, while retain-
ing 'truth' as a pejorative term for false claims to have direct
access to reality, let's partially rehabilitate the word 'knowledge' in order to refer to a positive phenomenon that unmis-
takably does exist: the superior expertise that can be found
to a greater degree in some human masters, places or historical periods than in others. Indeed, I write this sentence from
a hospital ranked number one in the United States in a particular specialty, which is precisely why a family member of
mine has chosen to be a patient here instead of elsewhere. It
is axiomatic for OOO that no direct access to the reality of
this hospital is possible, since that would require that my
own relation to its excellence would be the same thing as
that excellence itself: as if carbon were nothing more than
the role it plays for oxygen in carbon dioxide. Stated differently, there is no *truth* available about this hospital: but not
because everything is relative and therefore just a matter of
opinion or of the way our specific culture constructs reality.
Instead, it is because the reality of the hospital – just like the
reality of anything else – will always be a surplus beyond any
possible opinion. But we have now deliberately decided to
split the word 'knowledge' away from truth and acknowledge
its possibility, in the sense of a form of expertise that is
somehow better than non-expertise, even though it cannot

consist of correct literal paraphrase of whatever subject matter concerns it. We do have a certain knowledge of the knowledge possessed by the specialists in this hospital. Yet neither of these forms of knowledge is a form of overmining, since neither can claim direct access to the reality of the situation itself. Even more than the official printed rankings, what bolsters our sense of the excellence of this hospital is our tacit familiarity with a range of other well-reputed institutions that seem not quite up to the level of this one; something in the manner of the doctor inspires confidence, though we cannot quite place our finger on it. Nor does the knowledge of the doctor herself count as a case of exhaustive overmining; there is somehow more art than science in her interpretation of MRI results, in the assessment of whether surgical or non-surgical options are better suited to the case, in the weighing of known procedural risks that range from the merely annoying to the downright blood-curdling. This can be stated in more technical terms as follows. Undermining and overmining are both ways of replacing a real object with sensual building blocks: whether it be the components of which it is built or the effects it has on other things, in both cases the 'miner' claims to have adequate direct access to these replacements, and thus makes a claim to possess the truth. But that is not what is happening here in the hospital. Instead, we have a sensual object (a medical disorder with a familiar name) made up of elusive *real* qualities that are somewhat known by the doctor without any claim to access them directly or exhaustively. The fact that the qualities are real rather than sensual instantly shows that it is not a question of undermining, overmining or duomining here. The object is not being confused with its components or its effects, as happens in undermining and overmining, since both are regarded by the doctor as not quite sufficient for diagnosis.

We move now to a related problem, which arises from the claim that the real qualities of an object such as a medical disorder come not from the object itself – which is withdrawn from access – but from qualities belonging to me the beholder. An ultra-relativist account of the medical object has already been developed by Annemarie Mol in her influential book *The Body Multiple*. From a OOO standpoint, the obvious deal-breaker in Mol's account is that her position is a case of unapologetic overmining: for Mol there is no unified disease called atherosclerosis (her chosen example), since this disease manifests itself in different ways through different symptoms and diagnostic procedures, and in her view there is no reason to think that a single, unified disease lurks behind its numerous different manifestations. Much of the appeal of this view to those who hold it is that it seems to offer a less rigid view of truth in medicine and elsewhere. By claiming that each medical practice generates its own truth about a disease, this Body Multiple Ontology (I do not use this name sarcastically) seems to let a thousand flowers blossom rather than handing over knowledge to a rationalistic police force cracking down on all dissidents. Yet anyone who has read this far into the book will already know the OOO arguments against overmining, and will know as well that OOO is interested in the *reality* of the disease as that which opposes any exhaustive truth about it. Other than the obvious difference that OOO is a realist position and Mol's an anti-realist one, there is a further distinction. Mol argues that since each diagnostic practice defines a different atheroscler-osis, and since for this reason the number of diseases in play is literally infinite, new practices can always arise in a limit-less number of different cultural contexts. By contrast, OOO is inclined to think that every reality supports multiple types of knowledge, but not an infinite number. More concretely, there may be five or six different ways to interpret a medical condition, and a similar half-dozen or so ways to approach a political dilemma, interpret *Hamlet*, or follow Immanuel Kant with a new philosophy of one's own. The customary postmodernist jump from one truth to infinite truths misses the more interesting option of a finite plurality of them.

Returning now to the main thread of the argument, we need to know what it means that the real qualities in know-ledge come from the beholder rather than the sensual object of knowledge itself. The negative side of this claim should be clear enough: when we observe the sun and theorize about it, the actual real qualities that belong to the sun are not dir-ectly accessible, since – despite Husserl's assertions to the contrary – real qualities withdraw just as much as real objects do. The positive part of the claim might seem more perplex-ing: in what sense does the beholder supply real qualities for a sensual object? Practically speaking, the real qualities of any sensual object we encounter can be found in the unnoticed background assumptions that make it visible to us. What is a good name for such an object, built of unknowable real qualities that cannot be stated literally, and which also come from our own side of the fence rather than from the object directly? It seems to me that we can use the term *paradigm*, made famous in the philosophy of science by

Thomas Kuhn, who tried to replace the gradualist model of scientific progress with one of sudden dramatic 'paradigm shifts' in which the entire course of a science changes suddenly: Darwin in biology, Newton or Einstein in physics.[29] At times, even Kuhn's enemies unwittingly repeat central features of his own position: for example, in my view a surprisingly similar thing is going on with the term 'research programmes' of Imre Lakatos, who presents himself as a committed opponent of Kuhn.[30] What both authors share is the view that there is a hard core to any scientific paradigm or program, one that the scientist does not immediately abandon in the face of occasional contradictory evidence. Against Karl Popper's claim that one falsifying experiment can lay waste to a scientific theory, Kuhn and Lakatos agree that this is not in fact what happens.[31] In any case, the usual reason for rejecting Kuhn is his supposed view that science involves the 'irrational' replacement of one paradigm by another on 'sociological' grounds that trigger scientists into making something like a religious conversion.[32] But there is no need for a paradigm shift to be irrational at all. Abundant good reasons can usually be found to explain why these shifts happen, though since new paradigms are never as broad or well-developed as older ones, something like a 'leap of faith' is usually needed to adopt the new one in its early days. More importantly, Kuhn is on to something important when he distinguishes between historic paradigm shifts in knowledge and the more piecemeal work that he calls 'normal science'. A paradigm is real without being easily translatable into words, whereas the puzzles of normal science can always be stated literally. But a paradigm is not real in the OOO sense of being absent, since it is both real and present in the manner of a *background medium*. Marshall McLuhan famously argued that a medium has a deeper effect on us than any of its content: recall his famous catchphrase, 'the medium is the message'.[33] In similar fashion, Kuhn's paradigm is a set of unarticulated background assumptions about the scientific object, ones that only gradually become literalized and in this way enter their teachable but also their decadent phase. A paradigm (or scientific research programme, to use Lakatos's term) only works for as long as its assumptions are not well understood, much as we saw with the case of symbioses in social theory. Those periods in science that are remembered as 'heroic' are the ones when the most crucial features of a new theory are successively unlocked, and the steadier periods are those in which well-established literal orthodoxy is used to crack down on outliers and renegades. Indeed, this phenomenon goes well beyond the natural sciences and covers the entire sphere of human knowledge, in philosophy as elsewhere.

Kuhn's idea of paradigms gives us a preliminary springboard for the OOO model of knowledge, which does not refer to the direct presence of verified specific facts. Instead, we mean the underlying paradigm or medium, its basic conditions never literally stated, of which the scientific object is composed. The paradigm itself cannot be said to be real, since we are speaking of a sensual object instead of a real one. Nonetheless, it is literally built of real qualities: the vague, initially unstated background assumptions on which the paradigm is based. The paradigm is an *untrue* belief since it does not mirror the world exactly and is doomed to be replaced by something better, yet it is a *justified* belief to the extent that its unstated principles have been able to empower a great deal of fruitful work. This criterion is even clearer in the case of Lakatos's research programmes, which are termed 'progressive' for as long as they make new predictions possible, and 'degenerating' once they are only kept afloat by *ad hoc* hypotheses and predictions of events that have already occurred. Instead of theatricality we might speak here of *commitment*, since a paradigm does not require our individual attention to exist in this moment in the way that a metaphor or artwork does, though we continue to live our lives in accordance with it nonetheless. The relevant authority here would not be Stanislavski as with aesthetics, but the philosopher Søren Kierkegaard, who is famous for urging that we will never have enough proof to justify our life-choices, but must make a decision despite incomplete evidence.[34]

Perhaps it will now also be clear why I argued that *truth* is not the right word to invoke against Donald Trump. From a OOO perspective, there is no truth: not because nothing is real, but because reality is *so* real that any attempt to translate it into literal terms is doomed to failure. We can invoke *knowledge* against Trump's deceptions and evasions, but only insofar as we adopt a new definition of knowledge that incorporates elusive real qualities rather than directly masterable sensual ones. None of us can point to an instrument that clearly displays global warming or the world refugee crisis on a luminous screen, as patent truths that compel specific strategies for dealing with these issues. What we can do, however, is hold the Trumps of the world accountable for taking no account of reality, by which I mean the genuine disturbances in our world that indicate that climate and refugee problems must somehow be incorporated into the body politic. And here as with medical ontology, we suspect that any political problem supports multiple approaches but not an infinite number of them.

# Object-Oriented Ontology and its Rivals

For more than a century, philosophy in the West has been polarized between two parallel traditions: the Anglo-American and the continental European, usually called 'analytic' and 'continental' for short. Despite the recent fashion of claiming that this familiar distinction is either illusory or 'merely sociological' – as if social phenomena had nothing to do with reality – the analytic/continental rift is alive and well today. This can be seen from the simple fact that the adherents of each tradition often do not read the major authors of the other, and in some cases are not even aware of the existence of those authors. Now, despite the markedly interdisciplinary character of OOO, it originally emerged from the discipline of philosophy, and more specifically from the subdiscipline of continental philosophy. This means that OOO has largely been ignored by analytic philosophers, and when not ignored has been quickly dismissed, like virtually all continental trends of sufficiently recent origin.[1]

Nor has the reception of OOO been much more favourable on the continental side of the fence, despite having its birthplace there. One major difficulty is that continental philosophy has usually been either agnostic on the question of realism or outright anti-realist in character, while OOO advocates a robust form of realism that continental readers are quick to treat as a relic of oppressive olden times in philosophy.[2] Furthermore, although cutting-edge continental philosophy since the 1980s has been under the influence of a mostly French avant-garde, the most important recent French thinker for OOO is Latour: widely read by sociologists and anthropologists, but hardly at all by continental philosophers. Those mainstream continental critics who have not simply ignored OOO have sometimes tried to claim OOO's insights as coming originally from their own heroes. The Derridean scholar Peter Gratton, for instance, has claimed that OOO has an 'anxiety of influence' directed at – no surprise – Jacques Derrida himself![3] The purpose of this chapter is to indicate some of the most obvious differences between OOO and those recent French authors who have remained the most dominant over the past thirty to forty years: Derrida and Foucault. Here we will leave out other relevant figures who possibly share more points in common with OOO, such as Badiou, Deleuze and Lacan.

## Jacques Derrida

Few figures in the humanities over the past century have been as controversial as Derrida, the most iconic figure of the intellectual period known as 'postmodern'. His unorthodox style and strange charisma have rubbed many observers the wrong way, to the point that he is sometimes dismissed as a charlatan or a fraud. One example of such negative reactions was when his 1992 nomination for an honorary doctorate at Cambridge University was publicly opposed by a number of prominent analytic philosophers, though he eventually received the degree.[4] While I have personally never been a great fan of Derrida (in the OOO community, Timothy Morton is alone in owing him an intellectual debt) he was certainly not a charlatan or a fraud. Derrida has a cogent philosophical case to make, even if it is not one that I have found compelling or even especially fateful for our discipline. Nonetheless, efforts have sometimes been made to show that OOO has borrowed more from Derrida than it wishes to admit, with Gratton merely providing the least openly hostile version of the claim. Despite his many detractors, Derrida remains adored by many as still the most advanced thinker in the continental tradition of philosophy, a verdict I can in no way accept. This is why I want to explain the major difference that separates Derrida and his still-active tradition with object-oriented currents of thought.

Though already famous in both France and the United States by the mid-1960s, Derrida came into his own as an author in 1967 with the publication of three landmark works.[5] One of these, *Of Grammatology*, remains by far the most frequently cited of his writings. The word 'grammatology' refers to a proposed 'science of writing', though he claims that the momentum for such a science has long been building outside his own work. Let's consider one of Derrida's most interesting interpretations of a classic work of philosophy: Plato's *Phaedrus*, treated in a remarkable essay entitled 'Plato's Pharmacy'.[6] One aspect of the *Phaedrus* is a discussion between Socrates and the title character about the invention of writing. Socrates refers to an ancient Egyptian myth in telling us that writing is a *pharmakon* (the root of our word 'pharmacy'), which in Greek means both poison and cure. What Socrates tries to convey is that while the invention of writing allowed for the preservation of much information that used to be lost to time, we also become reliant upon it in a way that damages our natural power of memory. Perhaps the most unique feature of Socrates as a thinker was that he never put his philosophy in writing, purportedly because he feared his works might be misunderstood after death, since he would no longer be there to explain them in person. More generally, Socrates seems to favour the in-person *presence* of philosophers speaking in their own voice; by contrast, written works would be merely derivative forms of the direct presence of the speaking master.

This is where Derrida inserts himself into the discussion. He dissents from Socrates' views on the privilege of the living voice, since for Derrida the worship of presence is the cardinal error of the entire Western intellectual tradition. As he sees it, there is no pure presence anywhere. The literal meaning of a word or a text is always impossible to pin down, since it cannot be isolated from the numerous possible contexts in which it might be interpreted. The 'misunderstandings' of written work that Socrates fears are, for Derrida, inevitable for every written or spoken utterance; he rechristens them as 'disseminations', referring to the unstoppable spread of meanings in unpredictable ways. Derrida associates presence with what he calls the *logocentrism* of Western metaphysics, and with its kindred terms *phonocentrism* and *phallogocentrism*. The last-mentioned term has often provoked vicious mockery, though the point seems to be that the phallus is often taken to be the ultimate example of pure presence as opposed to the apparent 'lack' represented by the female genitalia. In any case, it would be no exaggeration to say that the fight against presence makes up the whole of Derrida's intellectual career.

The question will now arise as to how Derrida and OOO differ on the theme of presence. OOO can in one respect be viewed as a development of the philosophy of Heidegger, and it is also often said – not without some justice – that Derrida's thought is a development of Heidegger. An introductory book I wrote on Heidegger some years ago even contains the following words on its opening page: 'It was [Heidegger's] view that every great thinker has a single great thought. For Heidegger, that thought can be expressed as follows: *being is not presence*.' Derrida might well have recognized himself in this sentence too, and all the more so given that I continued as follows: 'Being is not present, because *being is time* . . .'[7] Derrida often appeals to *time* as an escape from presence, and Gratton's critique of OOO amounts to the claim that it is a static philosophy unable to handle the innate flux of temporal reality.[8] Yet all of this misses the important point that there are at least *two* different ways of countering presence. One of them is the route taken by OOO, and – I have argued – by Heidegger as well, though OOO would persist on this path even if its interpretation of Heidegger were somehow refuted. This is the route of saying that presence fails because it is merely a translation of an absent real object that can never appear in the flesh without becoming something other than it really is. The real hammer never becomes present even when it breaks or when we deliberately stare at it, since breaking and staring are both relations to the hammer, and the hammer in its own right is something non-relational. In short, OOO follows a philosophically *realist* recipe for outflanking the relational presence of beings, which we have already termed the *sensual* realm. Gratton claims that OOO is merely repeating Plato's philosophy in this way, but such a claim is baseless: whereas Plato's perfect forms are otherworldly and eternal, OOO's real objects are this-worldly and fully destructible. For these reasons, Aristotle would be a much more accurate comparison with OOO.

By contrast, Derrida has nothing in common with philosophical realism, which can be provisionally defined as the view that there is a reality independent of the human mind. Now, it is true that some Derrideans have recently insisted that their hero is a 'realist'. Yet it is important to note that in doing so, they are not making a surprising claim about Derrida and attacking previous Derrideans for misinterpreting him. Instead, they are simply redefining and deflating the word 'realism' to the point where it can no longer pose a threat to Derrida's blatant anti-realism. Let us not mince words: this is a bad-faith effort that does nothing to advance the underlying philosophical dispute, and resembles public relations spin more nearly than scholarship.[9] For it is clear that Derrida's way of opposing presence, unlike OOO's, is *simply not* the realist path of saying that there is a reality independent of how it is accessed in thought, perception, practical action, or even causation. Derrida even dismisses such independent identity and existence as a kind of 'self-presence' that remains a prisoner of logocentric Western metaphysics. His proposed alternative is that the true reason nothing is present is because nothing can ever be pinned down in any *specific* context or as having any *particular* meaning. To defeat presence in a Derridean manner, we do not descend vertically into a non-relational kingdom of things-in-themselves, which is exactly what OOO does. Instead, we slip, slip, slip away *horizontally* into a multitude of other contexts, so that the thing itself not only never appears (as for OOO) but never exists at all. This is the root of the deconstructive method in philosophy, literary criticism, architecture and other fields where Derrida has had significant impact. Remembering our previous discussions of real and sensual objects, we can see that if Derrida makes room for objects at all in his philosophy – and this is already dubious – then they are *sensual* objects, never real ones. For this reason, I see Derrida as a successor less of Heidegger than of Husserl, given that Derrida joins Husserl in decisively rejecting the thing-in-itself in a way that Heidegger never fully does.

Perhaps the quickest way to see Derrida's main differences from OOO is to consider his remarks on metaphor in *Of Grammatology*. Near the end of Part I of that now classic book, we read as follows: 'Thus the name, especially the so-called proper name, is always caught in a chain or a system of differences . . . Metaphor shapes and undermines the proper name. The literal meaning does not exist, its "appearance" is a necessary function . . . in the system of differences and metaphors.'[10] For Derrida, everything is caught up in a chain or system of differences; contra OOO, there is no autonomous reality apart from this system, which is a purely immanent surface with nothing 'deep' hiding behind it. When he speaks of 'metaphor', he refers to the supposed contamination of every individual reality by every other. By contrast, he tells us that the 'literal' (or 'proper') meaning of a name would have to give us that thing directly, outside of any entanglement with other things. Yet this is precisely what Derrida thinks is impossible, since his ontology rules out the possibility of anything existing in isolation from anything else at all. From this he concludes that all names – indeed, all words – are metaphorical and none are literal. As seen in Chapter 2 above, OOO's account of the metaphorical and the literal is completely different from Derrida's. Though we certainly agree with him that there is no literal access to the thing-in-itself, we do not agree that this is because no thing-in-itself exists. For us, the difference between the metaphorical and the literal has to do with whether the bond between the object and its qualities is successfully severed (metaphorical) or whether the object is loosely or explicitly identified with those qualities (literal). From the standpoint of OOO, metaphor is precisely *not* a discourse that belongs to the surface system of differences, one that would scoff at any notion of a hidden depth in things. Instead, metaphor is precisely what points us *towards* the depth of things, despite the fact that this depth can never be encountered directly. One important consequence of Derrida's outright denial of any difference between literal and metaphorical language (since he denies that the former even exists) is that he provides us with no tools at all for examining the difference between them. From a Derridean standpoint, for instance, the phrase 'wine-dark sea' is no different in kind from 'dark purple sea', though OOO sees a powerful distinction between the two. Another way of putting it is that Derrida tries in advance to cancel one axis of OOO's fourfold structure while completely ignoring the other (though since he died in 2004, it is highly unlikely that he ever even heard of OOO). Namely, he (1) tries to abolish the real object in favour of a collection of differential sensual qualities and (2) completely ignores the difference between the thing as object and the thing as qualities, without which genuine metaphor is impossible.

Throughout the book *Of Grammatology* (I refuse to follow the affected guild mannerism of calling everything Derrida wrote a 'text') he shows ample evidence of possessing the usual continental philosophy gene that causes extreme intolerance towards realism. For instance, he accuses Louis Hjelmslev (1899–1965) and his Copenhagen School of linguistics of something called 'naive objectivism'.[11] What this refers to is the 'naive' belief that individual objects exist outside the human mind, or at least outside what Derrida calls 'the game of the world'.[12] For despite the 'fundamental progress' accomplished by Hjelmslev in recognizing the 'immanence' of the system of objects within language, Hjelmslev is 'plagued by a scientificist objectivism, that is to say by another unperceived or unconfessed metaphysics'.[13] But here Derrida adds inaccuracy to insult. The insult came with the word 'naive', as if any realist standpoint on the world were inherently gullible; Derrida leaves no room for any form of un-naive objectivism. The inaccuracy comes with the word 'scientificist', since there are other ways to take a realist approach to objects than via the natural sciences, which I already criticized in Chapter 1 for an overly *literal* approach to objects. The situation as Derrida sees it is that everything that exists refers immediately to something else that exists: 'from

the moment that there is meaning there are nothing but
signs. *We think only in signs.*'[14] Here he is too quick to equate
'we only *think* in signs' with '*there are* nothing but signs', as
if the realm of being were one and the same as the realm
of thinking. To do so he appeals to the authority of the
American semiotician C. S. Peirce, who 'goes very far in the
direction that I have called the de-construction of the transcendental signified, which . . . would place a reassuring end
to the reference from sign to sign'. In other words, Peirce
opposes the notion that a chain of signs ultimately comes to
an end in some ultimate resting point where the referent of
the sign stares us directly in the face: 'there is thus no phe-
nomenality reducing the sign or the representer so that the
thing signified may be allowed to glow finally in the luminos-
ity of its presence.'[15] The argument, in short, is that we never
reach some final thing that shines in 'luminous presence',
and therefore everything must be a sign. What Derrida never
considers is the OOO option: that signs do have an ultimate
signified whose nature is precisely *not* to become present.
The fact that a dog or tree can never become fully present
does not mean that we are confined to a surface of the world
where sensual dogs and trees are intertwined with everything
else. It suggests, instead, that the signified is evoked not with
specific attributes, but with a proper name referring to something deeper than all surface attributes: as in the theory of
names as 'rigid designators' in Saul Kripke's *Naming and
Necessity*, and even Husserl's account of 'nominal acts' in the
*Logical Investigations*.

But not only does Derrida dislike the idea that something
could be signified without also being a sign pointing to

something else: he is not even happy with the notion of individual objects at all. We have already seen that Derrida thinks of the world as a holistic web of signifiers which are bound, 'like all signifiers, to other written and oral signifiers, within a "total" system open, let us say, to all possible investments of sense'.[16] Here we should be very suspicious of the scare-quotes around the word 'total', like all of Derrida's scare-quotes, since he truly holds that everything belongs to a total system of sense and must not be allowed to flee the consequences of that view by divorcing himself from his own words. We should be equally suspicious of the disingenuous qualifier 'let us say', as if Derrida were just loosely entertaining the idea that all possible sense belongs to a holistic web, when in fact he is claiming it bluntly outright. Accompanying Derrida's rejection of isolated individual entities is his rejection of *words* as the basic units of language. He is distrustful of the 'atomic unities that are the written and the spoken word', which he views as 'constituted' unities, meaning that they are not naturally present in the world. Writing, which Derrida always treats as philosophically more interesting than speech, will have no choice in its phonetic form but to 'necessarily operate from already constituted units of signification, in the formation of which it has played no part'.[17] This is not to say that he conceives of words as true pre-existent units: 'the thing is itself a collection of things or a chain of differences . . .'[18]

I would like to close with what I regard as Derrida's fateful misreading of Heidegger, whose philosophy was one of the original inspirations for OOO.[19] This misreading is visible early in *Of Grammatology*, when Derrida speaks inaccurately of Heidegger's insistence that 'being is produced as history only through the logos, and is nothing outside of it . . . all this clearly indicates that fundamentally nothing escapes the movement of the signifier and that, in the last instance, the difference between signified and signifier is *nothing*'.[20] Stated in simpler terms, Derrida thinks that Heidegger makes the case that being is nothing outside the various ways in which it manifests itself to human existence (*Dasein*) over the course of history. While this interpretation does fit nicely with Derrida's crusade against 'naive objectivism', it makes a poor fit with the actual writings of Heidegger, for whom being is that which withdraws absolutely from any relation to humans or anything else. To summarize, Derrida has such animus against realism that he misses the considerable dose of it that can be found in Heidegger's philosophy. The same can be said for Derrida's dislike of what he calls 'the meta-physics of the proper', meaning a metaphysics which holds that things actually exist in their own right with their own properties, outside any holistic web of signifiers. For the sake of argument, let's agree with Derrida that there is no such thing as a proper *meaning* for every word, since every word does become entangled in a chain of further signifiers. Even so, it does not follow from this that nothing has its own proper *being*, as if reality itself were nothing but a holistic web. OOO holds the contrary: even if we were to agree that language is a continuum not broken up naturally into parts, there are no grounds for holding that reality itself is struc-tured in such a 'lava-lampy' way, to use Timothy Morton's phrase.

We might now summarize the difference between Derrida

and OOO as follows. Derrida is a holistic anti-realist who thinks that all language is metaphorical; OOO is an anti-holistic realism which views the distinction between the literal and the metaphorical as one of the key oppositions for philosophy and for everything else. Derrideans are of course free to continue honouring Derrida's legacy for as long as they wish. What they are not in a position to do is claim that Derrida beat OOO to the punch on its central insights, given that the two have stunningly little in common. Derrida as a writer always shows unusual aversion to stating his position clearly and letting the chips fall where they may. His followers too often nurse this aversion by trying to pretend that Derrida is saying everything and its opposite simultaneously, so that any critique is devoured and internalized as quickly as if Derrida had built it into his position in advance. In my opinion it is this unfortunate factor, even more than a suppressed craving for hardcore political Leftism, that lifted the plainspoken Žižek and Badiou to the pinnacle of continental philosophy during the decade following Derrida's death.

# Michel Foucault

Whatever one thinks of the works of Foucault, he is surely the most influential philosopher of the past half-century if we consider his effect across all disciplines, despite his not having survived to the age of sixty. Some of his best-loved books are case studies of the development of various modern institutions, such as *The Birth of the Clinic*, *History of Madness*, *Discipline and Punish*, and his unfinished multi-volume *History of Sexuality*. Alongside these are some more general and technical works, including *The Order of Things* and *The Archaeology of Knowledge*. But perhaps the best introduction to Foucault for newcomers is to read any collection of his interviews, in which the brilliance and rapidity of his mind come through even more clearly than in his books. My own favourite interview collection is the humorously entitled *Foucault Live*, which at nearly 500 pages can still be read with pleasure in less than a day. Nonetheless, when it comes to those French philosophers who pretend to be merely social scientists, I have always preferred Latour to Foucault, and suspect that the intellectual world may soon come to agree with me. The reason for this is Latour's far greater ability to deal with inanimate reality alongside the human sphere. Though Foucault is often described as a 'materialist', and has inspired much scholarship on 'material culture' through the school known as New Historicism, he really invokes non-human entities only in the service of his true intellectual project: a historicism of the human subject. Though Latour describes himself aptly as a 'non-modern' thinker, Foucault is clearly very much a modern one ('postmodernism' being just another form of modernism). For this reason, OOO finds less of immediate interest in Foucault's work than in Latourian actor-network theory. Nonetheless, self-styled materialists of Foucauldian inspiration often claim to have preceded OOO in discussing the non-human world. Here I want to show why such claims are false, and establish briefly that OOO and Foucault have little to do with each other.

Although Foucault is worth book-length treatment from a OOO standpoint someday, we can focus here on the opening chapters of *The Archaeology of Knowledge*, where the tenets of Foucault's ontology become clear, even though his ostensible subject is 'discourse' rather than reality. Much like Derrida, Foucault is sceptical of the concept of 'unity' that we find in any object-oriented philosophy in the widest sense: the unity of the object not just in OOO, but also the unity of the monad for Leibniz or of the primary substance for Aristotle. When speaking of intellectual figures, 'the unities that must be suspended above all are those that emerge in the most immediate way: those of the book and the *oeuvre*.'[21] Though a book seems like the most obvious sort of unified object, Foucault rejects its unity insofar as it 'is caught up in a system of references to other books, other texts, other sentences: it is a node within a network.'[22] Once its unity is challenged, 'it loses its self-evidence; it indicates itself, constructs itself, only on the basis of a complex field of discourse.'[23] The same objection holds if we are speaking of the *oeuvre* or entire written output of a single famous author. For instance: 'the same relation does not exist between the name Nietzsche on the one hand and the youthful autobiographies, the scholastic dissertations, the philological articles, *Zarathustra*, *Ecce Homo*, the letters, the last letters signed "Dionysos" or "Kaiser Nietzsche", and the innumerable notebooks with their jumble of laundry bills and sketches for aphorisms.'[24] Such unities, Foucault holds, 'do not come about of themselves, but are always the result of a construction the rules of which must be known, and the justification of which must be scrutinized . . .'[25]

Although Foucault manages to convince many people with these sorts of arguments, when viewed from a OOO standpoint the reasoning looks weak. We might concede the point that everything ever penned by Nietzsche, in youth or later, might need to be included in his collected works in the name of erring on the side of completeness. Even then – Foucault is right to say – it does not follow that all of these works have the same status. Scholars will tend to reach a consensus as to which writings by Nietzsche are a truly essential part of his philosophical career as a whole, or of his mature period, or of some other more or less well-reasoned periodization of his work. Of course, sometimes consensus is lacking. Many Heidegger scholars long avoided a serious reading of the philosopher's 1933 Nazi-inspired rectoral address, 'The Self-Assertion of the German University', which they viewed as an unfortunate and embarrassing piece of political hack-work. But this was not the case for Derrida, whose remarkable work *Of Spirit* treats the rectoral address as an important piece of Heidegger's intellectual output. There will always be scholarly struggles over which is the best text we have of works by Homer, Virgil or Shakespeare, and further struggle over what to include or exclude as concerns the collected works of any important intellectual figure. From these indisputable phenomena, Foucault hastily concludes that such decisions are 'constructed', meaning that they are constructed by *people* rather than provided directly by the object of study itself. But this conclusion sets the bar much too high for the object, and too low for the human subject. For on the one hand it is true in the most trivial sense that without human labour there would be no books left to us at all. A certain degree of scholarly diligence and judgement was required for us to inherit the reasonably accurate collected dialogues of Plato or plays of Shakespeare, as well as an ongoing (and apparently flawed) project like the Heidegger *Gesamtausgabe*.[26] The work of human intelligence is always needed to establish such collections, especially in a case like Plato's where there are so many possibly spurious dialogues floating around under his name, or a case like Heidegger's where even the handwriting poses obstacles to accurate transcription. But from the fact that those texts truly authored by Plato do not flash golden light once we select them properly, it does not follow that there is no unity to the works of Plato. The 'constructions' made by human scholars are not arbitrary or motivated solely by concerns on the human side of the equation, but are made in the service of a search for Plato's genuine texts. The impossibility of ultimately *knowing* which of those texts are really his does not entail that no true corpus of Plato's writing exists, just as the impossibility of *knowing* all the features of an apple does not mean that the apple is just a so-called unit constructed by the work of human habit.

The point I am criticizing here is not a small one for Foucault, but is the basis for his entire intellectual career. After resolving aloud that 'I will not place myself inside these dubious unities', Foucault enthusiastically reports that in this way 'an entire field is set free'.[27] It is 'a vast field, but one that can be defined nonetheless: this field is made up of the totality of all effective statements (whether spoken or written), in their dispersion as events and in the occurrence that is proper to them.'[28] In other words, what Foucault offers is not an object-oriented ontology, but one of its most frequently proposed alternatives: an *event*-oriented ontology.

He continues: 'Before approaching, with any degree of certainty, a science, or novels, or political speeches, or the *oeuvre* of an author, or even a single book, the material with which one is dealing is, in its raw, neutral state, *a population of events in the space of discourse in general.*'[29] An event is never indeterminate, but always consists of a completely definite set of relations. For example, if we decide to view the Cuban Revolution as an event rather than an object, what this means is that we focus on all of the specific *actions* that occurred, and not anything that might be imagined to lie deeper than those actions. This is why Foucault urges that no one try 'to rediscover beyond the statements themselves the intention of the speaking subject, his conscious activity, what he meant, or, again, the unconscious activity that took place, despite himself, in what he said or in the almost imperceptible fracture of his actual words . . .'[30] Instead, 'we do not seek below what is manifest the half silent murmur of another discourse . . .'[31] Now, in some cases it might prove to be an ingenious *method* to focus only on statements that were actually made and things that actually happened, in order to avoid all speculation as to the true intentions or deeper moving forces of any historical event. Powerful insights might result from this decision, just as actor-network theory (by also looking only at actions) has given us powerful interpretations of everything from the career of Louis Pasteur to the failure of a proposed new automated Metro system for Paris.[32] But methods are forms of *knowledge*, and as such they are either overmining methods (as with Foucault and Latour) or undermining methods (as with Dennett's preference for exact chemical formulae over more poetic methods of wine tasting). Philosophy, however, is a counter-knowledge or counter-method, and as such it must oppose any attempt to conflate useful methods for studying reality with reality itself. In this respect, Foucault is wrong when he tells us that 'a statement is always an event that neither the language nor the meaning can ever exhaust.'[33] Quite the contrary. As soon as something has been defined as an event, it is already defined as a very specific set of relations between various entities, and as such it is already exhausted by being reduced to a set of determinate features. The fact that historians and other speakers can explore this event from an infinite number of different viewpoints does not mean that the event itself is inexhaustible: for only objects, deeper than all relations, are truly inexhaustible, and it is the chief merit of OOO to have pressed this point.

This is not to say that Foucault's work is without importance. In point of practice, he has an unusual gift for uncovering merely *apparent* historical unities that may turn out to be false ones. In his classic *History of Madness*, Foucault does his best to show that there is no unified object called 'madness', and thus that 'it would certainly be a mistake to try to discover what could have been said of madness itself, its secret content, its silent, self-enclosed truth . . .'[34] He holds that human discourses *constitute* their objects rather than speaking about them as pre-given units. And indeed, it cannot be denied that philosophy is produced and developed through philosophical discourse, that societies can be redesigned thanks to the insights of sociologists, or that psychoanalytic patients often find themselves having Freudian or Lacanian dreams. The problem is that for Foucault, all of the work seems to be done on the human side of the fence, given the inherent 'non-identity [of objects] through time' and their 'internal discontinuity that suspends their permanence'.[35] Foucault even claims that the noun/verb distinction is an artifact of 'Classical grammar', and here we must keep in mind that for French philosophers of the 1960s the word 'Classical' is always meant to be one of the most devastating of adjectives.[36] In the cases of disciplines such as medicine, economics or grammar, Foucault does not see their unity as constituted by 'a full, tightly packed, continuous, geographically well-defined field of objects'.[37] For 'it would be quite wrong to see discourse as a place where previously established objects are laid one after another like words on a page.'[38] Speaking of words, Foucault is careful to insist that he is not simply retreating to an analysis of language rather than an analysis of the world. For as he notes, in 'the kind of analysis that I have undertaken, *words* are as deliberately absent as things themselves . . .'[39] And true enough, Foucault's 'events' are broader than words, though they are certainly not broader than the network of relations in which they always take place. As Foucault rather poetically puts it: 'the object does not await in limbo the order that will free it and enable it to become embodied in a visible and prolix objectivity . . . It exists under the positive condition of a complex group of relations.'[40] And once again: 'it is not the objects that remain constant, nor the domain that they form . . . but the relation between the surfaces on which they appear, on which they can be delimited, on which they can be analysed and specified.'[41]

All this attention to relations, to networks, to events of

which unified objects can only be a derivative, might make Foucault sound a bit like an actor-network theorist involved in precisely the same sort of overmining project as ANT. But as hinted previously, ANT is superior to Foucault in a crucial respect. Latour begins with a 'flat ontology' that erases the distinction between subject and object as an obsession of modern philosophy. This is precisely what makes Latour a *non-modern* thinker, to use a valuable term he coined himself. Retroactively, we can say the same of Alfred North Whitehead, who also steadfastly refused to see the human perception of a tree as anything radically different in kind from the wind's interaction with that tree. In Foucault's case, the object is weakened to such an extent that we are tempted to say it disappears entirely, with 'discursive formations' doing all of the work. But this claim is not essential; if it makes Foucauldians angry, we can drop it for now. What is more important at present is that his ontology is not flat, and thus he is very much a modern (though in the guise of a 'postmodern') rather than a non-modern. His thinking shows no respect for objects, and especially not for inanimate objects. As the role of inanimate objects in philosophy continues to increase, we might expect Latour to replace Foucault at some point as the standard default reference in the humanities and social sciences: by which I mean someone cited repeatedly even by those who have never read him.

# Varying Approaches to Object-Oriented Ontology

In the late 1990s I whimsically coined the term 'object-oriented philosophy' to refer to my own work, first delivering a conference lecture under that title in September 1999.[1] It took nearly a decade before others rallied to the banner and began to see their own work in similar terms. In the summer of 2009, Levi Bryant began to use the phrase 'object-oriented ontology' (OOO) as a broader umbrella term including variant forms of object-related thought with independent features differing from my own. Initially OOO referred only to Bryant, Ian Bogost and me; we were joined the following year by the prominent ecological writer Timothy Morton, who had initially been a OOO sceptic.[2] This became the original core group of object-oriented ontology, often still listed together whenever OOO is mentioned in various intellectual fields. In this chapter I will briefly introduce the thought of Bogost, Bryant and Morton, but will also speak briefly about two important outsiders who came to compatible views of their own in complete independence of the core OOO group: Jane Bennett in the United States, and Tristan Garcia in France. I will also discuss some of the key figures responsible for importing OOO into architecture, the field outside philosophy where it perhaps enjoys its greatest influence at present.

# Ian Bogost

Bogost (b. 1976) is the Ivan Allen College of Liberal Arts Distinguished Chair in Media Studies at Georgia Tech. He is a prominent videogame designer and critic, as well as a frequent columnist for *The Atlantic*. Among his most important books in connection with OOO are *Unit Operations*, *Persuasive Games*, *Alien Phenomenology*, and the more recent *Play Anything*. Bogost's writing is marked by a cultivated style pointing to his background as a literary scholar. He is also known for his lethal wit, as seen in his Facebook game Cow Clicker (a ruthless parody of the popular Farmville), and his widely followed and uproariously funny @ibogost Twitter account. In his debut book *Unit Operations*, Bogost employs the term 'unit' in much the same way as my own work uses 'object' or Leibniz uses 'monad'. Bogost's influential *Persuasive Games* focuses on the concept of 'procedural rhetoric' in a manner congenial to OOO's interest in rhetoric more generally. The subtitle of *Alien Phenomenology*, 'What It's Like to Be a Thing', points to another key concern of OOO: that non-human entities be treated philosophically in the same way as human ones. Since all of these books have already been widely discussed, I will focus my brief remarks on his new work *Play Anything*.

Bogost begins with what looks like a charming anecdote of fatherhood, recalling an incident in which he was pulling his four-year-old daughter too quickly through an Atlanta mall. While doing so he felt strange contrary forces coming from his daughter's tiny arm: 'When I looked down I saw why: she was staring straight at her shoes, timing her footfalls to ensure she stepped within the boundaries of the square, white tiles lining the floor. The sensations I interpreted as pulls and tugs had been caused by shifts in her weight as she attempted to avoid transgressing the grout lines, while I pulled forward and sideways around crowds.'[3] Starting from this anecdote, Bogost spends his entire book developing something like a OOO ethics, or at least a OOO art of living. For despite his frustration with the current 'gamification' of everything in our midst, whether through checking in at various businesses on the Foursquare mobile phone app or amassing banal point totals on a multitude of rewards cards, there is something to be said for treating oppressive consumerist situations as games.[4] Bogost contrasts his standpoint with that of the late novelist David Foster Wallace, who advised us to approach the miserable dullness of our everyday lives with *empathy* for those who provoke our anger in small ways: 'everyone else in the supermarket's checkout line is just as bored and frustrated as I am, and . . . some of these people probably have much harder, more tedious or painful lives than I do, overall.'[5] Despite the obvious good intentions of Wallace's advice, Bogost sees it as merely exacerbating the problem: for Wallace's 'alternative to the madness of default selfishness is an equally soul-destroying, utterly boundless hypothetical empathy. He advises us to retreat *further* into the self, which makes it more difficult truly to accept the woman at the checkout – or anything else, for that matter.'[6]

Already we see the main outlines of Bogost's ethics of play. Dreariness can be escaped by *exiting* the self rather than focusing on it, in contrast with philosophies of a Stoic inspiration that advise us to ignore the superficialities of an uncontrollable outside world and focus instead on our own *attitude* towards that world. Whereas modern thought in all its variants tries to *purify* human consciousness from the world, Bogost makes the blatantly non-modernist gesture (typical of OOO) of taking the world ever more seriously. As he puts it: 'We've trained ourselves to see commitments as affectations, and only to pursue a commitment ironically so that we can cast it aside if fear overtakes us. But foolishness signals that you're on the right track. Fun comes from the attention and care you bring to something that imposes arbitrary, often boring, even cruel limitations on what you – or anyone – can do with them.'[7] Such limitations also bring with them an important dose of humility, 'for they force us to treat things *as they are* rather than *as we wish them to be*'.[8] This amounts to 'the gratification of meeting the world more than halfway, almost *all* the way, and reaping the spoils of our new discoveries made under the sail of generosity rather than selfishness'.[9] It contrasts sharply with what Bogost calls 'the mania of selfish irony: the world can never fully satisfy me, so I will hold it at arm's length forever.'[10] To be endlessly ironic about everything, an attitude that follows directly from modern philosophy's clean split between thought and world, is to fail to recognize that we are necessarily amidst things, taking them seriously at every moment. Though Bogost does not use this example himself, the tendency is wonderfully parodied by a brilliant fake editorial in the satirical newspaper *The Onion*, entitled 'Why Can't Anyone Tell I'm Wearing This Business Suit Ironically?', authored by a fictitious character named Noah Frankovitch. As Frankovitch tells us, he began by attending parties in bland business suits while carrying an attaché case, only to discover that his friends missed the joke and angrily called him a 'sell-out'. Nonetheless, he pushed the irony further by taking a job in a law office, buying a 'lame-ass TAG Heuer' luxury watch, and taking the morning commuter train along with all of the un-ironic workers. Ultimately, Frankovitch goes so far as to dedicate his intimate personal life to the spirit of irony: 'I even married this clueless girl from Connecticut – loves shopping and everything – and we have two ironic kids. I swear, they look like something out of a creepy 1950s Dick And Jane reader – I even have these hilarious silver-framed pictures of them in my cheesy corner office. But still, the humor is lost on everybody but me.'[11] In a sense, Bogost's ethical proposals ask us to do nothing more than avoid Frankovitchism. The point is not that self-awareness has no value, because of course it does. The point is that ironic detachment from one's own views and even one's own life has, through the joint workings of postmodern theory and pop culture, become a miserable cliché: an idea once but no longer liberating. We are now awash in what Bogost – by analogy with paranoia – calls 'ironoia', defined as follows: 'If paranoia is the mistrust of people, ironoia is the mistrust of things . . . Zooming out a level with irony is far easier than reconciling the conflict between sincerity and disdain, so as to reconnect with the world we miss by wavering endlessly between them.'[12]

Real fun, Bogost holds, is found in the world rather than in us.[13] An object as simple as a steering wheel still has a definite range of possible movements to be explored, and the same holds for a guitar or anything else.[14] Whereas modernism puts all freedom on the side of an alienated human subject, estranged from the world, Bogost's non-modernist approach shifts much of the interest of life back into the things themselves. Supporting this case is the important twentieth-century Dutch thinker Johan Huizinga, whose classic work *Homo Ludens* 'shows that the rituals and practices of human culture, from law to religion to war to politics, all rely on the elements of play as fundamentals'.[15] Perhaps Bogost's most distinctive contribution to the discussion is his idea of play as *submissive* rather than *subversive*, since despite the high regard in which subversion is held by intellectuals today, it is really just another form of irony.[16] To think of play as subversion is already, Bogost notes, 'to contain and sterilize [it] under the plastic-wrap of commentary or sabotage'.[17]

Perhaps the culminating insight in Bogost's book, which occurs in Chapter 5, is the difference he sees between 're-straint' and 'constraint'. Restraint is a way of rejecting objects so as to remove oneself of their taint. For Bogost this is just another form of irony and the pre-eminence of the self as the wise rejecter of what lies outside: 'Perhaps all exercises of restraint are actually ironizing acts, symptoms of our fundamental boredom: holding something at arm's length, refusing it, and disposing of it all fashion a phantasmal copy, a ghost that we can then pride ourselves on having spurned. "Well, *I* didn't eat any cake."'[18] Constraint, by contrast, comes from accepting the limitations of one's situation and trying to do something new within their confines: 'Artists and designers have long known that creativity does not arise from pure, unfettered freedom. Little is more paralyzing than the blank canvas or the blank page.'[19] Whereas Kant thought of ethics as something unfolding entirely within the sphere of human subjectivity, so that any external objects or consequences were beside the point, Bogost's position is much closer to that of Scheler, who – as we saw earlier – treated ethics as occurring in the subject's passionate dealings with the world rather than in isolation from it.

## Levi R. Bryant

Bryant (b. 1974) is a member of the faculty at Collin College in Frisco, Texas, a suburb of Dallas. He is a prolific author of blog posts, and in my opinion his 'Larval Subjects' blog is home to the most serious philosophy ever done online.[20] He was also the conceiver and lead editor of *The Speculative Turn*, the most influential anthology of early twenty-first century philosophy in the continental tradition. Before his involvement with OOO, Bryant was known primarily for *Difference and Givenness*, his highly regarded debut book on the philosophy of Deleuze. The most famous work of his early object-oriented period is surely the 2011 book *The Democracy of Objects*. And while Bryant has declared his increasing distance from OOO in recent years, accompanied by a heightened number of references to his original philosophical hero Deleuze, the themes of OOO remain central even in his most recent book: the 2014 *Onto-Cartography*. His success has been aided by the remarkable lucidity and pedagogical skill of his writing, not to mention the wealth of detail at his command in multiple fields as a result of his omnivorous reading habits.

Here I will focus on *Onto-Cartography*, since it is Bryant's latest book, the subject so far of much less commentary than the already established *The Democracy of Objects*. In *Onto-Cartography*, Bryant claims to partly abandon OOO in favour of what he calls a 'machine-oriented ontology'. In one sense this might signal a simple return to his Deleuzian roots, since Deleuze and Guattari frequently speak of 'desiring machines' as well as other types of machines.[21] Yet Bryant also makes a specific complaint about the term 'object'. His primary reservation is that objects are usually opposed to human subjects, and hence the term OOO is doomed to perpetual misunderstanding. Nonetheless, we cannot help noticing that his classification of the six different types of machines uses the name 'object' for no less than four of them.[22] And quite aside from this inconsistency, 'machine' carries historical baggage at least as heavy as 'object', which Bryant tacitly recognizes by spending more than ten pages trying to distance his own sense of 'machine' from various possible misreadings.[23] All this aside, what Bryant seems to like best about the term 'machine' is its suggestion of a composite entity built of further sub-machines, and so on downward indefinitely. He also takes care to deny that 'machine' entails some sort of robotic mechanism that achieves automatic and predictable results each time (a self-imposed danger from which the term 'object' was already free). On the whole, the most characteristic tendency of Bryant's new term 'machine' is its emphasis on actions and effects. This fits well with his claim that what a machine *does* is more important than what it *is*, though this argument strikes me as a form of 'overmining', the term I've employed for philosophies that reduce a thing upward to its tangible appearances or effects.

Be that as it may, *Onto-Cartography* does the important work of attempting a theory of six different types of objects: dark objects, bright objects, satellites, dim objects, rogue objects and black holes. Or rather, it is a theory of six different kinds of *roles* that any object might fill at different times: 'a machine can pass from being a dim object to being a bright object. One machine can be a black hole for one machine, but a satellite for another machine.'[24] Here, as with any typology, our first task is to assemble Bryant's six proposed relational roles of objects into a plausible structure, though he already does the job so well himself that there is little to add to his account. In the first place, we find a continuum of machines ranging from least to most influential: dark objects, dim objects, bright objects and black holes. It should be noted that black holes in Bryant's usage, despite the occurrence of the word 'black', are even *brighter* than bright objects, since the metaphor 'bright' refers to degrees of influence rather than visibility. A purely dark object would exist without having an effect on anything else, and would thus be the sort of thing of whose very existence Latour would be sceptical. Dark objects are Bryant's version of what in my own work are called 'dormant' objects, which exist despite not yet (or not ever) influencing anything else.[25] Bryant reserves judgement as to whether these exist, 'because if dark objects do exist, they would be so thoroughly unrelated to other machines – most importantly, ourselves – that we would have no idea of their existence whatsoever.'[26] Yet he does point usefully to the existence of *relatively* dark objects, such as magnetic fields that may only be perceptible to birds, or the Dead Sea Scrolls prior to their discovery.

Dim objects refer to those entities that barely leave a trace on others, such as the homeless in most political contexts, or even those with disabilities if steps are not taken to ensure their inclusion. Bryant skilfully links such objects to the terminology of some well-known contemporary French thinkers: namely, to Jacques Rancière's proletariat or 'part of no part', and Badiou's mention of objects that 'appear only faintly' in a given world.[27] As politically the most Leftist member of the original OOO group, Bryant is occupied with the idea that much of politics has to do with giving voice to previously dim objects: as in the emancipation of slaves, women's suffrage, LGBTQ rights, and so forth. By contrast, bright objects are those with so much power that some or all humans must organize their lives according to them, for better or worse: the sun for all Earth life, oil for contemporary humans, parents for their children, rice for Asian farmers, university administrations for their professors, and the Supreme Court for (normal) American Presidents. Those objects that depend on bright objects are termed satellites, with children being one of Bryant's most moving examples: 'Children are caught in a web of the parents' desires, regrets, neuroses, beliefs, obsessions, values, and quirks.'[28] Next in order are black holes, the most dismally bright of bright objects, since their gravity is so strong that nothing can escape them: a terminal illness, paralysis following an accident, or confinement in prison under a Kafkaesque legal system. In the wary words of Bryant, 'let us hope that black holes are rare'.[29]

That leaves just one remaining type in Bryant's roster of machines: the *rogue* object, or one that comes from nowhere and disrupts the current world. After explicitly linking Rancière's politics with dim objects, Bryant ties Badiou's highly influential political theory more strongly to the rogue object: for surely the famous Badiouian *events* are the perfect case of something arriving from outside the world and shaking it to its core. Nonetheless, Bryant rightly complains that Badiou restricts events to a fourfold taxonomy of art, politics, love and science, deliberately excluding events such as natural disasters, to which we might also add the discovery of new continents, the arrival of extraterrestrials, or any event that does not hinge primarily on the human subject's attitude to a revolutionary occurrence in art, politics, love or science. For despite Badiou's careful insistence that not all individual humans are subjects and not all subjects are human individuals, all he means by the latter point is that a *human collective* can also be a subject. Nowhere does Badiou entertain the notion that an event might involve purely inanimate agents, and Bryant remains sufficiently OOO in spirit to regret this typical modernist downgrade of everything outside the human sphere.

# Timothy Morton

Morton (b. 1968), a native of London, is Rita Shea Guffey Professor of English at Rice University in Houston, and had already come into his own as a public figure before joining forces with OOO. Originally a scholar of English Romanticism, he channelled this interest into two ground-breaking works on environmental themes: *Ecology without Nature* and *The Ecological Thought*. Here already he showed an uncanny gift for introducing new terms that stick, such as 'the mesh', 'the strange stranger', and 'hyperobjects'. The latter term provided the title for his briskly selling 2013 book, which refers to objects deployed so massively in space or time that human beings cannot engage with them in any reciprocal way. This should be obvious once we think of radioactive waste, plastic garbage, or global warming itself, all of them having effects at a scale we can hardly begin to conceive. Also in 2013, Morton published his controversial *Realist Magic*, whose controversy stemmed mostly from its spirited defence of the OOO thesis that physical causation itself has a metaphorical structure. In 2016 came the long-awaited release of Morton's *Dark Ecology*, based on the transcripts of his prestigious Wellek Lectures several years earlier at the University of California at Irvine. Morton is active as a visiting speaker around the world, and has received growing attention due to his timely work on ecological themes.

Having just recounted Bryant's six different types of roles that can be filled by machine-objects in their mutual relations, let's consider another interesting classification found in Morton's *Hyperobjects*, one of his most widely read books. The concept is defined on the opening page:

> In *The Ecological Thought* I coined the term *hyperobjects* to refer to things that are massively distributed in time and space relative to humans. A hyperobject could be a black hole. A hyperobject could be the Lago Agrio oil field in Ecuador, or the Florida Everglades. A hyperobject could be the biosphere, or the Solar System. A hyperobject could be the sum total of all the nuclear materials on Earth; or just

the plutonium, or the uranium. A hyperobject could be the very long-lasting product of direct human manufacture, such as Styrofoam or plastic bags, or the sum of all the whirring machinery of capitalism. Hyperobjects, then, are 'hyper' in relation to some other entity, whether they are directly manufactured by humans or not.[30]

By book's end, Morton will conclude that in light of our environmental crisis, there is a sense in which *every* object is a hyperobject.[31] As he puts it: 'Nonhuman beings are responsible for the next moment of human history and thinking . . . The reality is that hyperobjects were already here, and slowly but surely we understood what they were already saying. They contacted us.'[32] Like Bogost, Morton rejects the modernist idea of thought as taking a distance from the world or rising above it in jaded or ironic transcendence. In Morton's words: 'If there is no metalanguage, then cynical distance, the dominant ideological mode of the left, is in very bad shape, and will not be able to cope with the time of hyperobjects.'[33] To begin to cope with it, Morton invokes a list of five features belonging to hyperobjects: viscosity, nonlocality, temporal undulation, phasing and interobjectivity. He summarizes these properties as follows:

> Hyperobjects have numerous properties in common. They are *viscous*, which means that they 'stick' to beings that are involved with them. They are *nonlocal*; in other words, any 'local manifestation' of a hyperobject is not directly the hyperobject. They involve profoundly different temporalities than the human-scale ones we are used to

[*temporal undulation*] . . . Hyperobjects occupy a high-dimensional phase space that results in their being invisible to humans for stretches of time [*phasing*]. And they exhibit their effects *interobjectively*; that is, they can be detected in a space that consists of interrelationships between aesthetic properties of objects. The hyperobject is not a function of our knowledge: it's *hyper* relative to worms, lemons, and ultraviolet rays, as well as humans.[34]

We should now give a brief account of these features, an activity that occupies Morton for the whole of Part I of his book.

Viscosity was already subjected to beautiful philosophical treatment in the 1940s by the existentialist Jean-Paul Sartre, who compares our absorption in viscous media to 'that of a wasp which sinks into the jam and drowns in it'.[35] Whereas modern philosophy views humans as transcendent and ironic beings, not made entirely of the same stuff as the cosmos in which they dwell, viscosity teaches the opposite lesson: that 'we are [not] forever floating in outer space, but quite the opposite: we are glued to our phenomenological situation.'[36] All viscosity, Morton argues, is really just a watered-down version of its greatest possible intensity: death. As he puts it: 'When the inside of a thing coincides perfectly with its outside, that is called *dissolution* or *death*. Given a large enough hyperobject . . . all beings exist in the jaws of some form of death, which is why the Buddhist thangkas of the Wheel of Life depict the six realms of existence cycling around within the open, toothy mouth of Yama, the Lord of Death.'[37] Now, a critical reader might complain that viscosity is already a well-worn theme for which Morton and OOO can take no credit. For not only does Sartre treat the theme explicitly, but numerous other philosophers in the modern period have realized that self and world are entangled in a sticky manner, in particular through the fact that our mind is always *embodied* in the world. Yet such claimants to priority nearly always miss the really original point of OOO: namely, 'that *one can extend this insight to nonhuman entities*. In a sense, all objects are caught in the sticky goo of viscosity, because they never ontologically exhaust one another even when they smack headlong into one another.'[38] Citing a term that is crucial for OOO despite the sneers it often evokes, Morton speaks as well of 'the truth of what phenomenology calls *ingenuousness* or *sincerity*'.[39] For Morton as for Bogost, the sincerity of any human or nonhuman agent stems from the fact that it is inevitably wrapped up in whatever it is doing right now: much like Noah Frankovitch, the 'ironic' fictional lawyer, who expends his life in lawyering even while claiming to mock the practice.

We turn next to what Morton calls the nonlocality of hyperobjects. He openly acknowledges the scientific origins of this concept: '*Nonlocality* is a technical term in quantum theory. Alain Aspect, Einstein's student David Bohm, Anton Zeilinger, and others have shown that the Einstein–Podolsky–Rosen [EPR] Paradox concerning quantum theory is an empirical fact.'[40] What this means is that two particles can be 'entangled', so that when information is sent to one of them, the other will immediately act in opposite or complementary fashion – even if they are already separated by a distance that ought to make rapid communication impossible. Morton continues: 'According to the accepted view, this should fail to happen, since it implies signals travelling faster than light.

[Yet] Zeilinger has demonstrated nonlocal phenomena using entangled particles on either side of Vienna, between two Canary Islands, and between orbiting satellites.[41] Unless we want to question Einstein's axiom that the speed of light is the maximum speed for any information transfer, we seem compelled to accept nonlocality as a basic feature of our universe. From this, Morton draws conclusions extending beyond the sphere of contemporary science, linking it to Bryant's ontology: none of the surviving witnesses of Hiroshima experienced the entire event, but only 'local manifestations' of it.[42] Morton ties this insight to his views from *Realist Magic* on the aesthetic structure of causation in general and perception more specifically: 'birds perceive not some traditional material lump [when navigating], but an aesthetic shape', which can also be treated as a local manifestation of the earth's magnetic field, ungraspable in itself or as a whole.[43] Returning to the environmental concerns that are central to his book, Morton reminds us that all we ever experience of earth systems are local manifestations as well: 'When you feel raindrops falling on your head, you are experiencing climate, in some sense . . . But you are never directly experiencing global warming as such.'[44] Or more poetically, 'when I look for the hyperobject oil, I don't find it. Oil is just droplets, flows, rivers, and slicks of oil.'[45]

With his notion of *temporal undulation*, Morton harvests additional fruit from the concept of nonlocality. For hyperobjects exist at scales that make them difficult if not impossible to perceive. In an especially vivid example, Morton cites the sound art piece *Air Pressure Fluctuations* by Felix Hess, for which Hess recorded five days' worth of sound in New

York and then played it at 360 times the speed of the original. The results are breathtaking: 'Traffic begins to sound like the tinkling of tiny insects. A slow, periodic hum begins to become audible . . . the standing wave caused by pressure changes in the air over the Atlantic Ocean. I am hearing the sound of the air over the Atlantic.'[46] Here, a previously inaudible hyperobject has become available to the human ear. Morton credits the medieval Arab philosopher ar-Razi with the discovery of hyperobjects, given his (ultimately correct) view that many of the objects viewed in his time as eternal and incorruptible are nonetheless created, and must therefore be subject to decay: 'ar-Razi writes that gold, gems, and glass can disintegrate, but at much slower speeds than vegetables, fruits, and spices.'[47] This leads Morton to a fine insight about how very large finite amounts of anything are somehow more threatening than supposed infinite amounts of the same thing. For 'these gigantic timescales [of hyperobjects] are truly humiliating in the sense that they force us to realize how close to Earth we are. Infinity is far easier to cope with. Infinity brings to mind our cognitive powers . . .' And later on the same page: 'There is a real sense in which it is far easier to conceive of "forever" than very large finitude. Forever makes you feel important. One hundred thousand years makes you wonder whether you can imagine one hundred thousand anything.'[48]

As we saw earlier, Morton introduces *phasing* by telling us that 'hyperobjects occupy a high-dimensional phase space that results in their being invisible to humans for stretches of time.'[49] For those readers who are interested, the philosophy of phase space has been covered lucidly by the philosopher Manuel DeLanda in his 2002 book *Intensive Science and Virtual Philosophy*. Although data from a weather reading in some place always takes some discrete value for temperature and air pressure, patterns often emerge that show all the detailed readings to be governed by some underlying 'attractor' deeper than any specific reading. This was first discovered by the American meteorologist Edward Norton Lorenz, pioneer of Chaos theory, famous today for his musing that the tiny flapping wings of a butterfly might eventually lead to the formation of a hurricane.[50] Speaking of hurricanes, Morton continues his discussion as follows: 'A high enough dimensional being could see global warming itself as a static object . . . As it is, I only see brief patches of this gigantic object as it intersects with my world. The brief patch I call a *hurricane* destroys the infrastructure of New Orleans. The brief patch I call *drought* burns the plains of Russia and the Midwestern United States to a crisp.'[51] Despite the mathematical origin of attractors, Morton agrees with me – in opposition to Badiou and Meillassoux – that mathematics is not quite enough to do justice to the phased nature of objects: 'This doesn't mean that I am supplementing "hard" math with something warm and fuzzy . . . the mathematical entity is the "warm and fuzzy" one, on the hither side of human meaning.'[52] If human understanding can master it, then it is not yet sufficiently weird to do justice to reality: 'hyperobjects are disturbing clowns in an Expressionist painting, clowns who cover every available surface of the painting, leering into our world relentlessly . . . The psychotic intensity of Expressionist painting, poetry, and music thus expresses something about the hyperobject much more effectively than a cool mathematical diagram of phasing flows.'[53] Morton concludes his chapter on phasing with the one philosophical point on which we perhaps disagree most: announcing his agreement with the philosopher Graham Priest that true contradictions do exist, something I have not been prepared to endorse in my own work.[54]

We now come to the fifth and final feature that Morton ascribes to hyperobjects: interobjectivity. As we have seen, modern philosophy begins in Descartes with a radical split between thought on one side and physical matter on the other. This has brought about too many 'revolutionary' attempts to claim that thought and matter are entangled with each other from the start; the notion of 'the body' is frequently invoked as a supposed middle ground between these two modern extremes. What this repeated false solution misses is the central claim of OOO: that philosophy must also account for relations *between objects* even when there are no humans anywhere on the scene, without simply leaving it to science to calculate the outcome of such relations. Here Morton puts a clever twist on the philosophically overexposed theme of the 'intersubjectivity' of communicating human beings: '"intersubjectivity" is really human interobjectivity with lines drawn around it to exclude nonhumans.'[55] Referring to Heidegger's tool-analysis, Morton invokes his own term 'mesh'. Whereas Heidegger himself uses the system of meaningful tools to claim that humans are always at the centre of things, Morton puts an 'interobjective' spin on his mesh, which is replete with object–object relations that have nothing to do with people at all.[56] The imperfect translation of objects is not something that is done solely by finite human minds, as Kant held; rather, objects do this to each other as well. As Morton puts it, in typically beautiful prose: 'The bamboo forest is a gigantic wind chime, modulating the wind into bambooese. The bamboo forest ruthlessly bamboo-morphizes the wind, translating its pressure into movement and sound. It is an abyss of bamboo-wind.'[57]

## Fellow Traveller: Jane Bennett

Bennett (b. 1957) is Professor of Political Science at Johns Hopkins University in Baltimore. She came to the attention of OOO readers with her fourth book, *Vibrant Matter*, published in 2010. This beautifully written work opposes the modernist spirit in philosophy by stressing the agency of non-human materials, including inanimate ones. In response to the critique that this amounts to an 'anthropomorphic' projection of human qualities on to non-human entities, Bennett has often said that a bit of anthropomorphism is sometimes needed to counter the much more prevalent anthropocentrism. I once published an appreciative review of *Vibrant Matter*, and two years later Bennett was the invited respondent to a pair of articles by me and Morton in *New Literary History*, whose editor Rita Felski has been sympathetic to OOO.[58] Though often critical of the specific arguments of OOO, Bennett fully endorses its attention to the life of non-human things.

A brief glance at Bennett's *Vibrant Matter* should make it clear why the authors of OOO have reacted so strongly to her work. For Bennett is nothing if not a flat ontologist: 'I am a material configuration, the pigeons in the park are material compositions, the viruses, parasites, and heavy metals in my flesh and in pigeon flesh are materialities, as are neurochemicals, hurricane winds, E. coli, and the dust on the floor.'[59] Such wonderful prose is the norm in Bennett's work, as is her innate resistance to the standard anthropocentrism of modern philosophy: 'I will emphasize, even overemphasize, the agentic contributions of nonhuman forces . . . in an attempt to counter the narcissistic reflex of human language and thought.'[60] This leads Bennett to insights that she is not afraid to turn against some of the major political philosophers of our time. For instance: '[Rancière's] description of the [political] act increasingly takes on a linguistic cast . . . It is an "objection to a wrong", where a wrong is defined as the unequal treatment of beings who are equally endowed with a capacity for *human* speech.'[61] This goes hand-in-hand with her frustration at the intellectual method of demystification, which 'assumes that at the heart of any event or process lies a *human* agency that has illicitly been projected into things'.[62] Yet for all these points of agreement with OOO, Bennett is ultimately suspicious of our view that the world is home to pre-existent unified entities that have individual shapes prior to being encountered by some observer. Her allegiance to the philosophies of Baruch Spinoza, Henri Bergson and Deleuze lead her to conclude that the model of 'a world of fixed entities . . . [is a] distortion . . . necessary and useful because humans must use the world instrumentally if they are to survive in it.'[63] This attitude culminates at the end of *Vibrant Matter* with a new 'Nicene Creed', as Bennett playfully puts it. This creed begins as follows: 'I believe in one matter–energy, the maker of things seen and unseen. I believe that this pluriverse is traversed by heterogeneities that are continually *doing things*.'[64] The words in this credo that show Bennett's ultimate disagreement with OOO are 'one', 'matter', and 'doing things'. For OOO does not view the world as a unified whole that is only secondarily broken up into individuals; it does not endorse the concept of matter at all, with the possible exception of Bryant; and again with the exception of Bryant, OOO does not think the ultimate role of objects is *doing*, which for most of us can only count as a form of overmining.

In 'Systems and Things', Bennett made her first direct response to me and Morton, showing the same mixture of sympathy and unease towards our philosophies that we felt towards hers in turn. But the sympathy predominates. Bennett correctly notes that 'Morton and Harman and I and our objects are all in the game together.'[65] She also takes care to note that she *likes* the OOO point that 'communication via proximity is not limited to that between *human* bodies.'[66] Yet her ontology is not quite as flat as this might make it sound. For Bennett seems to think that it must at least be a question of *bodies*, as when she worries about my own 'philosopher's concern to always include *objects of thought* in the category of objects', as if the non-physical were excluded from the ranks of all that is vibrant for her.[67] We have seen that Bennett prefers the model of flowing, dynamic liquids to that of discrete entities, though she is gracious enough to acknowledge Morton's argument that this is 'biased toward the peculiar rhythms and scale of the human body'.[68] Yet again we are brought back to something resembling Bennett's 'Nicene Creed', recommending that we 'understand "objects" to be those swirls of matter, energy, and incipience that hold themselves together long enough to vie with the strivings of other objects, including the indeterminate momentum of the throbbing whole'.[69] Although Bennett says this in a purported effort to do justice both to objects *and* relations, it is hard to see how this could be the case. If objects are nothing but 'incipient swirls', then it is difficult to see how they can ever have more than derivative status by contrast with relations. This differs from OOO, which leaves abundant room for relations by treating them as irreducible objects in their own right.

## Fellow Traveller: Tristan Garcia

Garcia (b. 1981) teaches at the Université Jean Moulin in Lyon, France. A former student of the prominent French philosophers Alain Badiou and Quentin Meillassoux, he first gained public acclaim as a fiction writer, winning the Prix de Flore for his debut novel in 2008.[70] In 2011 he made waves in French philosophy with a massive systematic book entitled *Form and Object: A Treatise on Things*, available in English since 2014. Though Garcia wrote *Form and Object* before becoming familiar with the work of OOO authors, the points of resonance are sufficient that he addressed the similarities and differences with my own work in a 2013 essay entitled 'Crossing Ways of Thinking'. Garcia has continued to alternate between periods devoted to fiction and to philosophy, but is currently in the midst of publishing a fresh philosophical trilogy in French, with English translations planned for the near future.[71]

*Form and Object* is an ambitious work that presents us with a total system of philosophy. Book I, entitled 'Formally', runs to roughly 150 pages in English. It gives us a rather technical meditation on what Garcia calls *things*, in the sense of anything whatever: the rules that hold for a thing no matter what it is. The chief enemy of this first segment of *Form and Object* is what Garcia calls the 'compact', which means the same thing in both French and English: that which is compressed into its own self. For Garcia, things are always outside themselves in the world, and thus (unlike OOO) he rejects the Kantian thing-in-itself, which supposedly is what it is regardless of any relations with outside things.[72] Whereas in 'The Third Table' I argued that a table is reducible neither to its components nor to its relations, Garcia takes a different approach: for him, the table is the *difference* between the two. In any case, in his Introduction to *Form and Object* he agrees with OOO and DeLanda about the necessity of beginning with a 'flat ontology'.[73] Indeed, he begins the book with his own example of a 'Latour Litany', Bogost's term for the long lists of random objects at which Bruno Latour particularly excels. Garcia's litany runs as follows: 'We live in this world of things, where a cutting of acacia, a gene, a computer-generated image, a transplantable hand, a musical sample, a trademarked name, or a sexual service are comparable things.'[74] Book II of *Form and Object* shifts its focus from things to objects, which Garcia defines as specific things inscribed in specific systems of relations, as opposed to anything no-matter-what. While Book I might seem forbidding to some readers due to its sometimes abstract precision, Book II cuts into the juicy pulp of the world in seventeen consecutive chapters building logically from one to the next. It is worth listing all of the chapter topics here, in case it inspires some of my readers to attempt a reading *in toto* of Garcia's marvellous book: Universe, Objects and Events, Time, Living Things, Animals, Humans, Representations, Arts and Rules, Culture, History, Economy of Objects, Values, Classes, Genders, Ages of Life, Death. A great number of concrete insights are won in these chapters, of which several in particular have stayed in my memory. The first is Garcia's argument against vegetarianism in the name of flat ontology, though as a vegetarian since childhood I was not convinced by it. The second is his claim that artworks remain artworks even if humans are nowhere on the scene, with which I also disagree. The third is Garcia's spirited claim that it is never true to say that friendships and relationships are beyond any possible price, and that it is not actually a compliment to say that they are. The fourth, even more persuasive point is his beautifully developed view that adolescence has become the dominant age of life in our era. Some readers might actually prefer to begin their reading of *Form and Object* with Book II, especially those who lack formal training in philosophy. In any case, Garcia is surely one of the most promising philosophers in the world under the age of forty, and is well worth following closely in the years to come. For those who are interested, Jon Cogburn's 2017 book *Garcian Meditations* is highly recommended for its explanation of Garcia's importance, and its account of how Garcia resembles and differs from various OOO philosophers.

# Object-Oriented Ontology and Architecture

As mentioned above, architecture even more than the visual arts is the field outside philosophy where OOO has been adopted the most rapidly and enthusiastically (though here too it has detractors). There are several likely reasons for this. The first is that architects have long had an attentive awareness of theoretical currents from the humanities and the social sciences. In the late twentieth century, the most striking example was probably Derrida's influence on 'deconstructivist' architecture, as featured in a heralded 1988 show on the topic at the Museum of Modern Art in New York.[75] Among many other things, this led to collaboration and eventual disagreement between Derrida and the prominent American architect Peter Eisenman.[76] But architecture did not stay with Derrida forever. Beginning in the early 1990s, architects took an increasing interest in the philosophy of Deleuze, with Sanford Kwinter one of the most prominent Deleuzean voices in architectural criticism, and Jeffrey Kipnis another early advocate of Deleuze's entry into the field.[77] But to some extent Deleuze was the victim of his own success, with too many people quickly embracing his preference for becoming over being, for continuous gradients and curves over sharply defined articulations of corners and apertures, and in some cases for an all-too-literal adoption of Deleuze's concept of 'the fold' in incorporating actual physical folds in buildings.[78] For all these reasons, OOO's entry into architecture may have been unusually well-timed, given its disagreement with Derrida and Deleuze on most theoretical questions just as many practitioners were becoming sated with their influence.

Much of the credit for importing OOO into architecture goes to David Ruy, now of the Southern California Institute of Architecture (SCI-Arc), who seems to have seen OOO as a possible counterweight to trends he disliked in architecture itself: 'Since the mid-nineties, architecture has accelerated its move away from the discourse of the architectural object towards the discourse of the architectural field.' In this way architecture loses its specificity and treats itself 'as a byproduct of socio-cultural milieus, as a conditional component of technocratic systems and networks, or even as the provisional end calculations of measurable parameters within the literal or constructed environment'.[79] Erik Ghenoiu, also of SCI-Arc, agrees with Ruy that this trend has become overly dominant: 'The manipulation of relations has favored the distraction technique of making the built place seem like the result of forces and considerations over which the designer had no control.'[80] Some of the pressure for this shift has come from an increasing concern with the 'carbon footprint' of buildings amidst what is taken to be the holistic web of nature, now widely agreed to be in danger from global warming. Yet OOO challenges the notion of nature as holistic, viewing the world instead as a partially non-communicating system in which only certain *specific* relations yield dangerous positive feedback loops. This seems to be what Ruy has in mind when he says that 'object-oriented ontology would have to throw the being of any relational model into doubt. Though networks and fields may continue to be eminently useful models of understanding, they carry with them a flawed ontology.'[81] While professional opinion has recently turned against the celebrity 'starchitects' of the profession in favour of collectives and shareable methods (as seen in the recent choices of recipients for the Pritzker Prize – the Nobel of architecture – which have largely favoured those who emphasize sustainability and social responsibility over dramatic design styles), Ruy is correct to note that OOO leaves more room open for the fruits of individual excellence: 'There is something about the master craftsman, as object, that cannot be reduced to a set of qualities and is irreproducible.'[82]

In this brief discussion we have already mentioned three faculty members from SCI-Arc in Los Angeles: Kipnis, Ruy and Ghenoiu. Since I myself was also hired by the school in 2016 to teach OOO to their students, it can be inferred that interest in the movement runs high at SCI-Arc. But we have not yet even mentioned one of the most important names in this context: the architect Tom Wiscombe, also of SCI-Arc, who has made some of the most concrete efforts to import OOO into discussions of design strategy.[83] Wiscombe is especially concerned with the possibilities opened up for architecture by OOO's 'flat ontology', its wish to treat all objects as equally objects, whether small, large, human, non-human, natural or artificial. Though he concedes that there have been some disastrous attempts to import philosophy into architecture, Wiscombe notes that 'the framework for a flat ontology to some extent *already* exists inside architecture', by allowing for a reconceptualization of how part–whole relationships work within architectural composition.

In short, 'a flat ontology confronts the possibility of radically de-stratifying architecture without resorting to smoothing on the one hand or disjunction on the other.'[84] Flat ontology undercuts the vertical hierarchization of wholes and parts insofar as everything is already both whole and part, depending on whether we look downward or upward from it. 'In [the OOO flat ontology] model, everything exists side by side, like a collection of treasures laid out on a table.'[85]

This immediately leads Wiscombe to a number of promising implications. As he puts it: 'Three examples of models that push this project forward include the *figure in a sack*, the *implied outer shell*, and the *supercomponent*.'[86] The figure in the sack owes something to Tristan Garcia, who is cited by Wiscombe in the opening pages of his article.[87] In Wiscombe's words, the purpose of the sack in architecture is that 'hints are given as to the contents of the "sack", but the contents are never revealed in full. Inner objects push out like a fist through a rubber sheet, creating strange formal inflections in the sack, and a strange simultaneity of inner and outer silhouettes.'[88] The implied outer shell, which Wiscombe sees as foreshadowed in certain works by Le Corbusier and Bernard Tschumi, concerns 'the spatial effects of a partial secondary enclosure, which shrouds but does not completely obscure inner objects'.[89] And whereas the figure-in-the-sack model gives us partly concealed objects bumping slightly into the building envelope, the supercomponent model works in the opposite direction: 'objects are instead pressed into an enclosure from the outside. As if vacuformed together and then released, objects can be nestled into one another, implying a coherent new object without producing a

fused monolith.'[90] Wiscombe closes the article with two additional suggestions for design strategies possibly entailed by
flat ontology. The first is that architects might reconsider the
relation between the ground and the building mass, a relation that is often simply taken for granted. 'Building mass
[should] not fuse or otherwise disappear into ground, but
rather maintain distinction from it.'[91] Methods of achieving
this would include 'hovering', 'nestling', and what Wiscombe
calls the 'ground object', meaning 'the total objectification of
the land underneath the building. Ground is re-cast as mass
rather than surface.'[92] Rather than using pedestal or plinth
techniques, in which the building support is simply a new
surface extruded from the earth, Wiscombe imagines 'a
strong ground object . . . characterized by undercuts to the
landscape, [which] would appear dug-up and loose and
would empathize actively with the building mass.'[93] The article closes with the idea of the surface tattoo, whose 'primary
architectural role is to produce mysterious cross-grain
formal effects, which can emphasize or obscure the discreteness of the objects into which they are inscribed'.[94] While
initially this might sound like nothing more than arbitrary
surface decoration, Wiscombe notes that it is less a purely
visual matter than a way of articulating the new construction
techniques, now that 'the age of tectonic articulation based
on bricks, sticks, and panels is past.'[95]

Outside the walls of SCI-Arc, one of the most prominent
defenders of OOO has been Mark Foster Gage, Assistant
Dean of the Yale School of Architecture. Gage has been
involved in an important and ongoing critical interchange
with Patrik Schumacher of Zaha Hadid Architects, in which

Gage took the side of OOO against Schumacher's 'parametric' philosophy of architecture as developed in a huge two-volume manifesto.[96] But Gage has also written another clear article on OOO in architecture entitled 'Killing Simplicity', whose title points directly to Gage's own architectural style.[97] Near the end of that article, Gage tells us that 'what architecture needs is a philosophical reset of its underlying assumptions – not new shapes or a new style, but a deep and meaningful inquiry into the nature of the profession today, what it can do and what it cannot, what it should do and what it should not, and, most important, what is worth doing and why.'[98] While there is nothing wrong with such a call, it might mislead readers into thinking that Gage merely wishes to lead a meta-debate about the future of architecture rather than propose a definite new style linked in some way to the concerns of OOO. But in fact, Gage has developed as memorably individual a style as one could hope to find, as in his proposed skyscraper for the West Side of Manhattan, which is covered with feathered wings, cog-shaped structures, and long brass and bronze strips. In the words of the website *De Zeen*: '[Gage's] proposal features four enormous cantilevered balconies, supported by concrete carved wings that extend outwards from the structure's exterior.'[99] It is certainly not the minimalistic sort of modernist architecture that Gage dismisses as 'just tall boxes covered in selected glass curtain wall products'. But neither is it the postmodernist architecture that recycles dead historical forms in a contemporary pastiche. Instead, it startles the viewer much as one of horror writer H. P. Lovecraft's narrators was unsettled by a strange tiara in a sleepy museum:

All other art objects I had ever seen either belonged to some known racial or national stream, or else were consciously modernistic defiances of every recognized stream. This tiara was neither. It clearly belonged to some settled technique of infinite maturity and perfection, yet that technique was utterly remote from any . . . which I had ever heard of or seen exemplified.[100]

In theoretical terms, Gage holds that OOO 'has the potential to reconfigure the theoretical foundation on which most architectural movements of the 19th and 20th centuries have been based'.[101] What seems to him most promising is OOO's distinction between the real and the sensual, which 'puts architects in the business of designing qualities that wrap around and allude to the existence of deeper realities lurking below the perceivable surface . . . This strange proposition represents a shift away from the theoretical foundations of modern and contemporary architecture, which emerged from Enlightenment values of discovery and knowable absolutes as opposed to sense and inference.'[102] The alternative envisaged by Gage is the design of sensual qualities in such a way as to suggest complex realities.[103] Shifting to the use of 'encrusted qualities', one of the OOO synonyms for sensual qualities, Gage recommends 'designing encrusted qualities towards the goal of inference via sense rather than truth via isolated, singular concept'.[104] This would be 'to imagine architecture that . . . *alludes* to a deeper or alternate view of reality', one running counter to 'the simplification of big, singular ideas through reductive diagrams', a practice that Gage sees as plaguing architectural practice today.[105]

# Object-Oriented Ontology in Overview

You have now reached the end of the first comprehensive book on OOO aimed at a wide general readership. Even if you do not yet feel like a master of all the ideas presented so far, you can safely say that you know more on the topic than most of its critics. There are several different ways to view the meaning of OOO in historical terms, depending on which seems most interesting to the individual reader. One way is to treat OOO as a revival of the covertly object-oriented trend that has intermittently arisen to oppose the excesses of undermining and overmining methods, with some of the key moments being Aristotle's substances, Leibniz's monads, Kant's things-in-themselves, Whitehead's and Latour's flat ontologies of entities/actors, and the object-oriented impetus in the works of Husserl (intentional objects) and Heidegger (the thing). Another way to look at OOO is that it takes the other fork in the road after Kant than the one taken by German Idealism (Hegel, Fichte, Schelling): which eliminated Kant's things-in-themselves while affirming his prejudice that philosophy must talk primarily about the interplay between thought and world, leaving any object–object interactions apart from humans to the mathematizing methods of natural science. By contrast, OOO endorses the things-in-themselves and asks instead why Kant treated them as the sole and tragic burden of human beings, rather than as the ungraspable terms of *every* relation, including those between fire and cotton or raindrops and tar. Third, the interdisciplinary success of OOO allows us to view it instead as an extremely broad method in the spirit of actor-network theory, but one that rescues the non-relational core of every object, thus paving the way for an *aesthetic* conception of things. In differing moods, I favour each of these conceptions in turn, and the reader is free to do likewise.

It may now be useful to finish this book with a brief survey of some of the main principles of OOO as covered above. A number of these contributions were first made by others, and I will try to indicate the cases in which this is so.

*Flat Ontology* (Chapter 1). This is the idea that philosophy must *begin* by casting the widest possible net in aspiring to talk about everything. The chief enemy of flat ontology is the taxonomical prejudice which assumes in advance that the world must be divided up between a small number of radically different *types* of entities. Medieval philosophy orbited around the difference between God on one side and everything else on the other. Modern philosophy simply exchanged God for human thought, without giving up the notion that one extra-important type of being was so vastly different from everything else that it deserved to occupy half of ontology. This modern taxonomy continues today in the work of leading European philosophers such as Žižek, Badiou and Meillassoux. This is why OOO, using Latour's term, calls itself a 'non-modern' philosophy, since we have no wish to return to the pre-modern era and merely reject thought/world or human/non-human as a purportedly basic distinction that wrongly cuts the universe in half. It is DeLanda who inspired OOO's use of the term 'flat ontology', though the tendency this phrase describes can be found throughout the history of philosophy, especially in Aristotle's claim that while humans, animals and plants may be different, a human is not more a human than a plant is a plant. That is to say, both are equally substances.

*Anti-mining* (Chapter 1). An object is whatever cannot be reduced to either of the two basic kinds of knowledge: what something is made of, and what it does. Too many philosophies in the West have tried to claim that it is simply one of these, the other, or both. Another way of saying it is that OOO is strongly committed to an *anti-literalist* view of objects, literalism being the notion that we can paraphrase an object, as if it were truly equivalent to a sum total of qualities or effects and nothing more. In terms of contemporary philosophy, the model of a swirling, dynamic whole that only temporarily gives rise to transient objects (Henri Bergson, Jane Bennett) counts for OOO as a form of undermining, since it treats individual entities as shallow by comparison with an underlying unity. On the other side of the coin, OOO cannot endorse philosophies of actions or events, since these merely overmine objects. This criticism holds good in different ways of Latourian actor-network theory, of Foucault's theory that discursive events precede objects, and of Derrida's view that nothing is identical to itself (a.k.a. 'self-presence') but that everything exists in dissemination. A few days ago I saw another variant of such theories on an internet comment thread, where an anonymous critic of OOO praised Karen

Barad and Donna Haraway instead, due to their defence of 'relations without relata'.[1] While there is much of value in the writings of Barad and Haraway, I do not see how the idea of relations that generate their terms out of nothing is feasible: as if a marriage generated both partners out of thin air, rather than joining and changing them. It is hard to imagine a more severe form of overmining, which as we have seen has the problem of not being able to explain change.

*OOO is not a form of materialism* (Chapter 1). Any new theory will tend to attract a number of different misunderstandings. By far the most common mistake pertaining to OOO is the claim that it is a form of 'materialism'. In fact, OOO has no interest whatsoever in the concept of 'matter', let alone materialism. The notion of matter as unformed physical stuff in which forms can be stamped has no basis in experience, and is simply unhelpful in theoretical terms. The difference between a horse, an imaginary horse and a unicorn is not that the former 'inheres' in matter and the latter two do not. Instead, the difference is that the real horse has a *different form* from the imaginary horse, and certainly a different one from the unicorn. One of the implications of this is that we cannot 'extract' a form from a thing and express this form in mathematical or other directly knowable terms; or rather, we can do this, but only by paying the price of changing the form into something else. There is no translation of anything without energy loss, and hence it is impossible to grasp anything perfectly.

*Objects withhold themselves not just from human access, but from each other as well* (Chapter 1). This is the important way in which OOO differs from Kant, and from important

Kantian heirs such as Heidegger. Most post-Kantian philosophies have accepted some version of the German Idealist critique of Kant: it is impossible to think a thing outside thought, and therefore the concept of a thing-in-itself beyond thought is incoherent. By contrast, OOO fully accepts the Kantian thing-in-itself, and merely denies that it is something that haunts human thought alone. Fire and cotton are also opaque to each other even if they are not 'conscious' in the same way as humans or animals. If we consider two great recent philosophers who masquerade as sociologists (Latour and Luhmann), we will see that communication is not quite as easy as Latour holds. Relations are incidental in the life of things, rather than the stuff of which they are constituted; furthermore, not all relations leave a lasting trace on the relata that enter them. Conversely, communication is not as difficult as Luhmann holds. Humans can interact with and affect their societies and political systems, though here too not all such interactions leave any trace. Communication between objects is neither easy nor impossible, but both possible and difficult.

*The fracture in things* (Chapter 2). Most debates about realism obsess over the single gap between reality and our representations of it. Along with broadening this question so that thinking humans are no longer the sole locus of these representations, OOO adds another twist to the problem. There is also a gap *within* things, and we call it the object/qualities rift. Neither the sensual object nor the real one is just a bundle of qualities. Instead, the object precedes its qualities despite not being able to exist without them. In combination, these two separate axes of the world (withdrawn/present and objects/qualities) yield a fourfold structure (as shown in Figure 1) that is the basis of the OOO method in every field where it has found relevance.

*Aesthetics as first philosophy* (Chapter 2). Aesthetic experience is crucial to OOO as a form of non-literal access to the object. It occurs when sensual qualities no longer belong to their usual sensual object, but are transferred instead to a real object, which necessarily withdraws from all access. For this reason, the vanished real object is replaced by the aesthetic beholder herself or himself as the new real object that supports the sensual qualities. Thus we can speak of the necessary *theatricality* of aesthetic experience, despite the art critic Michael Fried's forceful condemnation of theatre.

*Objects act because they exist, rather than existing because they act* (Chapter 3). Social theory must be based on the *reality* of objects, not on their *actions*, since the latter can only overmine the objects themselves. Of the countless relations into which a thing enters during its lifespan, only a small number of them are pivotal, and these are the ones we call symbiotic. Symbioses are often non-reciprocal, meaning that thing A can relate to thing B without the reverse being true. And all symbioses are asymmetrical in the same way that metaphors are: wine-dark sea is not sea-dark wine.

*There is no political knowledge* (Chapter 3). Political theory cannot be based on a claim to knowledge: whether it be the supposed knowledge of what the best polity is, or merely the cynical claim that it's all just a struggle for power. Along with the need to recognize itself as a non-knowledge, political theory must give a much larger role to non-human entities than has previously been the case.

OOO is still a living theoretical movement, and thus we certainly hope that it continues to make new discoveries. My hope for this book is that it has succeeded in giving the reader a vivid sense of the substantial progress already made by this school of thought.

# Further Reading

Aristotle. *The Art of Rhetoric*, trans. H. Lawson-Tancred. London: Penguin, 2005.

—— *The Metaphysics*, trans. H. Lawson-Tancred. London: Penguin, 2004.

—— *Physics*, trans. R. Waterfield. London: Penguin, 1996.

—— *Poetics*, trans. A. Kenny. London: Penguin, 2013.

Badiou, Alain. *Logics of Worlds: Being and Event II*, trans. A. Toscano. London: Continuum, 2009.

Barad, Karen. *Meeting the Universe Halfway: Quantum Physics and the Entanglement of Matter and Meaning*. Durham, NC: Duke University Press, 2007.

Bennett, Jane. 'Systems and Things: A Response to Graham Harman and Timothy Morton', *New Literary History* 43 (2012), pp. 225–33.

—— *Vibrant Matter: A Political Ecology of Things*. Durham, NC: Duke University Press, 2010.

Berkeley, George. *A Treatise Concerning the Principles of Human Knowledge*. Indianapolis: Hackett, 1982.

Bhaskar, Roy. *A Realist Theory of Science*. London: Verso, 2008.

Black, Max. 'Metaphor', in *Models and Metaphors*. Ithaca, NY: Cornell University Press, 1962.

Bogost, Ian. *Alien Phenomenology, or What It's Like to Be a Thing*. Minneapolis: University of Minnesota Press, 2012.

—— *Persuasive Games: The Expressive Power of Videogames*. Cambridge, MA: MIT Press, 2010.

—— *Play Anything: The Pleasure of Limits, the Uses of Boredom, and the Secret of Games*. New York: Basic Books, 2016.

—— *Unit Operations: An Approach to Videogame Criticism*. Cambridge, MA: MIT Press, 2006.

—— 'Why Gamification Is Bullshit', in *The Gameful World: Approaches, Issues, Application*, ed. S. Walz & S. Deterding. Cambridge, MA: MIT Press, 2015; pp. 65–80.

Branch, John. 'Fright Nights in the NBA', *New York Times*, 19 April 2014. http://www.nytimes.com/2014/04/20/sports/basketball/hotel-leaves-oklahoma-city-thunder-opponents-telling-ghost-stories.html?_r=0

Brassier, Ray, Iain Hamilton Grant, Graham Harman & Quentin Meillassoux. 'Speculative Realism', *Collapse* III (2007), pp. 306–449.

Braver, Lee. *A Thing of This World: A History of Continental Anti-Realism*. Evanston, IL: Northwestern University Press, 2007.

Brentano, Franz. *Psychology from an Empirical Standpoint*, trans. A. Rancurello, D. B. Terrell & L. McAlister. New York: Routledge, 1995.

Brooks, Cleanth. *The Well Wrought Urn*. New York: Harcourt, Brace & World, 1947.

Bryant, Levi R. *The Democracy of Objects*. Ann Arbor, MI: Open Humanities Press, 2011.

—— *Difference and Givenness: Deleuze's Transcendental Empiricism and the Ontology of Immanence*. Evanston, IL: Northwestern University Press, 2008.

—— Larval Subjects blog, https://larvalsubjects.wordpress.com/

—— *Onto-Cartography: An Ontology of Machines and Media*. Edinburgh: Edinburgh University Press, 2014.

——, Nick Srnicek, & Graham Harman (eds.), *The Speculative Turn: Continental Materialism and Realism*, Melbourne: re.press, 2011.

Bub, Jeffrey. *Interpreting the Quantum World*. Cambridge, UK: Cambridge University Press, 1997.

Buchanan, Mark. *Ubiquity: Why Catastrophes Happen*. Portland, OR: Broadway Books, 2002.

Butler, Judith. *Gender Trouble: Feminism and the Subversion of Identity*. London: Routledge, 1990.

Caputo, John D. 'For Love of the Things Themselves: Derrida's Phenomenology of the Hyper-Real', in *Fenomenologia hoje: significado e linguagem*, ed. R. Timm de Souza & N. Fernandes de Oliveira. Porto Alegre, Brazil: 2002; pp. 37–59.

Cerf, Bennett. *Book of Riddles*. New York: Beginner Books, 1960.

Chang, Ha-Joon. *Economics: The User's Guide. A Pelican Introduction*. London: Pelican, 2014.

Churchill, Winston S. *The Gathering Storm: The Second World War*, Vol. 1. Boston: Mariner Books, 1986.

Cogburn, Jon. *Garcian Meditations: The Dialectics of Persistence in Form and Object*. Edinburgh: Edinburgh University Press, 2017.

Colebrook, Claire. 'Not Kant, Not Now: Another Sublime', *Speculations* V (2014), pp. 127–57.

Coleman, Sam. 'Mind Under Matter', in *Mind that Abides: Panpsychism in the New Millennium*, ed. D. Skrbina. Amsterdam: John Benjamins, 2009; pp. 83–108.

DeLanda, Manuel. 'Emergence, Causality and Realism', in *The Speculative Turn: Continental Materialism and Realism*, ed. L. Bryant, N. Srnicek & G. Harman. Melbourne: re.press, 2011; pp. 381–92.

—— *Intensive Science and Virtual Philosophy*. London: Continuum, 2002.

—— *Philosophical Chemistry: Genealogy of a Scientific Field*. London: Bloomsbury, 2015.

——, in conversation with Christoph Cox, 'Possibility Spaces', in *Realism Materialism Art*, ed. C. Cox, J. Jaskey & S. Malik. Berlin: Sternberg Press, 2015; pp. 87–94.

—— & Graham Harman, *The Rise of Realism*. Cambridge, UK: Polity, 2017.

Deleuze, Gilles. *The Fold: Leibniz and the Baroque*, trans. T. Conley. Minneapolis: University of Minnesota Press, 1992.

—— & Félix Guattari. *Anti-Oedipus: Capitalism and Schizophrenia*, trans. R. Hurley, M. Seem & H. R. Lane. Minneapolis: University of Minnesota Press, 1983.

Dennett, Daniel C. 'Quining Qualia', in *Consciousness in Modern Science*, ed. A. Marcel & E. Bisiach. Oxford: Oxford University Press, 1988; pp. 381–414.

Derrida, Jacques. 'Appendix: Letter from Jacques Derrida to Peter Eisenman', in Peter Eisenman, *Written into the Void: Selected Writings, 1990–2004*. New Haven, CT: Yale University Press, 2007; pp. 160–68.

—— *Of Grammatology*, trans. G. Spivak. Baltimore: Johns Hopkins University Press, 1997.

—— *Of Spirit: Heidegger and the Question*, trans. G. Bennington & R. Bowlby. Chicago: University of Chicago Press, 1991.

—— 'Plato's Pharmacy' in *Dissemination*, trans. B. Johnson. Chicago: University of Chicago Press, 1983; pp. 61–171.

—— *Voice and Phenomenon*, trans. L. Lawlor. Evanston, IL: Northwestern University Press, 2010.

—— *Writing and Difference*, trans. A. Bass. Chicago: University of Chicago Press, 1978.

Descartes, René. *Meditations on First Philosophy*, trans. D. Cress. Indianapolis: Hackett, 1999.

Dewey, John. *The Public and its Problems: An Essay in Political Inquiry*. University Park, PA: Penn State University Press, 2012.

Dunbar, Robin. *Human Evolution: A Pelican Introduction*. London: Pelican, 2014.

Eisenman, Peter. *Written into the Void: Selected Writings, 1990–2004*. New Haven, CT: Yale University Press, 2011.

Eldredge, Niles & Stephen Jay Gould. 'Punctuated Equilibria: An Alternative to Phyletic Gradualism', in *Models in Paleobiology*, ed. Thomas J. M. Scopf. New York: Doubleday, 1972; pp. 82–115.

Evens, Aden. 'Object-Oriented Ontology, or Programming's Creative Fold', *Angelaki*, 11 (1), 2006, pp. 89–97.

Fakhry, Majid. *Islamic Occasionalism and its Critique by Averroes and Aquinas*. London: Allen & Unwin, 1958.

Ferraris, Maurizio. *Manifesto of New Realism*, trans. S. De Sanctis. Albany, NY: SUNY Press, 2015.

Foote, Shelby. *The Beleaguered City: The Vicksburg Campaign, December 1862–July 1863*. New York: Modern Library, 1995.

Foucault, Michel. *The Archaeology of Knowledge* and *The Discourse on Language*, trans. A. M. Sheridan Smith. New York: Pantheon Books, 1972.

—— *The Birth of the Clinic: An Archaeology of Medical Perception*, trans. A. Sheridan. New York: Vintage, 1994.

—— *Discipline and Punish: The Birth of the Prison*, trans. A. Sheridan. New York: Vintage, 1995.

—— *Foucault Live: Interviews, 1961–84*, ed. S. Lotringer. New York: Semiotext(e), 1996.

—— *History of Madness*, trans. J. Murphy. New York: Routledge, 2006.

—— *History of Sexuality, Vol. 1: An Introduction*, trans. R. Hurley. New York: Vintage, 1990.

—— *The Order of Things: An Archaeology of the Human Sciences*. New York: Vintage, 1994.

Frankovitch, Noah [fictitious person]. 'Why Can't Anyone Tell I'm Wearing This Business Suit Ironically?', *The Onion*, November 30, 2005. http://www.theonion.com/blogpost/why-cant-anyone-tell-im-wearing-this-business-suit-11185

Freud, Sigmund. *Introductory Lectures on Psycho-analysis*, trans. J. Strachey. New York: Liveright, 1999.

Fried, Michael. *Art and Objecthood: Essays and Reviews*. Chicago: University of Chicago Press, 1998.

Gabriel, Markus. *Fields of Sense: A New Realist Ontology*. Edinburgh: Edinburgh University Press, 2015.

Gage, Mark Foster. 'Counterpoint: A Hospice for Parametricism', in *Parametricism 2.0*, ed. Patrik Schumacher. Hoboken, NJ: Wiley, 2016; pp. 128–33.

—— 'Killing Simplicity: Object-Oriented Philosophy in Architecture', *Log* 33 (Winter 2015), pp. 95–106.

Garcia, Tristan. 'Crossing Ways of Thinking: On Graham Harman's System and My Own', trans. M. A. Ohm. *parrhesia* 16 (2013), pp. 14–25.

—— *Form and Object: A Treatise on Things*, trans. M. A. Ohm & J. Cogburn. Edinburgh: Edinburgh University Press, 2014.

—— *Hate: A Romance*, trans. M. Duvert. New York: Farrar, Straus and Giroux, 2010.

—— *Nous*. Paris: Bernard Grasset, 2016.

—— *La Vie intense: Une obsession moderne*. Paris: Autrement, 2016.

Gettier, Edmund L. 'Is Justified True Belief Knowledge?', *Analysis* 23:6 (June 1963), pp. 121–3.

Ghenoiu, Erik. 'The World Is Not Enough', *tarp Architecture Manual* (Spring 2012).

Granovetter, Mark S. 'The Strength of Weak Ties', *American Journal of Sociology* 87:6 (1973), pp. 1360–80.

Gratton, Peter. 'Interviews: Graham Harman, Jane Bennett, Tim Morton, Ian Bogost, Levi Bryant and Paul Ennis', *Speculations* 1:1 (2010), pp. 84–134.

—— *Speculative Realism: Problems and Prospects*. London: Bloomsbury, 2014.

Greenberg, Clement. *Art and Culture: Critical Essays*. Boston: Beacon Press, 1989.

—— *The Collected Essays and Criticism, Vol. 4: Modernism with a Vengeance, 1957–1969*, ed. J. O'Brian. Chicago: University of Chicago Press, 1993.

—— *Homemade Esthetics: Observations on Art and Taste*. Oxford: Oxford University Press, 1999.

Greene, Brian. *The Elegant Universe: Superstrings, Hidden Dimensions, and the Quest for the Ultimate Theory*. New York: Norton, 1999.

Grousset, René. *The Empire of the Steppes: A History of Central Asia*. New Brunswick, NJ: Rutgers University Press, 1970.

Hägglund, Martin. *Radical Atheism: Derrida and the Time of Life*. Stanford, CA: Stanford University Press, 2008.

Haraway, Donna. *Simians, Cyborgs, and Women: The Reinvention of Nature*. London: Routledge, 1990.

Harman, Graham. 'Autonomous Objects', *new formations* 71 (2011), pp. 125–30.

—— *Bruno Latour: Reassembling the Political*. London: Pluto, 2014.

—— *Dante's Broken Hammer: The Ethics, Aesthetics, and Metaphysics of Love*. London: Repeater Books, 2016.

—— 'Dwelling with the Fourfold', *Space and Culture* 12.3 (2009), pp. 292–302.

—— 'Entanglement and Relation: A Response to Bruno Latour and Ian Hodder', *New Literary History* 45:1 (2014), pp. 37–49.

—— *Guerrilla Metaphysics: Phenomenology and the Carpentry of Things*. Chicago: Open Court, 2005.

—— *Heidegger Explained: From Phenomenon to Thing*. Chicago: Open Court, 2007.

—— *Immaterialism: Objects and Social Theory*. Cambridge, UK: Polity, 2016.

—— 'Object-Oriented France: The Philosophy of Tristan Garcia', *continent* 2.1 (2012), pp. 6–21. http://continentcontinent.cc/index.php/continent/article/viewArticle/74

—— 'Objects and Orientalism', in *The Agon of Interpretations: Towards a Critical Intercultural Hermeneutics*, ed. M. Xie. Toronto: University of Toronto Press, 2014; pp. 123–39.

—— 'On the Undermining of Objects: Grant, Bruno, and Radical Philosophy', in *The Speculative Turn: Continental Materialism and Realism*, ed. L. Bryant, N. Srnicek & G. Harman. Melbourne: re.press, 2011; pp. 21–40.

—— 'On Vicarious Causation', *Collapse* II (2007), pp. 171–205.

—— *Prince of Networks: Bruno Latour and Metaphysics*. Melbourne: re.press, 2009.

—— *The Quadruple Object*. Winchester, UK: Zero Books, 2011.

—— 'The Third Table', in *The Book of Books*, ed. C. Christov-Bakargiev. Ostfildern, Germany: Hatje Cantz Verlag, 2012; pp. 540–42.

—— 'Time, Space, Essence, and *Eidos*: A New Theory of Causation', *Cosmos and History* 6:10 (2010), pp. 1–17.

—— *Tool-Being: Heidegger and the Metaphysics of Objects*. Chicago: Open Court, 2002.

—— *Towards Speculative Realism: Essays and Lectures*. Winchester, UK: Zero Books, 2010.

—— 'Tristan Garcia and the Thing-In-Itself', *parrhesia* 16 (2013), pp. 26–34. http://www.parrhesiajournal.org/parrhesia16/parrhesia16_harman.pdf

—— 'Undermining, Overmining, and Duomining: A Critique', in *ADD Metaphysics*, ed. J. Sutela. Aalto, Finland: Aalto University Design Research Laboratory, 2013; pp. 40–51.

—— 'The Well-Wrought Broken Hammer: Object-Oriented Literary Criticism', *New Literary History* 43 (2012), pp. 183–203.

—— 'Zero-Person and the Psyche', in *Mind that Abides: Panpsychism in the New Millennium*, ed. D. Skrbina. Amsterdam: Benjamins, 2009; pp. 253–82.

Heidegger, Martin. *Being and Time*. New York: Harper & Row, 1962.

—— *Bremen and Freiburg Lectures: Insight Into That Which Is* and *asic Principles of Thinking*, trans. A. Mitchell. Bloomington, IN: Indiana University Press, 2012.

—— *Off the Beaten Track*, trans. J. Young & K. Haynes. Cambridge, UK: Cambridge University Press, 2002.

—— 'The Self-Assertion of the German University: Address, Delivered on the Solemn Assumption of the Rectorate of the University of Freiburg. The Rectorate 1933/34: Facts and Thoughts', trans. K. Harries, *Review of Metaphysics* 38:3 (1985), pp. 467–502.

—— *What Is Called Thinking?*, trans. J. G. Gray. San Francisco: Harper, 1976.

Hemingway, Ernest. *The Old Man and the Sea*. New York: Scribner, 1995.

Hobbes, Thomas. *Leviathan*. Oxford: Oxford University Press, 2009.

Hodder, Ian. *Entangled: An Archaeology of the Relationship Between Humans and Things*. Oxford: Wiley, 2012.

Huizinga, Johan. *Homo Ludens: A Study of the Play-Element in Culture*. Boston: Beacon Press, 1994.

Hume, David. *A Treatise of Human Nature*. Oxford: Clarendon, 1973.

Husserl, Edmund. 'Intentional Objects', in *Early Writings in the Philosophy of Logic and Mathematics*, trans. D. Willard. Dordrecht, The Netherlands: Kluwer Academic, 1994.

—— *Logical Investigations*, 2 vols., trans. J. N. Findlay. London: Routledge & Kegan Paul, 1970.

James, William. *Pragmatism*. New York: Dover, 1995.

Johnson, Philip & Mark Wigley. *Deconstructivist Architecture*. Boston: Little, Brown and Company, 1988.

Johnston, Adrian. 'Points of Forced Freedom: Eleven (More) Theses on Materialism', *Speculations* IV (2013), pp. 91–8.

Jung, C. G. *The Archetypes and the Collective Unconscious: The Collected Works of C. G. Jung, vol. 9*, trans. R. F. C. Hull. Princeton, NJ: Princeton University Press, 1980.

Kant, Immanuel. *Critique of Judgment*, trans. W. Pluhar. Indianapolis: Hackett, 1987.

—— *Critique of Pure Reason*, trans. N. K. Smith. London: Palgrave Macmillan, 2003.

—— *Groundwork of the Metaphysics of Morals*, trans. M. Gregor. Cambridge, UK: Cambridge University Press, 1997.

—— *Prolegomena to Any Future Metaphysics*, trans. G. Hatfield. Cambridge, UK: Cambridge University Press, 1997.

Kierkegaard, Søren. *Concluding Unscientific Postscript* to *Philosophical Fragments*, trans. H. Hong. Princeton, NJ: Princeton University Press, 1992.

Kipnis, Jeffrey. *A Question of Qualities: Essays in Architecture*. Cambridge, MA: MIT Press, 2013.

Kisiel, Theodore. 'Heidegger's *Gesamtausgabe*: An International Scandal of Scholarship', *Philosophy Today* 39:1 (1995), pp. 3–15.

Kripke, Saul. *Naming and Necessity*. Cambridge, MA: Harvard University Press, 1980.

Kuhn, Thomas. *The Structure of Scientific Revolutions*, 3rd edition. Chicago: University of Chicago Press, 1996.

Kwinter, Sanford. *Far from Equilibrium: Essays on Technology and Design Culture*. Barcelona: ACTAR Publishers, 2008.

Lacan, Jacques. *Anxiety: The Seminar of Jacques Lacan, Book X*, trans. A. R. Price. Cambridge, UK: Polity, 2016.

—— *The Ethics of Psychoanalysis (1959–1960): The Seminar of Jacques Lacan, Book VII*, trans. D. Porter. New York: Norton, 1997.

Ladyman, James & Don Ross, with David Spurrett, John Collier. *Every Thing Must Go: Metaphysics Naturalized*. Oxford: Oxford University Press, 2009.

Lakatos, Imre. *The Methodology of Scientific Research Programs*. Cambridge, UK: Cambridge University Press, 1980.

Latour, Bruno. *Aramis, or The Love of Technology*, trans. C. Porter. Cambridge, MA: Harvard University Press, 1996.

—— 'Can We Get Our Materialism Back, Please?', *Isis* 98 (2007), pp. 138–42.

—— *An Enquiry Into Modes of Existence: An Anthropology of the Moderns*, trans. C. Porter. Cambridge, MA: Harvard University Press, 2013.

—— *Facing Gaia: Eight Lectures on the New Climactic Regime*. Cambridge, UK: Polity, 2017.

—— 'Irreductions', in *The Pasteurization of France*, trans. A. Sheridan & J. Law. Cambridge, MA: Harvard University Press, 1988.

—— *Pandora's Hope: Essays on the Reality of Science Studies*. Cambridge, MA: Harvard University Press, 1999.

—— *The Pasteurization of France*, trans. A. Sheridan & J. Law. Cambridge, MA: Harvard University Press, 1988.

—— *Politics of Nature: How to Bring the Sciences into Democracy*, trans. C. Porter. Cambridge, MA: Harvard University Press, 2004.

—— *Reassembling the Social: An Introduction to Actor-Network-Theory*. Oxford: Oxford University Press, 2007.

—— 'Two Bubbles of Unrealism: Learning from the Tragedy of Trump', trans. C. Soudan & J. Park, *Los Angeles Review of Books*, 17 November 2016. https://lareviewofbooks.org/article/two-bubbles-unrealism-learning-tragedy-trump/

—— *We Have Never Been Modern*, trans. C. Porter. Cambridge, MA: Harvard University Press, 1993.

—— Graham Harman & Peter Erdélyi. *The Prince and the Wolf: Latour and Harman at the LSE*. Winchester, UK: Zero Books, 2011.

Leibniz, G. W. 'From the Letters to Des Bosses (1712–16)', in *Philosophical Essays*, pp. 197–206.

—— *Philosophical Essays*, trans. R. Ariew & D. Garber. Indianapolis: Hackett, 1989.

—— 'The Principles of Philosophy, or, the Monadology (1714)', in *Philosophical Essays*, pp. 213–25.

Lenton, Tim. *Earth System Science: A Very Short Introduction*. Oxford: Oxford University Press, 2016.

Levenson, Carl & Jonathan Westphal (eds.). *Reality*. Indianapolis: Hackett, 1994.

Linder, Mark. *Nothing Less Than Literal: Architecture After Minimalism*. Cambridge, MA: MIT Press, 2007.

Lingis, Alphonso. *The Imperative*. Bloomington, IN: Indiana University Press, 1997.

Lippmann, Walter. *The Phantom Public*. New Brunswick, NJ: Transaction Publishers, 1993.

Lovecraft, H. P. *Tales*. New York: Library of America, 2005.

Luhmann, Niklas. *Social Systems*, trans. J. Bednarz Jr. Palo Alto, CA: Stanford University Press, 1996.

Machiavelli, Niccolò. *The Prince*, trans. P. Bondanella. Oxford: Oxford University Press, 2008.

Margulis, Lynn. *Symbiotic Planet: A New Look at Evolution*. New York: Basic Books, 1999.

Marres, Noortje. 'No Issue, No Public: Democratic Deficits After the Displacement of Politics', Ph.D dissertation, University of Amsterdam, The Netherlands, 2005. http://dare.uva.nl/record/165542

Marx, Karl. *Capital*, vol. 1, trans. B. Fowkes. New York: New World Paperbacks, 1967.

McLuhan, Marshall. *Understanding Media: The Extensions of Man*. Cambridge, MA: MIT Press, 1994.

—— & Eric McLuhan. *Laws of Media: The New Science*. Toronto: University of Toronto Press, 1992.

Meillassoux, Quentin. *After Finitude: Essay on the Necessity of Contingency*, trans. R. Brassier. London: Continuum, 2008.

Meinong, Alexius. *On Assumptions*, trans. J. Heanue. Berkeley, CA: University of California Press, 1983.

Moeller, Hans-Georg. *The Radical Luhmann*. New York: Columbia University Press, 2012.

Mol, Annemarie. *The Body Multiple: Ontology in Medical Practice*. Durham, NC: Duke University Press, 2003.

Moreno Villa, José. *El pasajero*. Madrid: Renacimiento, 1924.

Morton, Timothy. *Dark Ecology: For a Logic of Future Coexistence*. New York: Columbia University Press, 2016.

—— *The Ecological Thought*. Cambridge, MA: Harvard University Press, 2012.

—— *Ecology Without Nature: Rethinking Environmental Aesthetics*. Cambridge, MA: Harvard University Press, 2009.

—— *Hyperobjects: Philosophy and Ecology After the End of the World*. Minneapolis: University of Minnesota Press, 2013.

—— 'An Object-Oriented Defense of Poetry', *New Literary History* 43 (2012), pp. 205–24.

—— *Realist Magic: Objects, Ontology, Causality*. Ann Arbor, MI: Open Humanities Press, 2013.

—— & Björk Guðmundsóttir, *This Huge Sunlit Abyss from The Future Right There Next To You*. New York: Museum of Modern Art, 2014.

Mumford, Stephen & Rani Lill Anjum. *Causation: A Very Short Introduction*. Oxford: Oxford University Press, 2013.

Nadler, Steven. *Occasionalism: Causation Among the Cartesians*. Oxford: Oxford University Press, 2011.

Nicholas of Cusa. *Selected Spiritual Writings*, trans. H. L. Bond. Mahwah, NJ: Paulist Press, 2005.

Nietzsche, Friedrich. *Beyond Good and Evil: Prelude to a Philosophy of the Future*, trans. W. Kaufmann. New York: Vintage, 1989.

Norwich, John Julius. *A History of Venice*. New York: Vintage, 1989.

Ortega y Gasset, José. 'An Essay in Esthetics by Way of a Preface', in *Phenomenology and Art*, trans. P. Silver. New York: Norton, 1975; pp. 127–50.

Peirce, Charles Sanders. *Philosophical Writings of Peirce*, ed. J. Buchler. New York: Dover, 1955.

Perler, Dominik, & Ulrich Rudolph. *Occasionalismus: Theorien der Kausalität im arabisch-islamischen und im europäischen Denken*. Göttingen: Vandenhoeck & Ruprecht, 2000.

Pinkard, Terry. *German Philosophy 1760–1860: The Legacy of Idealism*. Cambridge, UK: Cambridge University Press, 2001.

Plato. *Meno*, trans. G. M. A. Grube. Indianapolis: Hackett, 1980.

—— *Phaedrus*, trans. A. Nehamas. Indianapolis: Hackett, 1995.

—— *The Republic of Plato*, trans. A. Bloom. New York: Basic Books, 1968.

Popper, Karl. *The Logic of Scientific Discovery*. London: Routledge, 2005.

Priest, Graham. *Beyond the Limits of Thought*, 2nd edition. Oxford: Clarendon Press, 2003.

Pseudo-Dionysius. *Pseudo-Dionysius: The Complete Works*, ed.
C. Lubheid. Mahwah, NJ: Paulist Press, 1988.

Rousseau, Jean-Jacques. *Discourse on the Origin of Inequality*, trans.
D. Cress. Indianapolis: Hackett, 1992.

Ruy, David. 'Returning to (Strange) Objects', *tarp Architecture
Manual* (Spring 2012), pp. 38–42.

Sartre, Jean-Paul. *Being and Nothingness: An Essay on
Phenomenological Ontology*, trans. H. Barnes. New York:
Philosophical Library, 1984.

Sartwell, Crispin. 'Why Knowledge Is Merely True Belief', *Journal
of Philosophy* 89:4 (April 1992), pp. 167–80.

Saussure, Ferdinand de. *Course in General Linguistics*, trans.
R. Harris. Chicago: Open Court, 1986.

Scheler, Max. *Formalism in Ethics and Non-Formal Ethics of Values:
A New Attempt toward the Foundation of an Ethical Personalism*,
trans. M. Frings & R. Funk. Evanston, IL: Northwestern
University Press, 1973.

—— 'Ordo Amoris', in *Selected Philosophical Essays*, trans.
D. Lachterman. Evanston, IL: Northwestern University Press,
1992.

Schmitt, Carl. *The Concept of the Political: Expanded Edition*, trans.
G. Schwab. Chicago: University of Chicago Press, 2007.

Schumacher, Patrik. *The Autopoiesis of Architecture*, 2 vols. London:
Wiley, 2011/2012.

—— (ed.). *Parametricism 2.0: Rethinking Architecture's Agenda for
the 21st Century AD*. London: Wiley, 2016.

Sellars, Wilfrid. *In the Space of Reasons: Selected Essays of
Wilfrid Sellars*. Cambridge, MA: Harvard University Press,
2007.

Shapin, Steven, & Simon Schaffer. *Leviathan and the Air-Pump:
Hobbes, Boyle, and the Experimental Life*. Princeton, NJ:
Princeton University Press, 2011.

Smith, Barry, & Jeffrey Sims, 'Revisting the Derrida Affair with
Barry Smith', *Sophia* 38:2 (September–October 1999).

Smolin, Lee. *The Trouble with Physics: The Rise of String Theory, the Fall of Science, and What Comes Next.* New York: Mariner Books, 2007.

Stanislavski, Konstantin. *An Actor's Work.* New York: Routledge, 2010.

Stowe, Harriet Beecher. *Uncle Tom's Cabin.* New York: Norton, 2010.

Strauss, Leo. *Natural Right and History.* Chicago: University of Chicago Press, 1999.

Strum, S. S., & Bruno Latour. 'Redefining the Social Link: From Baboons to Humans', *Social Science Information* 26:4 (1987), pp. 783–802.

Tolstoy, Leo. *War and Peace.* New York: Vintage, 2008.

Tucker, Emma. 'Mark Foster Gage Proposes Elaborate Gargoyle-Covered Skyscraper for New York', *De Zeen*, 14 December 2015. https://www.dezeen.com/2015/12/14/mark-foster-gage-proposes-elaborate-gargoyle-covered-skyscraper-new-york-west-57th-street/

Twardowski, Kazimirz. *On the Content and Object of Presentations: A Psychological Investigation.* The Hague: Martinus Nijhoff, 1977.

Uexküll, Jakob von. *A Foray into the Worlds of Humans and Animals with A Theory of Meaning*, trans. J. D. O'Neil. Minneapolis: University of Minnesota Press, 2010.

Vogelin, Eric. *The New Science of Politics.* Chicago: University of Chicago Press, 1987.

Wallace, David Foster. *This is Water: Some Thoughts, Delivered on a Significant Occasion, about Living a Compassionate Life.* New York: Little, Brown & Co., 2009.

Whitehead, Alfred North. *Process and Reality.* New York: Free Press, 1979.

Wiscombe, Tom. 'Discreteness, or Towards a Flat Ontology of Architecture', *Project* 3 (2014), pp. 34–43.

Woit, Richard. *Not Even Wrong: The Failure of String Theory and the Search for Unity in Physical Law.* New York: Basic Books, 2006.

Zeilinger, Anton. 'Distributing Entanglement and Single Photons through an Intra-City, Free Space Quantum Channel', *Optics Express* 13 (2005), pp. 202–9.

Žižek, Slavoj. 'Afterword: Objects, Objects Everywhere', in *Slavoj Žižek and Dialectical Materialism*, ed. A. Hamza & F. Ruda. London: Palgrave Macmillan, 2015; pp. 177–92.

—— 'The Hillary Clinton Consensus Is Damaging Democracy', *Newsweek* online, 12 August 2016. http://www.newsweek.com/slavoj-zizek-hillary-clinton-donald-trump-us-presidential-election-bernie-489993

# Notes

*Full publication details for all works cited in the Notes can be found in Further Reading.*

---

## INTRODUCTION

1. Slavoj Žižek, 'The Hillary Clinton Consensus Is Damaging Democracy'.
2. 'post-truth' dictionary entry, https://en.oxforddictionaries.com/definition/post-truth
3. http://www.attn.com/stories/9613/neil-degrasse-tysons-latest-political-tweet-backfires
4. James Ladyman & Don Ross, *Every Thing Must Go*.
5. Slavoj Žižek, 'Afterword: Objects, Objects Everywhere'.
6. Bruno Latour, *An Enquiry Into Modes of Existence*, pp. 327, 337.
7. https://artreview.com/power_100/graham_harman/
8. I have heard this said by Dean Michael Speaks of Syracuse University in 2014, and by Michael Benedikt of the University of Texas in 2016.
9. Mark Foster Gage, 'Counterpoint: A Hospice for Parametricism'.
10. Timothy Morton and Björk Guðmundsóttir, *This Huge Sunlit Abyss from the Future Right There Next To You*.
11. Strictly speaking, I used the term 'object-oriented philosophy' for my own work beginning in 1997, and first introduced it in public in 1999, in a lecture called 'Object-Oriented Philosophy', later published in my book *Towards Speculative Realism*. In 2009, Bryant coined the term 'object-oriented ontology' as a piece of umbrella terminology capable of embracing object-oriented approaches other than my own. It should be noted that by that point the phrase 'object-oriented ontology' had already been used as an article title by philosopher Aden Evens (in 2006). But Evens' piece dealt

with the implications of computer programming for philosophy rather than with the sort of broad philosophical ontology envisioned by the OOO movement.

12. Martin Heidegger, *Being and Time*.

13. Graham Harman, *Immaterialism: Objects and Social Theory* and *Bruno Latour: Reassembling the Political*.

14. Jane Bennett, *Vibrant Matter*; Tristan Garcia, *Form and Object*.

15. Mark Foster Gage, 'Counterpoint: A Hospice for Parametricism'; Erik Ghenoiu, 'The World Is Not Enough'; David Ruy, 'Returning to (Strange) Objects'; Tom Wiscombe, 'Discreteness, or Towards a Flat Ontology of Architecture'.

---

## CHAPTER 1: A NEW THEORY OF EVERYTHING

1. Brian Greene, *The Elegant Universe*, p. 211.

2. Lee Smolin, *The Trouble with Physics*; Richard Woit, *Not Even Wrong*.

3. John Branch, 'Fright Nights in the NBA'.

4. C. G. Jung, *The Archteypes and the Collective Unconscious*.

5. Sam Coleman, 'Mind Under Matter'.

6. Manuel DeLanda, 'Emergence, Causality and Realism'.

7. G. W. Leibniz, 'The Principles of Philosophy, or, the Monadology'. The chief paradox of Leibniz's concept of the monad is that on the one hand it is said to be completely self-contained, having 'no windows' as Leibniz colourfully puts it. A monad cannot communicate with anything else directly, but only insofar as God allows for such communication to occur. But on the other hand, the Leibnizian God sees to it from the dawn of time that every monad is utterly *saturated* with relations to other monads. In one of his best-known examples, the fact that Julius Caesar effectively declared war on the Roman Republic by crossing the Rubicon River with his army was not the contingent result of a free decision by Caesar. Instead, this decision was contained in Caesar's monad from its creation at the beginning of the universe, billions of years before that monad was born as a human infant from the body of its mother. This obviously poses problems for an adequate Leibnizian account of free will, and I for one – though a great fan of Leibniz – have never found his efforts on this point to offer much more than nuanced contradiction.

8. Tim Lenton, *Earth System Science*, p. 15.

9. Jeffrey Bub, *Interpreting the Quantum World*, p. 34.

10. Jakob von Uexküll, *A Foray into the Worlds of Humans and Animals*, p. 47.

11. René Grousset, *The Empire of the Steppes*, p. 110.

12. John Julius Norwich, *A History of Venice*, p. 412.

13. Daniel Dennett, 'Quining Qualia', p. 384.

14. Martin Heidegger, *What Is Called Thinking?*, p. 8.

15. Aristotle, *The Metaphysics*, Book VII.

16. Wilfrid Sellars, *In the Space of Reasons*, p. 369.

17. Manuel DeLanda in conversation with Christoph Cox, 'Possibility Spaces', p. 93.

18. Martin Heidegger, 'Insight Into That Which Is', in *Bremen and Freiburg Lectures*.

19. Franz Brentano, *Psychology from an Empirical Standpoint*; Kasimir Twardowski, *On the Content and Object of Presentations*; Edmund Husserl, 'Intentional Objects'; Alexius Meinong, *On Assumptions*.

20. Martin Heidegger, *Being and Time*. For a critique of Heidegger's interpretation of his own thought-experiment on the hammer, see Graham Harman, *Tool-Being*.

21. A good, short collection of the sayings of the various pre-Socratics can be found in Chapter 2 of Carl Levenson & Jonathan Westphal (eds.), *Reality*.

22. Graham Harman, 'On the Undermining of Objects'.

23. René Descartes, *Meditations on First Philosophy*.

24. George Berkeley, *A Treatise Concerning the Principles of Human Knowledge*.

25. Alfred North Whitehead, *Process and Reality*; Bruno Latour, 'Irreductions'.

26. William James, *Pragmatism*; Charles Sanders Peirce, *Philosophical Writings of Peirce*.

27. Edmund Husserl, *Logical Investigations*.

28. Michel Foucault, *The Archaeology of Knowledge*.

29. Jacques Derrida, *Of Grammatology*, p. 158. It is fashionable among Derrideans to quibble over the proper translation of this phrase, and technically they are right that '*il n'y a pas de hors-texte*' should be translated as 'there is no outside-text'. But since both English translations seem to me to lead equally to anti-realism, I have stuck with Gayatri Spivak's now-classic choice of English wording.

30. Aristotle, *The Metaphysics*.

31. Graham Harman, 'Undermining, Overmining, and Duomining'.

32. Plato, *Meno*.

33. Manuel DeLanda & Graham Harman, *The Rise of Realism*, p. 58.

34. Karen Barad, *Meeting the Universe Halfway*.

35. Levi R. Bryant, *The Democracy of Objects*.

36. Roy Bhaskar, *A Realist Theory of Science*. For Bhaskar, a 'flat ontology' is one that flattens out everything by saying that everything is equally a human

experience. This leads to an empiricist philosophy of science that Bhaskar rejects, since he is interested in real causal mechanisms that never quite become evident in experience but are deeper aspects of the world itself.

37. Quentin Meillassoux, *After Finitude*.
38. Bruno Latour, *We Have Never Been Modern*.
39. Graham Harman, *Prince of Networks*.

---

## CHAPTER 2: AESTHETICS IS THE ROOT OF ALL PHILOSOPHY

1. Adrian Johnston, 'Points of Forced Freedom', p. 93.
2. Pseudo-Dionysius, *Pseudo-Dionysius: The Complete Works*, p. 30.
3. Bennett Cerf, *Book of Riddles*.
4. Cleanth Brooks, *The Well Wrought Urn*; Max Black, 'Metaphor'.
5. José Ortega y Gasset, 'An Essay in Esthetics by Way of a Preface'.
6. The book of poetry in question was José Moreno Villa, *El pasajero* (*The Traveller*).
7. It should be noted that Ortega's essay also includes some misogynistic and Anglophobic remarks that I do not endorse.
8. Immanuel Kant, *Groundwork of the Metaphysics of Morals*.
9. Alphonso Lingis, *The Imperative*.
10. Immanuel Kant, *Prolegomena to Any Future Metaphysics*.
11. Immanuel Kant, *Critique of Judgment*.
12. Ortega, 'An Essay in Esthetics by Way of a Preface', p. 136.
13. Graham Harman, 'Zero-Person and the Psyche'.
14. Ortega, 'An Essay in Esthetics by Way of a Preface', p. 133.
15. Ibid., p. 134.
16. Ibid., pp. 138–9.
17. Ibid., p. 139.
18. Ibid., p. 140.
19. Ibid., p. 141.
20. Ibid.
21. Ibid., p. 142.
22. Ibid., p. 143.
23. Ibid., p. 145.
24. David Hume, *A Treatise of Human Nature*, Book I, Chapter IV.
25. Edmund Husserl, *Logical Investigations*.
26. Kasimir Twardowski, *On the Content and Object of Presentations*.
27. Ortega, 'An Essay in Esthetics by Way of a Preface', p. 134.

28. Martin Heidegger, *Being and Time*; Graham Harman, *Tool-Being*.
29. Martin Heidegger, 'The Origin of the Work of Art', in *Off the Beaten Track*.
30. Ortega, 'An Essay in Esthetics by Way of a Preface', p. 139.
31. Konstantin Stanislavski, *An Actor's Work*.
32. Ortega, 'An Essay in Esthetics by Way of a Preface', p. 144.
33. Ibid., p. 148.
34. Ernest Hemingway, *The Old Man and the Sea*.
35. Claire Colebrook, 'Not Kant, Not Now: Another Sublime', p. 145.
36. Aristotle, *Poetics*.
37. Martin Heidegger, *What is Called Thinking?*, p. 8.
38. Heidegger, *Being and Time*.
39. Aristotle, *The Art of Rhetoric*.
40. Marshall McLuhan, *Understanding Media*.
41. Clement Greenberg, *Art and Culture*.
42. For a fuller treatment of this theme see Graham Harman, *Dante's Broken Hammer*.
43. Immanuel Kant, *Groundwork of the Metaphysics of Morals*.
44. Max Scheler, 'Ordo Amoris' and *Formalism in Ethics and a Non-Formal Ethics of Values*.
45. Immanuel Kant, *Critique of Judgment*.
46. Clement Greenberg, *Homemade Esthetics*, pp. 28–9.
47. Clement Greenberg, *The Collected Essays and Criticism, Vol. 4*, p. 293 (passage reworded slightly for clarity).
48. Michael Fried, 'Art and Objecthood'.
49. Mark Linder, *Nothing Less Than Literal*.
50. Harriet Beecher Stowe, *Uncle Tom's Cabin*.

## CHAPTER 3: SOCIETY AND POLITICS

1. S. S. Strum & Bruno Latour, 'Redefining the Social Link: From Baboons to Humans'.
2. Graham Harman, *Bruno Latour: Reassembling the Political*.
3. Graham Harman, *Immaterialism: Objects and Social Theory*.
4. Bruno Latour, *Reassembling the Social*.
5. Bruno Latour, *The Pasteurization of France*.
6. Bruno Latour, *Pandora's Hope*.
7. Niles Eldredge & Stephen Jay Gould, 'Punctuated Equilibria: An Alternative to Phyletic Gradualism'.

8.   Lynn Margulis, *Symbiotic Planet*.

9.   Ian Hodder, *Entangled*; Graham Harman, 'Entanglement and Relation'.

10.  Mark S. Granovetter, 'The Strength of Weak Ties'.

11.  Winston S. Churchill, *The Gathering Storm*.

12.  Terry Pinkard, *German Philosophy 1760–1860*.

13.  Harman, *Immaterialism*, p. 107.

14.  The story is told by Shelby Foote in his wonderfully written three-volume history of the war, excerpted in *The Beleaguered City*.

15.  Bruno Latour, 'Can We Get Our Materialism Back, Please?'

16.  Levi R. Bryant, *Onto-Cartography*, p. 2.

17.  For a good discussion of this topic, see Hans-Georg Moeller's *The Radical Luhmann*. For a sample of Luhmann's own mature work, see his *Social Systems*.

18.  Leo Strauss, *Natural Right and History*.

19.  Bruno Latour, *We Have Never Been Modern*, p. 27.

20.  See Bruno Latour, *Facing Gaia*.

21.  Eric Vogelin, *The New Science of Politics*.

22.  Bruno Latour, Graham Harman & Peter Erdélyi, *The Prince and the Wolf*, p. 96.

23.  G. W. Leibniz, 'From the Letters to Des Bosses (1712–16)'.

24.  Important steps towards a topology of the relations between objects can be found in Marshall & Eric McLuhan's *Laws of Media*, published long after the death of the elder McLuhan.

25.  Bruno Latour, 'Two Bubbles of Unrealism'.

## CHAPTER 4: INDIRECT RELATIONS

1.   Graham Harman, 'On Vicarious Causation'; Steven Nadler, *Occasionalism*.

2.   See Judith Butler, *Gender Trouble*, along with the works of the other authors already mentioned earlier.

3.   Martin Heidegger, 'Insight Into That Which Is', in *Bremen and Freiburg Lectures*.

4.   See also Graham Harman, 'Dwelling with the Fourfold'.

5.   Edmund Husserl, 'Intentional Objects'.

6.   In a 2014 article entitled 'Objects and Orientalism', I give a detailed treatment of the case of Middle Eastern peoples.

7.   Maurizio Ferraris, *Manifesto of New Realism*; Markus Gabriel, *Fields of Sense*.

8. For more on this topic see Majid Fakhry, *Islamic Occasionalism and its Critique by Averroes and Aquinas*, and (for those who read German) Dominik Perler & Ulrich Rudolph's *Occasionalismus*.

9. Graham Harman, 'Time, Space, Essence, and Eidos'.

10. Plato, *Meno*, 71b. I am quoting from Grube's translation, published by Hackett.

11. Ibid., 71e–72a.

12. Ibid., 73d.

13. Ibid., 77b.

14. Ibid., 78c.

15. Ibid., 80d–81a.

16. Ibid., 81d.

17. Ibid., 87c.

18. Ibid., 89e.

19. Ibid., 96a–d.

20. Ibid., 97b.

21. Ibid., 97c.

22. Ibid., 97e.

23. Ibid., 98a.

24. Ibid., 81e.

25. Nicholas of Cusa, *Selected Spiritual Writings*.

26. Plato, *The Republic*, Book VI, 509d–511d.

27. Plato, *Meno*, 99e.

28. Edmund Gettier, 'Is Justified True Belief Knowledge?', p. 121. The reference to Plato is contained in Footnote 1 on the same page.

29. Thomas Kuhn, *The Structure of Scientific Revolutions*.

30. Imre Lakatos, *The Methodology of Scientific Research Programs*.

31. Karl Popper, *The Logic of Scientific Discovery*.

32. For one critique along these lines, see Manuel DeLanda, *Philosophical Chemistry*.

33. Marshall McLuhan, *Understanding Media*, Part I, Chapter 1.

34. Søren Kierkegaard, *Concluding Unscientific Postscript*.

---

## CHAPTER 5: OBJECT-ORIENTED ONTOLOGY AND ITS RIVALS

1. An important exception is the remarkably open-minded Jon Cogburn of Louisiana State University, who taught the first known university seminar on OOO in spring 2012, and whose outstanding new book *Garcian*

*Meditations* does as much to negotiate the analytic–continental divide successfully as anything I have read.

2. For the most candid possible statement of continental anti-realism, see Lee Braver, *A Thing of This World*.

3. Peter Gratton, *Speculative Realism*, p. 5.

4. Barry Smith & Jeffrey Sims, 'Revisiting the Derrida Affair with Barry Smith'.

5. Derrida's three prominent works of 1967 are *Of Grammatology*, the important interpretation of Edmund Husserl entitled *Voice and Phenomenon*, and the great collection of essays *Writing and Difference*.

6. Plato, *Phaedrus*; Derrida, 'Plato's Pharmacy'.

7. Graham Harman, *Heidegger Explained*, p. 1.

8. For another example of the use to which 'time' can be put by a skilled Derridean, see Martin Hägglund, *Radical Atheism*.

9. See for example John D. Caputo, 'For Love of the Things Themselves'.

10. Derrida, *Of Grammatology*, p. 89.

11. Ibid., p. 61.

12. Ibid., p. 50.

13. Ibid., p. 61.

14. Ibid., p. 50. Postmodern philosophy in France often laid emphasis on the distinction between signifier and signified, under the influence of the Swiss linguist Ferdinand de Saussure (1857–1913), whose *Course in General Linguistics* had an extensive impact in French philosophical circles. Saussure taught that the relation between any given signifier and what it signifies is arbitrary, since for example different foreign languages have different words for 'dog' though all signify the same animal. Beyond this, French thinkers such as Lacan and Derrida liked to stress the idea of a relational play of signifiers that merely point to other signifiers rather than to any ultimate signified thing lying beyond the play of language itself. Note that this is an emphatically *anti-realist* strategy, since realism requires that something exists outside language: a claim that sounds commonsensical enough, but which is openly denied by Lacan and Derrida in their more candid moments.

15. Derrida, *Of Grammatology*, p. 49.

16. Ibid., p. 45.

17. Ibid., p. 31.

18. Ibid., p. 90.

19. For more on this topic see Graham Harman, *Guerrilla Metaphysics*, pp. 110–16.

20. Derrida, *Of Grammatology*, pp. 22–3.

21. Michel Foucault, *The Archaeology of Knowledge*, p. 23.

22. Ibid.
23. Ibid.
24. Ibid., p. 24.
25. Ibid., p. 25.
26. For an especially acerbic account of the problems with the Heidegger collection, see Theodor Kisiel, 'Heidegger's *Gesamtausgabe*: An International Scandal of Scholarship'.
27. Foucault, *The Archaeology of Knowledge*, p. 26.
28. Ibid., pp. 26–7.
29. Ibid., p. 27 (italics added).
30. Ibid.
31. Ibid., p. 28.
32. For the former, see Bruno Latour, *The Pasteurization of France*; for the latter, see Bruno Latour, *Aramis*.
33. Foucault, *The Archaeology of Knowledge*, p. 28.
34. Ibid., p. 32.
35. Ibid., p. 33.
36. Ibid., p. 34.
37. Ibid., p. 37.
38. Ibid., pp. 42–3.
39. Ibid., p. 48.
40. Ibid., p. 45.
41. Ibid., p. 47.

---

## CHAPTER 6: VARYING APPROACHES TO OBJECT-ORIENTED ONTOLOGY

1. Graham Harman, 'Object-Oriented Philosophy', in *Towards Speculative Realism*.
2. See Morton's remarks in Peter Gratton, 'Interviews: Graham Harman, Jane Bennett, Tim Morton, Ian Bogost, Levi Bryant and Paul Ennis'.
3. Ian Bogost, *Play Anything*, pp. 1–2.
4. Ian Bogost, 'Why Gamification Is Bullshit'.
5. David Foster Wallace, *This is Water*, p. 84; cited at Bogost, *Play Anything*, p. 8.
6. Bogost, *Play Anything*, p. 9.
7. Ibid., p. 13.
8. Ibid., p. 14.
9. Ibid., p. 20.

10. Ibid., p. 22.
11. Noah Frankovitch, 'Why Can't Anyone Tell I'm Wearing This Business Suit Ironically?'
12. Bogost, *Play Anything*, p. 42.
13. Ibid., p. 58.
14. Ibid., p. 95.
15. Ibid., p. 99.
16. Ibid., pp. 104–7.
17. Ibid., p. 106.
18. Ibid., p. 133.
19. Ibid., p. 146.
20. Levi R. Bryant, Larval Subjects blog, https://larvalsubjects.wordpress.com/
21. Gilles Deleuze & Félix Guattari, *Anti-Oedipus*.
22. Levi R. Bryant, *Onto-Cartography*, pp. 198 ff.
23. Ibid., pp. 15–25.
24. Ibid., p. 198.
25. Graham Harman, 'Time, Space, Essence, and *Eidos*'.
26. Bryant, *Onto-Cartography*, p. 199.
27. Ibid., p. 205, citing Alain Badiou, *Logics of Worlds*.
28. Ibid., p. 203.
29. Ibid., p. 208.
30. Timothy Morton, *Hyperobjects*, p. 1.
31. Ibid., p. 201.
32. Ibid.
33. Ibid., p. 6.
34. Ibid., pp. 1–2.
35. Jean-Paul Sartre, *Being and Nothingness*, p. 609, cited Timothy Morton, *Hyperobjects*, p. 30.
36. Morton, Hyperobjects, p. 36.
37. Ibid., p. 31.
38. Ibid., p. 36 (italics added).
39. Ibid., p. 35.
40. Ibid., pp. 41–2.
41. Ibid., p. 42. The reference to Zeilinger is to his co-authored article 'Distributing Entanglement and Single Photons through an Intra-City, Free Space Quantum Channel'.
42. Ibid., p. 49.
43. Ibid., p. 45.
44. Ibid., p. 48.
45. Ibid., p. 54.

46. Ibid., p. 56.

47. Ibid., p. 66.

48. Ibid., p. 60.

49. Ibid., p. 1.

50. Mark Buchanan, *Ubiquity*.

51. Morton, *Hyperobjects*, pp. 71–2.

52. Ibid., pp. 71–5.

53. Ibid., p. 76.

54. Graham Priest, *Beyond the Limits of Thought*.

55. Morton, *Hyperobjects*, pp. 81–2.

56. Ibid., p. 83.

57. Ibid., p. 81.

58. Graham Harman, 'Autonomous Objects'; Jane Bennett 'Systems and Things'.

59. Jane Bennett, *Vibrant Matter*, p. 112.

60. Ibid., p. xvi.

61. Ibid., p. 106.

62. Ibid., p. xiv.

63. Ibid., p. 128.

64. Ibid., p. 122.

65. Bennett, 'Systems and Things', p. 232.

66. Ibid., p. 228.

67. Ibid.

68. Ibid., p. 229.

69. Ibid., p. 227.

70. Tristan Garcia, *Hate: A Romance*.

71. The two parts of Garcia's trilogy already published in French are *La Vie intense* and *Nous*.

72. I have discussed these issues in two articles on Garcia's work: 'Object-Oriented France' and 'Tristan Garcia and the Thing-In-Itself'.

73. Tristan Garcia, *Form and Object*, p. 4.

74. Ibid., p. 1.

75. Philip Johnson & Mark Wigley, *Deconstructivist Architecture*.

76. 'Appendix: Letter from Jacques Derrida to Peter Eisenman', pp. 160–68, in Peter Eisenman, *Written into the Void: Selected Writings, 1990–2004*.

77. Sanford Kwinter, *Far from Equilibrium*; Jeffrey Kipnis, *A Question of Qualities*.

78. Gilles Deleuze, *The Fold*.

79. David Ruy, 'Returning to (Strange) Objects', p. 38.

80. Erik Ghenoiu, 'The World is Not Enough', p. 6.

81. Ruy, 'Returning to (Strange) Objects', pp. 40–41.

NOTES

82. Ibid., p. 42.
83. Tom Wiscombe, 'Discreteness, or Towards a Flat Ontology of Architecture'.
84. Wiscombe, 'Discreteness', p. 43.
85. Ibid., p. 35.
86. Ibid., p. 39.
87. Ibid., p. 35.
88. Ibid., p. 39.
89. Ibid.
90. Ibid.
91. Ibid.
92. Ibid., p. 41.
93. Ibid.
94. Ibid., p. 43.
95. Ibid.
96. Patrik Schumacher, *The Autopoiesis of Architecture*, 2 vols.
97. Mark Foster Gage, 'Killing Simplicity'.
98. Ibid., p. 106.
99. Emma Tucker, 'Mark Foster Gage Proposes Elaborate Gargoyle-Covered Skyscraper for New York'.
100. H. P. Lovecraft, 'The Shadow over Innsmouth', p. 595, in *Tales*.
101. Gage, 'Killing Simplicity', p. 100.
102. Ibid., p. 103.
103. Ibid., p. 104.
104. Ibid., p. 105.
105. Ibid., p. 106.

## CHAPTER 7: OBJECT-ORIENTED ONTOLOGY IN OVERVIEW

1. Karen Barad, *Meeting the Universe Halfway*; Donna Haraway, *Simians, Cyborgs, and Women*.

# Index